Frank Cowan

The Poetical Works of Frank Cowan

Vol. I.

Frank Cowan

The Poetical Works of Frank Cowan
Vol. I.

ISBN/EAN: 9783337181475

Printed in Europe, USA, Canada, Australia, Japan

Cover: Foto ©Thomas Meinert / pixelio.de

More available books at **www.hansebooks.com**

THE
POETIC WORKS

OF

FRANK COWAN.

It is the Poet's function to embody in his song,
The spirit of the age and clime to which he may belong;
To feel, with comprehensive heart, think, with constructive mind,
And voice the vital universe in numbers for mankind. —
From THE PLAIN OF TROY, *vol. 1, page 84.*

IN THREE VOLUMES.

I.

GREENESBURGH, PENNSYLVANIA:
THE OLIVER PUBLISHING HOUSE:
1892.

PREFACE AND ADVERTISEMENT.

As projected, the poetic works of the writer will be published in three volumes.

This, the first, contains three collections of poems, each of which is the subject of a paragraph below, revealing in a measure the relation between them and the writer, his evolving individuality, his peculiar investigations, and his ever-varying environment in the zigzag course of his travels in the northern and southern hemispheres twice around the globe — stitching together, with the thread of his life, the sibylline leaves of his poetic fancy and philosophy, scattered far and wide by the winds that wander around the world.

The second volume will contain SOUTHWESTERN PENNSYLVANIA IN SONG AND STORY: (severed from the compilation, entitled THE BATTLE BALLADS, AND OTHER POEMS, OF SOUTHWESTERN PENNSYLVANIA, with which it was published in 1878:) with prefatory notes, historic, anecdotic, and scientific: revised, and enlarged with the addition of several poems written since the publication of the original volume, notably, THE BATTLE OF THE BISON AND THE UNICORN, introducing the extinct bison, *Bos latifrons*, in conflict with the mythic unicorn of the early palæontologists of Pennsylvania, *Rhinoceroides Alleghaniensis*, and illustrating, (like THE LAST OF THE MAMMOTHS, the initial poem of the volume,) prehistoric life and the supremacy gained by Man over the savage beasts of his environment by availing himself of the multiform weapon of fire; THE LAST OF THE MOUND-BUILDERS, descriptive of the expulsion of the prehistoric semi-civilized, field-tilling and town-building, tribes of Southwestern Pennsylvania by the hunting savages found in possession of the territory by the Europeans on their arrival; THE BATTLE OF BUSHY RUN, read, August 6th, 1883, at an anniversary celebration of the decisive victory gained in 1763 by the British forces, under the command of Colonel HENRY BOUQUET, over the Redskins of Western Pennsylvania, under the leadership of GUYASUTHA, — a battle typical of the conquest of the savage New World by the civilized Old, and admitting a justification of the survival of the fittest in the struggle for existence among races as well as individuals; and WHEN MAMMON WENT A-FISHING IN THE LOCH OF CONEMAUGH, descriptive of the destruction of JOHNSTOWN, with an immediate loss of three thousand lives, on the 31st day of May, 1889, by the sudden descent of a sea of waters, suspended, as a summer plaything of a gilded coterie, until the fatal moment, in a mountain gorge above the city, by a deliquescent wall of earth and straw!

The third volume will contain FAUSTINA: A FANTASY OF AUTUMN IN THE HEART OF APPALACHIA. This is a poem descriptive of the mountainous parts of Pennsylvania during the months of September, October, and November — the American autumn; the succession of meteorologic phenomena, the characteristic flora and fauna, and the peculiar manners and customs of the people, every detail of which has been a special study, and its setting, in the poetic, philosophic, and fanciful mosaic of the comprehensive whole, the ultimate of the writer's art. FAUSTINA, the Fated One, the personification of the season, is represented as a wife and mother, who, as the life of summer passes into the death of winter, decays and dies, leaving her babe to survive her, the symbol of the season's self-incapsulating seeds. It is written in blank verse: the writer allowing himself, as a compensation for the exactions of accurate observation and precise expression, the latitude of a world-wandering sight-seer in the selection of his similes and images, and that of a lexicographer of the English language in its totality in the *scaling* of his words.

> And oh, that I could be the mirror of
> The moment that I would! a bubble filmed
> With subtle sight and filled with sentient soul,
> That, bursting in the audient air, might voice
> The whole within a comprehending word!—
> FAUSTINA, *Saturday, October, 16th.*

To recur now to the three collections contained in this, the first volume—

The first, THE RIME OF A RAMBLER TWICE AROUND THE WORLD, is a fragmentary resultant of two tours of the globe made by the writer in the expression of his ravenous and insatiate greed to devour in the raw and digest as much of the earth and as many of its involvings as possible and make them his own, a part of himself, organic, human—a thing of thought; that, haply, the phenomena of his ever-changing environment might become so many fancies; the facts of fire and water, earth and air around him, so many factors of fiction; the real, the ideal; form, formula ; thing, thought; the world, a word. In the first of these foraging expeditions, made in the years 1880 and 1881, the writer, traveling in general from west to east in the northern hemisphere, visited the following countries, or parts of the earth, in the order named—his appetite increasing with that which it fed upon, and his hunger becoming the more inappeasable with the indigested accumulations in his maw: Ireland, Scotland, England, France, Belgium, Holland, Germany, Austria, Italy, Switzerland, France, Switzerland, Germany, Russia, Finland, Sweden, Norway, Denmark, Germany, England, Portugal, Spain, Algeria, Tunisia, Sicily, Greece, Asia Minor, Turkey, Syria, Palestine, Egypt, India, the Malay Peninsula, the East Indian Archipelago, China, Japan, Chosen or Corea, Japan, and the United States from sea to sea. In the second, made in the years 1884 and 1885, traveling in general from east to west and mainly in the southern hemisphere, he visited Cuba, Yucatan, Mexico, several of the West Indian Islands, Northern or Amazonian Brazil, Eastern Peru, Southern Brazil, Uruguay, the Argentine Republic, Patagonia, Tierra del Fuego, Chili, Western Peru, Mexico, California, the Hawaiian Islands, New Zealand, New South Wales, Victoria, South Australia, Egypt, England, and France. A summary of the traveler's most noteworthy accidents and adventures is given in a series of antithetic lines in the poem entitled AT GETTYSBURG; and a portraiture of himself at the end of his travels, as he conceived himself to be in the exercise of his art, (remembering the while the limitations of the happy dicta of Cicero and Heine respectively, that the eye may see many things, but never itself, and the bird may fly high, but never above itself,) is given in the opening lines of AUSTRALIA: A CHARCOAL SKETCH.

The poems, comprised in the second collection of this volume, are conceived to be —

 LIKE FERN-LEAVES FOUND IN SHALE, outlining life
 Against a world turned into sunless stone,

and so are entitled. They are a product mainly of the years 1877, 1878, and 1879, during which, as well as a preceding lustrum, the writer was an enthusiastic laborer in the lampless past of America, digging and delving in the vast kjökkenmöddings of the prehistoric ages, decyphering the hieroglyphics of the glaciers, and following the footprints of his predecessors back to their primal appearance in the sands of time; till every potshard became a burning wick illuminating a long-vanished household of labor and love, every score, a scar of suffering and sacrifice, and the earth itself, the unbosomed heart of buried humanity. The series passes from the palæontologic to the archæologic or prehistoric, and thence to the historic. None has been in type before, except the first, THE ATLANTOSAURUS, in WARD'S *Natural Science Bulletin*, 1 Jan., 1884.

The third collection, SAGE, RUE, AND THYME, is an *olla podrida*, containing poems written betimes during the past quarter of a century and exhibiting a corresponding evolution — growth or decay, as the case may be — in the writer. Assuming the development has been from the local and contracted to the cosmopolitan and comprehensive, the reader may find an interest in the relations of these poems to one another and their author to compensate for what they lack in themselves. Assuming, also, the development has been from ignorance to knowledge, and from error to truth, the student of sex-symbolism may profit by the variations in the signification of the forms of prayer to be found in THE TWO TOWERS, written in 1871, CHAUTAUQUA, in 1875, [ATLANTIS, in 1878,] and THE MEANING OF THE MONUMENT, in 1887.

In conclusion, a paragraph or two with respect to the explanatory notes which either are prefixed or suffixed to several of the poems in these volumes.

When, presumably, the subject-matter of a poem is known to the reader, and the factors of the fiction are familiar, the poem should be its own interpreter in every respect; but when the subject is strange, its involvings many and complicated, and an understanding thereof a mental growth requiring research and reflection, the poem cannot be self-intelligible within reasonable bounds, and explanatory notes are indispensable and admissible perhaps to the point of being burdensome.

Like the rainbow that comes into being and beauty only as a relation between a sunlit shower and the eye of an observer, so the poetic comes into existence only as a relation between a theme and a poet, or a printed page and a reader. Without the prosaic facts, phenomena, and experiences of the writer, the reader cannot stand in his stead and become the possessor of his fancies — without the factors of the fiction, the page before him is a blank. There is no royal road around the world and into the head and heart of humanity to the reader any more than there is to the traveler and writer.

> Go where the trav'ler will, by land or sea,
> The world is void of all that thrills the heart,
> Or fills the fancy with delightful visions,
> Unless he, like another Atlas, bears
> A world of comprehension on his shoulders.
>
> The eye sees only what it brings with it
> The power to see, the wise Carlyle hath said :
> A simple saw of universal scope. — ALGERIA, *p.* 42.

It follows, hence, that, all men differing from one another in their powers of observation, one man may see more of the poetic in a theme than another, and one reader, more in a poem than another. Indeed, it is possible that a reader may see more in a poem than the maker of it. Aye, further, this is not only possible, but it is highly probable that a zoölogist of OWEN's comprehensiveness, in reading AUSTRALIA : A CHARCOAL SKETCH, will entertain a thousand thoughts and theories that never entered the head of its author, and rate the poem the rather from its subjective effect than as an objective cause. So, to a geologist of MARTIN's encompassing, THE TERRACES OF ROTOMÁHANA and THE HELL OF HÁLEMÁUMAU have a scope and significance far beyond the ken of the traveler who fashioned the complicated phenomena of these world's wonders into his fictions. So, to a critic of ZIMMERMAN's refined sensibility and boundless sympathy, THE LAND OF AULD LANG SYNE, DIE DEUTSCHER's FADERLAND, and OLD IRELAND — GOD BLESS HER! may contain a tenderness to which their author is a trilobite. To all which, the German proverb is a fitting colophon —

> Es steckt nicht im Spiegel, was man im Spiegel sieht.

FRANK COWAN.

GREENESBURGH, PENN'A.

CONTENTS.

THE RIME OF A RAMBLER TWICE AROUND THE WORLD.

VALE, VALHALLA! .	xvi
A FINLAND FANTASY, . .	17
THE LAND OF AULD LANG SYNE,	20
THE COGNIZANCE OF EUROPE, ...	21
THE CITY OF THE ROYAL PALM, (RIO DE JANEIRO,)	22
WILLIAM CULLEN BRYANT, . . .	24
A DUTCH FOG-SIGNAL, .	25
THE NIBELUNGENLIED, .	29
THE BALTIC, . .	30
ITALY, ...	30
A DRINKING-BOUT IN DENMARK,	31
THE IRISH CHANNEL, . .	34
NORWAY, . .	35
SCOTLAND,	40
FINLAND, ...	40
BELGIUM — THE GARDEN OF EUROPE, .	40
WOMAN, WINE, AND SONG, . . .	41
ALGERIA, . . .	42
THE FRENCH IN AFRICA, .	47

CONTENTS.

England,	48
Switzerland,	49
Object and Idea,	49
Hero and Leander,	50
On the Alps,	52
Amsterdam,	53
A Reverie in Rome,	54
My Castle in Spain,	56
In Holland,	58
In London,	59
The Tierra-del-Fuegian,	60
Old Ireland — God Bless Her!	63
Mont Blanc,	64
The Earth,	65
Psappha,	66
Die Deutscher's Faderland,	68
The Sea,	69
Corea, or Chosen,	70
Corea, — In Brief,	71
On Getting Drunk — In Parenthesis,	73
Exclusive Chosen,	75
The Funghwang, the Dragon, and the Feng-Shui,	75
The Mediterranean,	81
La Belle France,	82
The Plain of Troy,	83
Valhalla,	85
The Crystal Palace of the Czar,	89
The Title of the Czar,	90
A Captive in Sweden,	91
The Alhamra,	93
The German Empire,	93
In the Catacombs of Palermo,	94
The Crusades in Song,	99
The Camel Driver at Carthage,	105
John Chinaman,	107
In Norway,	110
London,	110
The Cannibal Islands,	111

GREECE,	113
VANDAL AND ANDALUSIA,	113
A PRINCESS OF THE ORIENT,	114
THE EASTERN HEMISPHERE,	116
THE WANDERING JEW,	117
THE GERMAN,	118
THE RIDDLE OF THE SPHINX,	119
MILITARY GERMANY,	120
DOWN THE ANDES IN A HAND-CAR,	121
HUMOR IN HOLLAND,	132
THE WORLD,	133
AT WATERLOO,	134
CHINA,	135
THE HUN,	135
THE GOTH AND THE HUN,	136
IN THE CITY OF MEXICO,	137
CAMOENS,	139
AT ILIUM,	140
AT CYPRUS,	140
ON THE PACIFIC,	141
JAPAN AND THE JAPANESE,	143
TUNISIA,	144
FUJIYAMA,	145
AT RHODES,	146
PORTUGAL,	146
WHAT IS POESY?	147
ATHENS,	147
IN A SILVER SHAFT OF NEVADA,	148
MOUNT ÆTNA,	149
COAL IN SITU,	149
THE TIDES,	150
SEA SICKNESS,	150
THE SEA,	150
THE GOLDEN CHERSONESUS,	151
BOUJIE,	154
PHILIPPEVILLE,	154
HOME ON THE HIMÁLAYAS,	155
CARTHAGE,	157

The Swedes,	157
Off the Coast of Abyssinia,	157
The Porpoise, or Dolphin,	158
The Sphinx,	158
The Ice-berg,	158
The Flying-fish,	158
Arabia,	158
The Taj Mahál,	159
Heliopolis,	166
The Red Sea,	166
Ivan Ivanovitch,	166
The Clepsydra,	166
A Storm at Sea,	167
Asia,	175
The Suez Canal,	175
The Hell of Hálemáumau,	176
The 180th Degree of Longitude,	190
The Ship's Lanterns,	190
The Terraces of Rotomáhana,	191
Australia: A Charcoal-Sketch,	221
At Beirut,	260
The German War-god,	260
New Jersey,	260
The Column and the Arch,	260
In Nagasaki,	260
The Brave, Old Burg of Greene,	261
At Gettysburg,	270

LIKE FERN-LEAVES FOUND IN SHALE.

The Atlantosaurus,	277
The Glacial Epoch,	279
The Savage Mother and the Cave Bear,	282
Atlantis,	286
Plot and Counterplot in the Palace of Palenque,	292

FREYDISA,	307
THE WITCH TRAGEDY OF SALEM,	322

SAGE, RUE, AND THYME.

THE LEGEND OF THE WEEPING WILLOW,	331
THE LOVE-LORN LADY'S LAMENT,	336
THE REBUKE OF THE SAGE,	337
THE TWO TOWERS,	338
THE JEWELS I PRIZE,	352
MAID OF MAHONING,	353
THE DEMON LOVER,	354
LOVE'S HOLY GRACE,	356
THE WITCH OF WESTMORELAND,	357
OH, I WOULD LOVE YOU ALWAY,	359
A LETTER TO A LADY,	360
THE VOICE OF THE ANVIL,	362
FATE,	363
AN EPIGRAM,	364
A POËT,	364
A TOAST TO WOMAN,	364
A REASON IN RHYME,	364
DESPAIR,	364
HER CHARACTER,	365
INDECISION,	365
TO ———,	365
TO A SILKWORM,	366
TO ———,	366
LOVE'S RULE OF THREE,	366
THE EYE AND THE IMAGINATION,	367
KATY-DID,	367
ASTRONOMICAL,	367
A FOURTH OF JULY ALTERNATIVE,	367
THE HEART ENTOMBED,	368
ON KISSING,	368

A Lover's Lament,	368
On a Ringing Bell,	369
A Lover's Prayer,	369
Loving and Longing,	369
On an Engagement Ring,	370
Literary Hermit Crabs,	370
A Simile,	370
Graveyard Grotesques,	371
The Last Kiss of Love,	372
To You, Man,	373
Jam Satis,	373
Once, and Once Only,	374
Niagara,	375
Chautauqua,	376
The Fiddler of Time,	390
The Last Man,	397
The Meaning of the Monument,	401

THE RIME OF A RAMBLER TWICE AROUND THE WORLD.

And therein of the strange, the wonderful,
And the sublime of every sea and land,
It was my good or evil hap to make
A part of my existence evermore:
A myriad of match-like memories,
Betimes to kindle feelings of delight,
Inflame the passions of my bosom, and
Illume the mystic midnight of my mind,
Now, with weird shimmering auroral dreams,
Anon, with flashing incandescent thoughts —
The lightning-scissored silhouettes of God
Within the storm-rack of the intellect. —
AT GETTYSBURG, p. 270.

VALE, VALHALLA!

It is the dawning of a day of June —
The twentieth — the rounding of the Summer
Into perfection; as the turning of
A score of years fills the organic measure
Of maidenhood, and, on the earth, is seen
The ultimatum of existence in
A red-lipped, round-limbed, mother-musing woman;
Her grey eyes glancing with departing fancies,
And gleaming with the facts forthcoming in
The future, e'en as now the eastern sky
Is spangled with the waning stars of night,
And radiant with the flashing beams of day;
Her white neck flushed with crimson, as
The floating cloud above the dim horizon;
And the world of humanities asleep
Beneath the fair folds of her bosom, as
The village in the vale, and all that it
Contains of vice and virtue, slumbering,
Beneath the soft white blanket of the fog, —
I look upon, ere my departure, from
My gabled homestead on the height, (yclept,
When heaven was nearer earth than now,)
    VALHALLA.

THE RIME OF A RAMBLER TWICE AROUND THE WORLD.

A FINLAND FANTASY.

When the world glows in the sunshine,
And all things appear objective,
Having size, and shape, and color,
Sight to man is all-sufficient.
      But when darkness dims the object,
      And the eyes of man are useless,
      Lo! within the mystic mirror
      Of organic cerebration,
Reäppears the world of sunshine
Shimm'ring in uncertain semblance,—
Till, evolving shape and likeness,
Forming the Imagination.

When the various vocations,
In the struggle for existence,
Scatter mankind in the sunshine,
Silence reigns among the severed.
    But at eve, when men and women
    Gather in the family circle,—
    Hark! the tongue hath found a function,
    And imagination language!
Then it is the father, mother,
Sister, brother, and the stranger,
Tell their haps to one another,
And the Story is invented.

When the summer and the sunshine
Have departed from the heavens,
And the winter and the darkness
Have enclosed the world within doors;
    When the oft-repeated story
    Falls unheeded into dull ears,
    And the sound of words outspoken
    Sinks into a senseless humming;
Then it is the story-teller,
Gifted with a voice melodious,
Sings an old tale in a new tone,
And invents the art of Music.

Then it is the feigning fancy
Is evolved to the creative,
In the rapt ecstatic vision
Of the soul-impassioned singer;
    Then it is the household story
    Is extended and expanded
    Into strange and unknown regions—
    Into past and future being;
Then it is the words are sounded
With recurrent intonation—
With a musical commingling,
And the Poet is created!

Happy Finland, in the far north,
Where the winter and the darkness,
Sinking and suspending eyesight,
Nurture the imagination;
  Where the callings of the people,
  Scatt'ring them o'er land and ocean,
  Multiply the story-tellers
  When they gather in the homesteads;
Where, in many a hall and hovel,
Hark! the wire-strung harp[1] resounding
In accord with sweetest voices
Molding Finland into music!

Happy, happy Suomema![2]
Ringing with the harp and voices
Of a thousand Runolainen[3]
Singing o'er the Kalevala —
  Singing o'er the people's love-songs,
  Singing o'er the people's hate-songs,
  Singing o'er the people's war-songs,
  Singing o'er the people's peace-songs,—
Singing o'er the wondrous medley
Wrought by Finland's peasant poets —
Gathered in a nation's epic,—
Gathered in the Kalevala![4]

---

[1] The favorite musical instrument of the Finns, the *Cantele*, is a kind of harp with five wire strings.

[2] Suomema, the Finnish name of Finland, signifying, Reion of Lakes.

[3] Runolainen, song-men, minstrels.

[4] The Kalevala was compiled and published in Helsingfors in 1835, by Elias Lönnrot, then a practicing physician, afterward professor of Finnish literature in the University of Helsingfors.

THE LAND OF AULD LANG SYNE.[1]

Loquitur — An old Scotch soldier, at Darjiling, a Sanitarium on one of the Indian foot-hills of the Himálayas.

Gude faith, my lads, I wadna gie a bawbee for a sang
That wadna tak' me ower the sea, whaur I may niver gang,
And gie me back the bluid o' youth, the heart, and hopefu' min',
Amid the wild enchantments o' the Land of Auld Lang Syne!

When a' the warl before me lay a straight and open road,
And I could rin and trip and dance, beneath a stark mon's load;
Fame's jeweled cross — the dewy cress was brighter i' the ditch,
And wi' a haggis i' the pat, I was aboon the rich!

When light o' foot and lang o' limb, amang the mountain rocks,
I boundit wi' the antlered stag, and skelpit wi' the fox;
Or, perched upon Ben Lomond's height, I liltit lang and loud,
To cheer the upward soarin' lark, beneath me i' the cloud!

When strang o' heart and fu' o' faith, wi' Jeanie by my side
I warkit frae the dawn till dusk, wi' pleasure and wi' pride;
I was a king and she a queen, aboon our happy hearth,
Until — the Lord forgie my tears! — Heaven went wi' her frae earth!

Hout, mon! this welt across my brow — it is a sabre
    scar;
And this sma' stump — I tint my leg i' the Crimean
    war;
But thae were wounds o' little weight that couldna
    sink within;
The sairest cuts and stabs are thae that niver break the
    skin!

Noo, gie me, lads, a cantic sang o' Scotland's rugged
    charms,
And let me close my bluidshot een, and sink in Jeanie's
    arms;
And what I hae o' this warl's gear that I can title
    mine,
I'll share wi' ye as brithers i' the Land of Auld Lang
    Syne!

---

[1] Recited on the anniversary of the birth of Robert Burns, at a commemorative festival in Pittsburgh, in 1884, and printed first the following morning in the Pittsburgh *Dispatch*, and other journals.

THE COGNIZANCE OF EUROPE.

The fairest of the women of the world
Should be the type and cognizance of Europe —
The only woman in the wide, wide world,
Compounded of the precious gems and metals:
Her skin, the white and lustrous pearl incarnate;
Her eyes, two sapphires in a living casket;
Her hair, the finest, fairest gold e'er spun;
Her heart, a thrilling, throbbing koh-in-oor!

THE CITY OF THE ROYAL PALM.[1]
(RIO DE JANEIRO.)

Canst fashion and then fix within thy mind
That thought of midnight in the form of fish
Evolved within the subterranean stream
Which never ray of light impinged, save that
Of the explorer's wick, revealing to
His wond'ring gaze, the sightless, eyeless thing?
Thou canst. Then close thine eyes, and, for the nonce,
Be to the sun-lit world as blind and blank;
That in the soul-lit world thou may'st discern
With keenest vision, and, as I descant,
Survey the City of the Royal Palm.

Behold an overarching sky, as blue
And clear and bright, as ever woman's eye
Appear'd to bending lover, prying through
The lace and lattice of a long-curv'd lash.

Behold, beneath this overarching sky,
A chaos of granitic mountains — cragg'd,
Storm-stained and weather-worn, fantastic,— like
An ocean-billow of enormous size,
Uprising o'er a reef, fix'd in mid-sky.

Amid this chaos of granitic mounts,
An ocean-inlet, scallop'd with a score
Of bays, and studded with a hundred isles;
An inlet so serene, that mirroring
The sky above, it seems to be in prayer —
The ocean in communion with high heaven.

Upon the shore of this communing sea,
An aggregation of the art of man,

Yclept a city, finite as a whole,
But infinite in its dissevered parts;
A city spreading far, and fair as far,
O'er hill and dale and mountain gulch and crag,
And housing half a million of mankind;
A city, in the belt of Capricorn
Around the world, the golden, jewel'd clasp.

Above the city's aggregated art,
Alone, in pairs, in groves, and endless rows,
A peerless palm in grandeur and in grace,
Uplifting, in its overarching fronds,
A royal crown, of God's own handiwork,
Unto itself and all that it o'ershadows —
The city spreading far, and fair as far,
Upon the shore of the communing sea,
Amid the chaos of granitic mounts,
Beneath the sky of love-lit blue-eyed glances,
The City of the Royal Palm!

Now, ope
Thine eyes; and when thou hearest merchants prate
Of Rio as a mart — a city in
A coffee-sack, — thou wilt review in prose
The self-same city thou hast seen in song.

---

[1] Printed first in the *Revue Commerciale, Financière et Maritime*, Rio de Janeiro, Brazil, 4th September, 1884; afterward as the initial poem in a small volume, entitled "THE CITY OF THE ROYAL PALM, AND OTHER POEMS," published in Rio de Janeiro, and dedicated to the Emperor, DOM PEDRO II.

[2] The Royal Palm, (*Oreodoxia regia*,) is first among the palmaceæ, in size, symmetry, and stateliness. It attains the perfection of its development in the celebrated Botanical Gardens of Rio de Janeiro. Here, planted in rows on each side of the principal avenues, the great symmetric files constitute one of the vegetable glories of the globe.

WILLIAM CULLEN BRYANT.

A meagre man of flesh and blood;
And yet, God wot, the while he stood,
In pensive and poetic mood,
   With age bowed down,
His head o'ertopped St. Patrick's Rood,
   Above the town.

Aye, rose to such a wondrous height,
That in the day or in the night,
He looked in the eternal light
   Above the clouds,
And saw with the supernal sight
   Ascribed to gods.

Now, glancing at the meadow star,
Anon, the globe that gleams afar,
Till, borne from the particular
   Unto the whole,
He saw and sang how all things are
   In subtile soul.

Good faith, his white-haired, wrinkled pate,
In phrenologic size and weight,
Was barely half again as great
   As mustard-pot,
Yet well did it accommodate
   A world of thought!

Whate'er, in fine and fact, the man,
As undertakers mortals span,
He was, as bards their forebears scan,
   A mental giant,
And worthily cleped among his clan,
   The Mighty Bryant!

I marvel, hence, New Yorkers fall
Before the Golden Calf of Wall,
The Brooklyn Bridge, the Gift of Gaul,
   The Obelisk,
The Giver of the Grandest Ball,
    The Bust of Fiske —

And never raise their heads to view
Above all these, within the blue
Of all that's good and all that's true,
   And death-defiant,
The hoary head of one they knew —
    The Mighty Bryant!

A DUTCH FOG-SIGNAL.

It is an old Dutch skipper,
 About as broad as long,
Sits in his cosy cabin,
 And sings his sailor's song,
And smokes his monstrous meerschaum,
 And drinks his can of grog,
Without a thought of danger
 In the increasing fog.

The while, the skipper's grandson,
 About as long as broad,
Sits at the oaken table
 And fills himself with cod;
Until he can't distinguish
 In the increasing gloom
A solitary object
 Within the little room.

D

Then up and speaks the grandson,
 To questioning inclin'd,—
The very world a wherefore
 To his enquiring mind,—
"Please tell me, Grandpa Skipper,
 How you can drink your grog
In absolute indiff'rence
 To danger in this fog?

"We are among a thousand
 Ships, brigantines, and barks,
Sloops, schooners, yacts, and steamers,
 Brigs, frigates, smacks, and arks,—
And yet you sit here smoking,
 When every mariner
Should be upon the look-out—
 Especially Mein Herr!"

Then up and speaks the skipper—
 "Come, sit upon my knee,
And I will tell you plainly
 The truth as it may be,
How I can smoke my meerschaum,
 And drink my can of grog,
In 'spite of all the dangers
 Of collision in a fog.

"Once, on a time, a wise man
 Discovered, with surprise,
That, like a raw potato,
 A skipper may have eyes;
And, forthwith, he invented,
 With colors red and green,
A special code of signals
 That might, perhaps, be seen!

"But alas! for his invention,
    Based on the sense of sight,
A fog was found to darken
    The brightest kind of light;
And many gallant vessels
    Went down into the deep,
Because, with their own eyelids,
    The eyes are closed in sleep!

" 'Twas then another wise man
    Discovered, it appears,
That, like an Indian corn-stalk,
    A skipper may have ears;
And, forthwith, he invented —
    As it to him occurred —
Another code of signals
    That might, perhaps, be heard!

" But alas! for his invention,
    Based on the sense of sound,
Collisions still were frequent,
    And may men were drowned;
The breakers bombed and bellowed
    Above the loudest bells,
And how the fog-horns fizzled,
    The City of Brussels tells!

"At last, a wondrous wise man
    Discovered, in a dose,
That, like a blacksmith's bellows,
    A skipper has a nose;
And, forthwith, he invented —
    And since, secure has felt —
A special code of signals
    That always can be smelt!

"Upon the vessel's mast-head,
    Exposed to every breeze,
He lashed with a good rope-yarn
    An old Limburger cheese!
And though, as thick as smearcase,
    The gathering fogs were blown,
The vessel by its savor
    For twenty leagues was known!

"And never, from that moment,
    A ship, the signal owns,
Has met with a collision
    And gone to Davy Jones;
For though both ears be plugged up,
    And both eyes closed in sleep,
The nose is always open
    To odors on the deep!"

"Who was the wondrous wise man
    This signal did devise?"
Th' interrogating grandson
    Enquires, with mouth and eyes;
"He is the good old skipper,
    Upon the stormy sea,
Commands the Flying Dutchman,
    With his grandson on his knee!

"Now, climb into thy hammock,
    Thou apple of my eye,
And drift away to dreamland,
    While I am sitting by;
And fear not, while thou'rt sleeping,
    And I am drinking grog,
The cheese upon the mast-head
    Will save us in the fog!"

THE NIBELUNGENLIED.

Hast read it?—Well, it seems to me, that, be it thing
 or thought,
Evolved into existence, or, in homely phrase, begot,
There is an age to one and all, within a wondrous
 womb,
In which a thousand monstrous shapes and shadows
 they assume.

Thus, in the womb of time and space, before the bliss-
 ful birth
Of the big, round, and dimpled babe, the planetary
 earth,
What meteoric maelstroms in the ether-ocean swirled!
What comets came and went in flame! what monsters
 filled the world!

Thus, in the womb of bird and beast, ere the organic
 worm
Through an infinity of shapes assumed the human
 form,
What whale-like lizards in the sea! what dragons in
 the air!
What crocodiles upon the land! what monsters every-
 where!

Thus, in the womb of fantasy, before the happy
 thought
Into the formal figure or similitude is wrought,
What monstrous and fantastic shapes into our vision
 creep!
What nightmares come and go betimes within our trou-
 bled sleep!

So, in the womb of German song, ere Goethe could create
The forms of Faust and Marguerite and forge their fearful fate,
The monstrous and misshapen must the beautiful precede
In the poetic nightmares of the Nibelungenlied.

THE BALTIC.

The civilizer of the north of Europe;
The avenue of interchange and commerce;
The impetus to daring enterprise;
The motive to adventure and the means;
The circumstance that made mild men bold sailors,
And, in the course of time, made sailors sov'reigns!

ITALY.

The Land of Beauty — color, form, proportion —
In fire and water, earth and air, combined:
The brightest, bluest skies; the fairest vales;
The loveliest of seas and waterfalls;
And mountains ranging from the peak of ice
Through every form unto the dome of fire!
And as in Nature so in Art: A Land
Of Beauty, the most rare and rapturous,
In architecture, sculpture, painting, and
The art of arts that weaves the wand'ring wind
Into the filmiest of fictile fabrics,
And yet the most enduring of man's works,—
The airy, soul-wrought art of Poesy!

A DRINKING-BOUT IN DENMARK.

Among the rare and interesting works of art and curiosities preserved in the Rosenborg Palace, at Copenhagen, the late Professor Carl Andersen, in an English translation of his Catalogue of "The Chronological Collection of the Kings of Denmark," refers to the glass goblet, which suggested the following ballad, in the following words: — " A very large glass goblet, (15 inches in height and 5 inches in diameter,) from which Frederik II., once, in the year 1568, drank with many princes and noblemen, to see who could drink the most, of which the names and marks of the king and his fellow-champions, scratched upon the glass, are a witness."— p. 12.

Of other drinking-cups in the collection, Mr. Andersen further remarks: — "Three goblets, of which the glass one with silver cover, on which the monogram of Christian IV. is engraved, was used, according to tradition, as his favorite drinking-vessel. Upon its sides the arms of the Danish provinces are cut. On the other two, which are silver (one gilded), the king's monogram appears; the ungilt silver one bears also an inscription denoting that the cup was made from money, which, in the year 1600, the king had won from four courtiers in a mutual bet, which of them first should become intoxicated between the 6th of February and Easter in the preceding year."— p. 19.

"A champagne glass 20 inches high with the following verse engraved upon it:

"'Wer mit Bacchus kompt ins Spiel,
Seh sich für und trau nicht viel,
Nimpt er dir dein Kopff nur ein,
So seind die Füsze nimmer dein.'"— p. 57.

It was the merry tide of Yule,
    A thousand years ago,
Where the Baltic roars on Danish shores
    When the winds of winter blow.

The king, among a score of lords
    Of high and low degree,
Sate at the board with wine well stored,
    In mirth and revelry.

Aha! oho! in the world without,
    The midnight sky may scowl,
And the blustering blasts from Norwegian wastes
    Like a thousand wolves may howl!

In the world within the castle's walls,
    A fire glows on the hearth,
And nothing is heard but the joyous word,
    And the song and laughter of mirth!

And oho! aha! in the world without,
    The drifting snow may chill,
And the ice may cut into many a hut
    With a sword's keen edge and kill!

In the world within the castle's walls,
    The warm wine gladly glows;
And, to many a toast and braggart boast,
    The warm wine freely flows.

Until upspake the heated king,
    "Go, fetch me the giant's bowl —
The Venetian vase of the clearest glass,
    The daring viking stole.

"And he, about this Yule-tide board,
    That, at a single draught,
The least can show in the bottom below,
    When thus he shall have quaffed —

"He shall be king of the Danes to-night,
    And sit at the table-head,
And wear a closed crown[1] till he topple down
    Among the drunken dead!"

The bowl was brought; and as each lord drank,
    With the diamond set in his ring,
The king, as the clerk, made a well-known mark,
    Signifying, Attest, the King.

A DRINKING-BOUT IN DENMARK.

And, as with varying results,
    The bowl was filled and drained,
And scratched by the king with his diamond ring,
    The contest in spirit gained.

Until, at length, a grizzled lord
    Of monstrous make and mien,
Reduced the score an inch or more
    Below the lowest seen!

And with a sudden burst of cheers
    That made the castle ring,
The lords, one and all, in the reeling hall,
    Began to hail him king!

But hold — there sate at the king's right hand,
    A lord as long and lank,
As if he had grown in skin and bone
    Into an enormous shank.

The lank lord took the bowl in his hands,
    And drank until, behold!
He can lay it down and take up the crown,
    As the king himself hath told!

Nay, not too fast — the king himself
    Has yet to leave his score
On the diamond-cut vase of the clearest glass,
    Ere the drinking-bout be o'er!

At last, the king took up the cup,
    Filled sparkling to the brim,
That all might see no favor should be
    Accorded unto him.

And, holding it firmly to his lips,
    He drank until the vase,
Turning up as he quaffed an enormous draught,
    Stood empty on his face!

Hurrah! hurrah! long live the king!
    Burst from the lips of all,
As the empty vase on the royal face,
    Was revealed in the glowing hall!

Aye, aye, hurrah! hip, hip, hurrah!
    Long live the king! the king!
And now once more, until with the roar
    The Danish realm shall ring!

But Christ! behold! the golden crown
    Has fallen from the king's head,
And the empty vase on his upturned face,
    Is on the face of the dead!

It was a thousand years ago,
    The merry tide of Yule,
But alas! the morrow was fraught with sorrow,
    And Denmark was in dool!

---

[1] In Denmark, when the succession of the crown was limited to a particular family, the fact was symbolized by drawing together the circle of points, and thereby closing an otherwise open crown, or one open to the competition of all. The event occurred in Danish history in 1660.

THE IRISH CHANNEL.

The ocean is whatever fancy wills:
A lonely, love-lorn lady, the Atlantic,
And this—the Irish Channel—a fair finger
Of an extended hand selecting gems:
Laying aside the Emerald of Erin
As the most pleasing to her downcast eyes—
A sacred souvenir, methinks, to give
A surcease to her sorrow—in the sigh—
The breath I feel upon my cheek, so close,
I turn to clasp the lady in my arms!

SCOTLAND.

A crag of granite rising from the sea;
Upon this crag a human habitation —
The home of Burns, the Poet of the Heart;
Upon the roof-tree of this humble cottage,
An airy perch above the earth, in cloudland —
In sight of castles, tents, and tournaments;
In sound of song and dance and minstrelsy;
In scent of steaming roasts of boar and ven'son;
In taste of wines of rich and rarest flavor;
In touch of heroes' hands and ladies' lips —
The realm of Scott, the Wizard of the North!

BELGIUM — THE GARDEN OF EUROPE.

Manured as it has been with human blood
For centuries, it is no marvel now
Abundance is synonymous with Belgium.

NORWAY.

Norway! where the tidal currents
Rushing, in their alternation,
Through an inter-islet channel,
Form a fierce engulfing whirlpool:
      Sweeping over sunken bowlders,
      Swirling in concentric circles,
      Seething, like a witch's cauldron,
      Foaming, like a maddened monster:
Tossing ships, like empty cockles,
Whirling whales, in giddy waltzes, —
In a roaring, raging passion,
Overwhelming all within it.

Aye, a mighty ocean-eddy,
Which, in the imagination
Of the terrified beholders,
Has evolved into another —
    An imaginary Maelström
    Of the world of waters swirling
    In an all-involving vortex
    Of delirious destruction!
By the side of which the circles
Of the classical Charybdis
Are but rings of bubbles bursting
In a summer-shrinking millpond!

Norway! where the whale, uprising
From the black depths of the ocean,
Blows into the air the water
Lying on its lidded nostril;
    And the waterspout, appearing,—
    To the whaler, in his vessel
    Laden deep with bone and blubber,
    Looking o'er the troubled waters,—
Like the lifting of the ocean
From above the lidded nostril
Of a greater whale than any
Ever struck by daring seaman.

Aye, a mighty whale-like monster,
Which, in the imagination
Of the fireside story-tellers,
Has evolved into the Kraken:
    Rising, like a huge volcano,
    From the billows of the ocean,
    And upheaving seas of water
    From a mighty belching crater!
When compared with the low island
Sindbad found to be a monster,
Not alone in bulk the greater,
But in grim and graphic grandeur![1]

Norway! where the mighty cuttle,
Rising from the lace-like spind-drift,
And, above the vessel's rigging,
Rearing tentacles, like serpents:
  Frighting him upon the masthead,
  Driving from his wheel the helmsman,
  And, perhaps, with might resistless,
  Seizing an astounded sailor:
Lifting him above the gunwale,
Strangling him in its enfoldings,
Sinking with him in the ocean,
And devouring him in secret.

Aye, a monster of the ocean,
Which, in the imagination,
Has commingled and united
With the mighty Midgard Serpent:
  An ideal serpent-circle
  Winding round and round the whole world,
  Symbolizing universal
  And eternal animation!
In the sight of which, the serpents
Twining round the writhing bodies
Of Laöcoön and children,
Are but pin-hooked squirming earthworms!

Norway! where the great winged eagle,—
Fearless with the pangs of hunger
Gnawing in herself and eaglets,—
Swooping down upon a lambkin,
  Fans the hot face of the shepherd,
  Battl'ing to protect the youngling,—
  Striking with the first-found weapon,
  Shouting till the wilds reëcho;
Till the great bird, in her talons,
Lifting o'er his head the lambkin,
Bears it to her lofty eyric
To devour it with her children.

Aye, a great winged fanning eagle,
Which, in the imagination
Of the mythopœic shepherds,
Has evolved into Hræsvelgur —
    Has evolved into the wind-god,
    In the guise of a great eagle,
    Sitting, on a mighty mountain,
    Far away in the wild northland:
Swooping from his lofty eyrie,
And, beneath his wide-spread pinions,
As they sweep and flap and flutter,
Fanning into life the tempests!

Norway! where the wolf of winter,
Gaunt and meagre as a spectre,
Stealing from its rocky fastness,
Ravages the frozen region:
    Running down the harnessed reindeer,
    Wearing out the shaggy horses,
    Slaughtering defenceless cattle,
    Butchering unguarded sheepfolds,—
Yea, attacking men and women
On the outskirts of the village,—
A remorseless and resistless
Monster of untold destruction.

Aye, a monster of destruction,
Which, in the imagination
Of the ever-watchful peasants,
Has developed into Fenrir:
    Of all monstrous wolves, the largest,
    Of all largest wolves, the fiercest,
    Of all fiercest wolves, the fellest,
    Monster of untold destruction!
In the universal ruin,
Prophesied by sage and singer,
Lapping up the mighty ocean
And devouring earth and heaven!

NORWAY.

Norway! wonderland of nature!
Where the earth and sky and ocean
Form, in their incessant jarring,
An environment of warfare:
  Reäppearing in the mental
  Mirror of the rugged people,
  As a wild and wondrous region
  Filled with mighty forms and monstrous:
Grim, primæval winter giants,
Grim, primæval summer war-gods,
In an all-involving struggle
For the boundless world's dominion!

Chief, among the monstrous giants,
Ymir, the primæval chaos,
Slain in battle by the war-gods,
And cut up to form the whole world:
  Of his flesh was made the mainland;
  Of his blood was made the ocean;
  Of his bones were made the mountains;
  Of his hair were made the forests;
Of his skull were made the heavens;
Of his brain, the clouds of vapor,—
Fitting image of the vague thoughts
Forming in a mind chaotic!

Chief among the mighty war-gods,
Thor, the lightning and the thunder
Of the animating summer,
Warring with the hosts of winter:
  Wielding only a huge hammer,
  In his conflicts with the giants!
  See it speeding through the storm-rack,
  Like a sun hurled through the heavens!
Hear it crashing through the brainbox
Of a fierce opposing giant!
And the world reverberating
With the heavy monster's falling!

Of the cosmical conceptions
Of the olden myth-creators,—
Comprehending naught in nature,
Till made concrete and objective,—
    This of Thor and his huge hammer
    Crashing through the skulls of giants
    In the lightning and the thunder,
    Is the grandest and sublimest!
Aye, of all the myth-creations
Of mankind through untold ages,
This, the grandest and sublimest,
Thor, the Thunderer of Norway![2]

---

[1] Commonly, the Kraken is regarded as an evolution of the Octopus. The object in nature, however, which is mirrored in the imagination as this ideal monster, is undoubtedly the whale supplemented by the waterspout, as set forth in the poem.

[2] In Norway, Thor was first among the gods; in Sweden, Odin.

FINLAND.

Heigho! the Finland of my fancy was
An ermine cloak upon the shoulders of
The shiv'ring, shudd'ring form of Northern Europe;
But this — it is a cape of dark green velvet,
Bespangled with a myriad of gems —
The little isles along the Baltic border.

FRANCE.

Rome's rival, France, as long as she includes
The Melos Venus and Mont Blanc within
The confines of her kingdom and possession;
Two types of the sublime and beautiful
Sufficient to redeem her from a world
Of dissipation, wickedness, and vice.

WOMAN, WINE, AND SONG.

„Wer nicht liebt Wein, Weib, und Gesang,
Der bleibt ein Narr sein Lebe=lang."—
Attributed to Martin Luther.

Come, fill to the brim the crystal cup with ruddy
    sparkling wine!
And let it flow until I feel its soul infused in mine—
Until, from the earthy of earth absolved, I live from
    my body apart,
A spirit of Heaven enshrined within a happy, happy
    heart!

Come, sit thee down, thou beauteous lass, and drain
    the cup with me,
And all that man may be to maid that will I be to
    thee;
Come, come, thou supplemental self, without whom I
    am naught,
But with whom I am all the world by man and wo-
    man wrought!

And while we sit and sip, fair maid, in happy uni-
    son—
In quivering throb and breathless thrill indissolubly
    one—
In the expression of our souls, loud let our voices rise
And mingle in melodious song, in the enraptured
    skies!

Then let the snows of winter fall, and midnight tempests roar,
And Wretchedness and Want in tears knock trembling at the door,
I shall be blest, and pray to God the moments to prolong —
There is no woe within the world of woman, wine, and song!

ALGERIA.

Go where the trav'ler will, by land or sea,
The world is void of all that thrills the heart,
And fills the fancy with delightful visions,
Unless he, like another Atlas, bears
A world of comprehension on his shoulders.

The eye sees only what it brings with it
The power to see, the wise Carlyle hath said:
A simple saw of universal scope.

So, stranger, ere thou sayest thou hast seen
Naught in Argier,[1] that, many a time and oft,
Thou hast beheld elsewhere — as fair a land,
As bright a sky, and Arabs just as brown,
And negroes just as black, and Jews as rich, —
Look once more from this ancient Moorish tower
Upon the panorama of the Tell.[2]

Nay, shut thine eyes — the power they bring to see
Is strongest when the lids are closed. Now, look.

Here, Masinissa lived and died of old,
A century of war incorporate!
As Ney to Bonaparte, Sherman to Grant,

So he to Scipio in the o'erthrow
Of Hannibal and the destruction of
The rival of imperial Rome, dread Carthage!
In yonder cloud of dust, methinks, I see
The warrior, at full four score and ten,
Upon his fiery steed, heading the charge
Of his renowned Numidian cavalry
Like an organic thunderbolt against
The cohorts of the Carthaginians!
And, in the sighing of the breeze, as well,
I hear the sobbing exhalations of
His four and fifty sons, about his bed,
When he gave up the ghost, at ninety-seven!
A mighty man, nor dwarfed, when placed beside
The giants Scipio and Hannibal!

Here, also, Génseric, the Vandal, came,
As dread a scourge within the Roman world
As his great compeer, Attila, the Hun!
Aye, here, this Bismarck of the olden time
From a chaotic world, amassed a might
To move resistless o'er the Midland Sea
And sack the very citadel of Rome!
Then was the world turned topsy-turvy, when
The white-skinned, blue-eyed, and red-bearded
    Norman
Came from the sunny regions of the South —
The land primæval of the sable Negro!
But though the earth hath many strange convul-
    sions,
The strangest of them are among mankind,
As witness the succession on this plain.

Here, also, Belisarius, the great,
The Glory of the Romans, came, to check
The triumph of the Vandals and regain
The world for the imperial Justinian;
And get, as his reward (if not, in fact,

At least, in fiction, for all time,) the chains
Of slavery, the sightless orbs of crime,
And an unheeded death in want and woe;
His name henceforth, howe'er, a synonym
Of the ingratitude of governments.
Immortal prototype of Barneveldt,
St. Clair, and many thousands more, accept,
I pray thee, as an earnest of the heart
That throbs for thee, this obolus of song!
The fame, thy ingrate master and the world
Denied thee in the flesh, shall not be wanting
As long as the great globe of history
Revolves in time around the hub of Rome.

Here, also, came Abdulla[3] and his horde
Of Arabs, like a whirlwind of the desert,
Destroying everything within its path;
And scarcely had the visitation passed,
When, like a countless swarm of locusts, came
Another host of Arabs to possess
The land and give it the impress of Asia.
Until, among them, lo! brave Tarik rose,
And gathering around him on this plain
An army of resistless might, set out,
And crossed the straits[4] that bear his name to-day,
And, sweeping o'er the beauteous land of Spain,
Above the Cross of Christ, the Crescent of
Muhammad reared, to gleam for centuries!—
Hast ever sighed within the halls of the
Alhamra?[5] Yea; know then that the great tide
That cast that paper-nautilus upon
The spur of the Sierras, for the world
To wonder at for ages, gathered here,
Within the scope of vision from this tower.

Here, also, Barbarossa[6] came, the first
Of the long line of pirate kings, to make
The mention of Argier throughout the world

A shudder to the boldest Christian heart!
Oh, for the word, the comprehensive word,
To compass in its airy metes and bounds
The world of woe these walls have witnessed!
    Hell! —
Nay, Hell is weak; for in the suffering
Of a damned soul, atoning for its sin,
There is a sense of justice that absolves
The comprehension from regarding it
An ultimate of agony and woe.
No other word, methinks, can half so well
Express the suffering upon this soil
As the accursed dissyllable Argier!
This bright blue sky o'erhead, oh, can it be
It arched so like a sapphire cup, o'erturned
By God above the rarest of his works,
The while it echoed with the sighs and groans
Of untold myriads of Christian slaves!"

Among the number, see the gifted man,
Whom to have borne and bred, a continent
May justly boast, Cervantes Saävadra,
The auther of —— Go, find the boy above
The age of twelve that knows not Don Quixóte,
And I will show you Sancho Panza's ass! —
What a resilient spirit to rebound
From the abyss of untold misery
Into the clouds, reëchoing henceforth
In thunder the explosions of his laughter!
And yet, methinks, without his trials here,
In the heart-breaking rack of slavery,
The world had never heard the joyful shout
That burst from his expanding chest, a freeman!

And in another group of slaves, behold,
The brave astronomer, who, to advance
The knowledge of the stars among mankind,
Feared not to put himself within the power

Of the accursed sea-rovers,— Arago.
Alas! the fate of many a noble soul,
Casting about to aid his fellow-man,
His eyes fixed on the gleaming globes of heaven,
And seeing not the pit-fall at his feet,
And the impatient barb within to pierce
His heart, as if he were a beast of prey.

Here, also, in the circle of our vision,
The Black Hawk of the Arabs, Abd-el-Kader,
Commanded, in the majesty of man
Involved within the purple of his blood,
The admiration of a startled world!
A warrior, as fierce and terrible
As ever caught the lightning in his grasp
And hurled it hissing through a foeman's heart!
A statesman, comprehensive, wise, and pure;
A priest, ennobling in his holiness
The stream of blood that coursed within his veins,
Although it issued from the heart of him
Whom untold millions symbolize within
The silver segment of the sun-lit moon,
Muhammad, the Apostle of the world
That turns about the Black-Stone[8] of the Kaaba!

O wondrous panorama of Argier!
Phœnicians, Romans, Vandals, Byzantines,
Arabians, and Turks, and now the French,
Appearing as successive conquerors;
Strutting awhile in triumph o'er the ruins
Of their enslaved or slaughtered predecessors,
And then o'erthrown and butchered in their turn!
Well may the aspect of the populace,
Compounding in its intermingling floods
The blood of Europe, Africa, and Asia,
Disport the mottled hues of Joseph's coat,
And shift, in countless combinations, like
The colored beads of a kaleidoscope:

I marvel at the masses and the men
I see, in fact and fancy, from this tower.

---

¹ Argier, an archaic form of Algeria, used by Shakespeare, *The Tempest*, i., 2, and other writers of his day.

² The Tell of Algeria is a strip of undulating cultivated land extending from the shore of the Mediterranean Sea to a distance varying from 50 to 100 miles inland.

³ Abdulla ibn Säad, in the reign of the Khalif Othman, in the year 647 of our era.

⁴ The Straits of Gibraltar, *i. e.*, *Djebel-al-Tarik*, signifying the Mount of Tarik.

⁵ Alhamra, in Arabic *Kal'-al-hamrah*, the Red Castle, from the reddish color of the stones of which it is built. Commonly but incorrectly written Alhambra.

⁶ Barbarossa, a name among Europeans borne by two brothers, albeit properly a corruption of the Turkish name of the elder, Baba-Arudj.

⁷ In 1646, the number of white Christian slaves held by the Algerines was estimated at 20,000. In 1768, 1500 were redeemed by Spain alone; and in 1816, when Lord Exmouth destroyed the last of the pirate ships, about 3000 were liberated. "These are some of the most striking instances; but hundreds of captives were annually ransomed by their respective nations, or by societies formed for the purpose. Many priests nobly devoted themselves to ministering to the slaves, even voluntarily going to the galleys for the sake of being with them. Several of these, who were killed among the other victims of the Turks, have been canonized."—R. L. PLAYFAIR.

⁸ Burton, one of the few Europeans who have seen the Holy Stone of Islamism, is of the opinion that it is an aërolite.

THE FRENCH IN AFRICA.

If France be resurrected Rome, why not
Dominion over Africa to-day?
And not alone in Mauritania,
But far within the bowels of the Niger,
And farther in out-lying Madagascar,—
As Africa has grown somewhat since Cæsar?

ENGLAND.

England! where the graphic Chaucer, in his panoramic page,
Fixed for aye the men and manners of his mediæval age;
As the ancient Grecian sculptor made a future time his own,
When he cut the frieze and tablets of the peerless Parthenon!

England! where the cosmic Shakespeare sate unseen in silent thought,
Till, behold! the English drama into shape and substance wrought;
As the Lotus-god[1] of India closed his eyes in reverie,
And, behold! the world created in his fertile fantasie!

England! where the musing Milton, with the in-sight of the blind,
Looked into the Court of Heaven from the midnight of his mind;
As the sailor, looking skyward, with the keenest worldly sight,
Sees the stars in all their glory only in the darkest night!

England! where the mighty Dryden, master of the English ode,
With majestic mien and motion in the realm of letters strode;
As a noble Roman consul, from the Rhine in triumph come,
Laden with a victor's trophies, walked within the walls of Rome!

England! where impassioned Byron, with intensest
    love and hate,
Wrought in rhyme his overwhelming, half-divine, half-
    demon fate;
Like a tropical tornado, whirling with resistless force,
A sublime sight in the distance, an appalling in its
    course!

England! where a thousand poets, gifted with a tuneful
    tongue,
Of the outer world and inner in successive ranks have
    sung;
Thee, I hail! with wild heart-beatings and ineffable
    delight,
As a pilgrim to St. Peter's when its dome appears in
    sight!

---

[1] One of the most sublime of the theological concepts of the Hindus is that the world as it appears to us an objective Thing is the subjective Thought of Brahma, sitting in eternal contemplation in silence and immovable in the corolla of the lotus, or water-lily, (*Nymphæa nelumbo*,) the symbolic seat of the Creator for ages wherever the plant is known in Asia, and the necessity was realized of focusing the infinite in the finite before it becomes a conceivable entity and unity.

SWITZERLAND.

The eyrie of the continent of Europe —
The eagle-nest of Law and Liberty! —
In fondled fiction, if not in firm fact.

OBJECT AND IDEA.

Next to the Sun and Sea and Sky, perhaps,
The Mountain, in the mirror of the mind,
Is wrought into the most sublime of thoughts.

HERO AND LEANDER.

When, in the course of the ascent of Man
From an amœboid, self-sufficient cell,
The waxing worm divided into twain,—
The opposite and supplemental sexes,—
It, by the act of severance, devolved
Upon the parted halves to join again
In order to compound the primal whole
And pass it thus in perpetuity.

The fatal consequence of man and woman
Remaining isolated and apart,
Being destruction unto both, the efforts,
Which each will make to bring about their union,
Evoke the ultimates of their existence
Involved in quiv'ring brawn and burning brain:
The terrors joined of fire and water, earth
And air, to them as individuals,
Being less potent in deterring from,
Than the annihilation of mankind
In moving them to meet and mate in love:
The little lumps, life-leavened, being but
The evanescent links of an eternal chain.

When, haply, Hero, the fair maid of Sestus,
Has ripened into perfect womanhood,
Although a priestess, vowed to chastity,
Incarcerated in a rocky tower —
In short, immaculate,— it is a fact,
Founded within her very flesh and blood,
That she will bud and blossom forth her being,
As well when she displays the lamp to guide
Her lover's course unto her in the night,
As when she, in despair after his death,

Leaps from her tow'r into the storm-swept sea :
The lustrous eyes and ruby lips of woman
Being the lamps by Nature lit within
Her beauteous body to the self-same end ;
And every instant's exhalation of
Expended feeling or exhausted force
Being an indistinguishable sigh
From the last breath of Hero as she sinks,
That fills a bubble on the Hellespont.

And so the youth, Leander, of Abydus,
Having attained unto the powers of manhood,
Albeit hedged about by household spies,
Will haply lie awake while others sleep ;
And, separated from the object of
His in-wrought and engrossing passion, by
The waters of a boatless, bridgeless river,
Will plunge into the cold and rapid stream
And cross and cross again, until he sinks
Within the whirlpool of a swirling storm :
The will to dare evolved within his brain,
The might to do developed in his muscle,
In view of the event e'en from his birth.

Again, Man being his environment
Involved into an organism, it follows
The formulæ of all his fictile dreams
Are in the world outside of him, objective,
Before they are, within the mirror of
His mind, subjective ideation.
The two approximating continents,
At Sestus and Abydus, symbolize
The fairer and the stronger halves of Man
As differentiated in his growth ;
And the swift waters of the Hellespont
That flow between the continental headlands,
The line of demarcation 'twixt the twain,
And all the woeful winds and wrecking waves

Encountered in the struggle to unite —
The struggle for existence of mankind.

I do not marvel, hence, the fabled fate
Of Hero and Leander, founded in
The absolute necessities of the
Organic halves of microcosmic Man,
And formulated by two continents
And a dividing stream, most happily,
Has been the poet's theme for untold time,
Already, as it will be evermore.

It is the lyric of organic love;
It is the song of the dissevered sexes;
It is the hymn of our humanity
Sung in the simplest and sublimest strain;
And he is fit to be a harem's slave,
And she, a nun in a sepulchral cell,
That sings it not until the morrow hears.

ON THE ALPS.

There are two ghosts upon the Alps, that like two
    statues stand,
Cut somehow from a crystal crag, by mighty Michael's
    hand;
The one, the ghost of Hannibal, the Spirit of the
    Sword,
The other, that of St. Bernard, the Spirit of the Word.

Of equal height and bulk are they, as they afar ap-
    pear,
But as unlike from top to toe as night and day, anear;
The soldier, mailed, pressing a spear into the dark
    earth driven,
The other, bared, intent upon a cross upheld in Heaven.

Upon the warrior's right hand, a gaunt and grizzly
    hound,
As if about to clutch a throat, upspringing from the
    ground;
And on his left, a rearing horse,— such as the Hun
    bestrode,
When, like a whirlwind from the east, he swept, the
    Scourge of God!

Upon the right hand of the saint, a mastiff, stark and
    stanch,
Howling for help above a wretch found in an ava-
    lanche;
And on his left, a spotless ox, decked with a symbol
    wreath,—
The victor's crown to him that will for others suffer
    death.

They are the two opposing halves of the composite
    Man,
The Slayer and the Savior, now, as when the world
    began;
The right hand and the left of God,— Jehovah, Brahm,
    or Jove,—
The dolor of disease and death, as well as life and
    love.

AMSTERDAM.

The centre of the trade in diamonds (coal
In its most perfect, pure, and precious form)—
A solitaire, the antitype of Pitt's
Black Diamond in the world beyond the sea:
The excellence of this expressed in water;
The very soul of that, in soot and smoke!

A REVERIE IN ROME.

Loquitur — A Pilgrim to the Shrine of St. Peter.

Rome! Ruin and Regeneration! Aye, as if the Fates,
I-was, I-am, and I-shall-be, who rule o'er men and
    states,
Here wrought in awful rivalry, each striving to excel,
Keeping a world chaotic, half in heaven, half in hell!

The Imperial City! Aye, supreme, commanding hom-
    age from
The wisest and the best of men, who, haply, hither
    come,
To see in Cæsar's sepulchre, the end of all in earth,
Or, kneeling at St. Peter's shrine, in death, a second
    birth.

The Mistress of the World! Aye, aye, the purple of
    her robe
Compounding with the boundless blue that wraps
    about the globe;
Wielding, throughout the universe, a weapon in the
    Word,
More potent and persistent than the pow'r of Cæsar's
    sword!

The Queen of Cities! Aye, her throne, a peerless work
    of art,
Wrought by a holy sculptor from the marble of the
    heart;
Her sceptre, the symbolic cross; and her resplendent
    crown,
The halo round the image of the Holy Mother thrown!

The Holy City! Aye, of all, the holiest of earth —
Above the boast of Bethlehem, the place of Jesus'
　　birth,—
Above Jerusalem, red with the life-blood of the
　　Lord,—
As long as it's the Oracle of His most Holy Word!

The Eternal City! Aye, evolved, like an organic form,
Through geologic ages, from a lowly, simple worm
To an erect and complex man — his hopeful skull
　　become
A symbol of Eternal Life in Holy Peter's Dome!

The City of the Seven Hills! Founded, for all the
　　years,
In firm substantiation of the music of the spheres [1]—
A symbol to the sentient soul, by the Creator given,
To hear the heart-beat of the Earth in harmony with
　　Heaven!

The Nameless City! Aye, a thought and feeling too
　　profound,
To be encompassed in a word and uttered in a
　　sound! —
As to the mystic of the East, the speechless symbol
　　OM,
So to the pilgrim of the West, the silent sign of Rome!

---

[1] According to the ancient astronomers, the planets were believed to be seven; and in accordance with this enumeration, the number Seven assumed a significance the value of which can be appreciated only in a measure to-day. It became the common divisor of the month and year in noting time, and of the octave in noting music. From the last, the phrase, "the music," or "the harmony of the spheres," arose; the number Seven, metaphorically, making music or harmony in the heavens as on earth.

MY CASTLE IN SPAIN.

LOQUITUR — A gentleman — such as a whole-souled gentleman should be at forty-nine.

My castle is a well-built house, with spacious rooms
    and halls,
Bay-windows, statues, open hearths, rare paintings on
    the walls,
Books, music, billiards, bath-tub — or, a residence, in
    fine,
Such as a whole-souled gentleman should have at
    forty-nine!

My Spain is an immense estate across the stormy
    water,
In Pennsylvania, Iowa, Ohio — or, no matter;
With a big barn, cribs, orchards, pens, and groves of
    oak and pine,
Such as a whole-souled gentleman should have at
    forty-nine.

My donjon is a cellar with a well-selected stock
Of Burgundy, Port, Malmosie, Champagne, Bordeaux,
    and Hock —
Or whiskey, brandy, rum, and gin, and California wine,
Such as a whole-souled gentleman should have at
    forty-nine.

My secret cell, a fire-proof vault, with combination
    locks,
And filled with filthy lucre in the form of bonds and
    stocks,
Certificates and mortgages — in short, a silver mine,
Such as a whole-souled gentleman should have at
    forty-nine.

My moat is a cool mountain stream, beyond the garden
  paling,
"With here and there a lusty trout, and here and there
  a grayling,"
Or other fish to take the bait and try the rod and
  line —
Such as a whole-souled gentleman should have at
  forty-nine.

My warden is a faithful wife, with a becoming wealth
Of good and generous qualities, including looks and
  health,
And "silver threads among the gold," in harmony
  with mine —
Such as a whole-souled gentleman should have at
  forty-nine!

My guard, a dozen boys and girls — alternating, of
  course —
And none a whit the better than their ancestors, or
  worse,
Nor older than their several years — a family, in fine,
Such as a whole-souled gentleman should have at
  forty-nine!

My butler is my eldest boy, to fill his father's place,
In public and in private, with his father's ease and
  grace,—
Collect the rents, and carve the ducks, when old friends
  come to dine —
Such as a whole-souled gentleman should have at
  forty-nine!

My page, the youngest of my girls, a little, lisping
  miss,
To spill my ink and spoil my pen, and get for all a
  kiss —

H

A fond, forgiving father's kiss, while loving arms en-
    twine —
Such as a whole-souled gentleman should give at
    forty-nine!

My dwarf, a round and rosy babe, a cute and cunning
    elf,
To banish from the breast of all a sullen, secret self,
And in the closest sympathy the family combine —
Such as a whole-souled gentleman should have at
    forty-nine!

In fine, my castle is a home, I trust, may yet be given,
To one not bad enough for hell, nor good enough for
    heaven —
A round, full man — a fair, square man — nor demon,
    nor divine —
Such as a whole-souled gentleman should be at forty-
    nine!

IN HOLLAND.

The myrmeleon in its hole should be
The Hollander's heraldic cognizance.

The Dutchman lives within his Hollow-land
Like an everted turtle in its box;
A "native" oyster in its own half-shell;
Or embryonic ostrich in its egg.

Within a fortnight of Dacota's plains,
In this the century of steel and steam,
It is astounding that the Dutch will filch
"The indigested vomit of the sea,"
And fight, as never mankind fought before,
To save it from the hunger of the beast.

IN LONDON.

Now may I see — and sing betimes — the lottery of life;
The ultimates of Fate and Chance in the eternal strife;
The differentiation wrought, since the great world began,
In its incorporated self, the Little World of Man.

Here sit two sisters side by side: the one in want and woe,
Debased by crime, debauched by vice, the lowest of the low;
The other — God of Heaven! keep her ever in Thine eye! —
The empress of a world-wide realm, the highest of the high!

And here two brothers in a booth: the one, as vile a worm
As ever wriggled by mischance into the human form;
The other — God of Heaven! smile forever in his face! —
The heir to the imperial crown, the noblest of his race!

And so — look as I will or may — the one, the most accursed;
Among mankind in wretchedness, beyond compare the worst;
The other blest beyond the best to mortal ever given —
His very name ne'er said nor sung, without a prayer to Heaven!

THE TIERRA-DEL-FUEGIAN.[1]

Crown-cropped; while, in a dank and matted fringe,
His black hair hangs around his brow and ears;
As if in mask or mimicry of the
Less densely clouded zenith overhead
And the obscuring curtain round about
Of dark, depending, dripping fog and mist.

Low-browed; with broad, flat face obscurely barred
With reddish-brown or smeared and daubed with
    white;
The counterfeit presentment of the band
Of shore surrounding, 'twixt the sea and clouds;
With dusky moss and lichens seamed; or flecked
With snow, low-lying in the dark ravines.

Broad-shouldered and big-bodied; brawny, bare;
With cramped and dwindled legs and slender arms;
With thongs around the wrists; small hands and
    feet —
So disproportionate unto his body,
The latter lapses in its likeness to
The limbless, glacier-smoothed and -rounded isles
Of quartz and gneiss and granite that appear
Above the line of the horizon, huge,
Unshapely,— weathered humpings, smooth and bare.

Subsisting on the shellfish of the shore —
The mussel, limpet, sea-egg, and the like,—
With now and then a duck-egg or a fish,
And rarer still, an otter, goose, or seal.
Incorporating aught and everything
Of life around him, till existing as
Subsisting, he embodies and expresses

The shore-line of mankind — the lowest level —
Or the horizon of humanity.

Within the frail walls of his birch-bark boat,—
With wicker strengthened and with crushed moss
    caulked,
With paddles crudely fashioned, and the skin
Of seal suspended in the bow for sail,—
Upon a hearth of clay, the ash and coals
Of an uncertain fire, fanned into flame
Before the bellows of the Long Reach gale;
Or spread and flattened into smothering smoke
By the descending williwaw; or whirled
Into a cloud of sparks and ashes by
The swift revolving gust; or, haply, quenched
By long continued rain or sudden splash
Of the foam-crested billow o'er the boat.

This fire the symbol of the slanting sun;
Now, glowing o'er the glaciers of the North
And scorching all upon the sheltered shore;
Now, frozen to a faint, vague, whitish spot
Beyond the overarching clouds, the while
An icy chill succeeds the dewy sweat;
Now, out of sight — its presence in the sky
Determined by a dim, diffusive light
Indissoluble from the mist and fog,
The rain and sleet and snow and hail, in which
It is involved,— revealed by that which veils.

This fire, as well, the symbol of the soul
Of the poor savage; now, aglow with joy
In the expression of incarnate greed
At the appearance of a coming ship,
With, haply, in exchange for eggs and pelts
And an inspection of his nakedness,
A string of beads or palm-length of tobacco;
Anon, a melancholy, wretched gloom,—

A sullen, silent, dark and dank despair,—
A deep and all-pervading murderous mood,—
In which the blear-eyed, gaunt and grizzled hag
That bare him in her womb, the rather than
His shiv'ring, cow'ring dog, falls at his feet
Beneath his club, to fill his hung'ring maw!
No mercy knows he than the south-pole wind;
No pity knows he than the south-pole wave;
No sympathy with mother, wife, and babe,
Than quartz and granite underneath his feet —
Than walls of ice-capped mountains on all sides —
Than sleet and hail upon his naked hide —
Than maws around as hungry, hands as strong,
And clubs as ready as his own to kill.

---

[1] Originally published in the Appendix to the author's "AUSTRALIA: A CHARCOAL-SKETCH," 1886, preceded by the following note:—

The Tierra-del-Fuegian and the Black of Australia are approximately equally low in the scale of humanity. They are so, however, not from the same but contrary causes. The Fuegian has never attained a higher stage of development than that in which he is found to-day; while the Black has degenerated from a higher stage than that in which he is disappearing at present. The Fuegian represents the babyhood of mankind in general; while the Black is the expression of the premature decay and second childhood of a race that at one time or elsewhere to-day might be set down as semi-civilized. The one is a resultant of the evolution of Growth; and the other, of Decay. The one is an overgrown baby; and the other, a stunted man.

Curiously, moreover, they are the organic expressions of opposite environments: the Fuegian, of winter and water; and the Australian, of summer and sand: extremes as great, perhaps, as may be found in the habitable globe. And that the contrast between them may appear in detail as well as in general, the following lines by the writer may serve. They were written from a study of several boat-loads of Fuegians encountered in November, 1884, in the Strait of Magellan and Smyth's Channel.

OLD IRELAND — GOD BLESS HER!¹

Loquitur — An Irish refugee, in the customs service of China, at Tien-Tsin.

There is an island in the sea, its name need not be spoken,
For man and woman everywhere may know it by this token:
It is the land that wheresoe'er her wand'ring sons address her,
Brings from the bottom of their hearts this fond appeal, God bless her!

It's there the stately Shannon flows beside a low, thatched cottage,
Where first I saw the light of day, and ate of poor-tith's pottage;
And by the spot my mother sleeps the sleep to virtue given,
Beneath St. Patrick's symbol of the Blessèd Three in Heaven!

It's there the Kerry Hills hang o'er the waters of Lough Leane,
And see themselves against the sky reflected in the sheen;
Where, looking into Kathleen's eyes, when we were forced to part,
I saw myself transfigured in the heaven of her heart!

It's there the beauteous Cove of Cork expands into the
    ocean,
Where, parting with the Blessèd Isle, I wept with wild
    emotion;
My trembling lips with envy pale at my old brogans'
    bliss,
That they should give the sacred sod my last, my fare-
    well kiss!

It's there the fairest scenes of earth my fancy fondly
    paints —
The land I love beatified, the Island of the Saints!
May Heaven's lightning blast the arm of him that
    would oppress her;
May Heaven's sunburst cheer the heart of him that
    prays, God bless her!

---

[1] Printed first in *The Post*, Pittsburgh, Pa., on St. Patrick's Day, 1883.

MONT BLANC.

But what, you ask, does Mont Blanc look like?
    Stranger, take a chair,
And fix your eyes upon a point till you see nothing
    there —
Till sight is sunk, and things are not, but, haply, as
    they seem
In an entrancing reverie or a delicious dream.

Hast ever seen St. Peter's? Well, Mont Blanc is like
    the dome
Upheaved by Michael Angelo above the walls of Rome;
As round and white — nay, fairer far, and infinitely
    greater,
A hemisphere of holiness upheaved by the Creator!

Or hast thou e'er seen Goethe? Well, Mont Blanc
    looks like the brow
Of the great sage and singer, dead and buried, yet
    somehow,
A living grandeur of the world — a deathless ghost,
    whose front
Has been engraved by God within the everlasting
    mount!

Or hast thou ever seen a storm in the Atlantic ocean —
The world of waters whirled into a white and wild
    commotion?
Well, well, Mont Blanc's the storm at rest; his face
    without a frown,
And his broad breast of billows stilled in silk and
    eider-down!

Or hast thou ever loved in youth a maid of truth and
    worth,
Expanding and exalting thee above the earth of earth?
Well, well, Mont Blanc's fair rounded mass of purest
    snow and ice
Is like a virgin's bosom bared by chance in Paradise!

Or hast thou ever felt, in fine, a great engrossing grief,
Or a pervading passion without purpose or relief?
Well, well, Mont Blanc is like the song that gives the
    surcease sought —
A world of feeling lifted up and crystallized in
    Thought!

THE EARTH.

This pendent sphere between infinities —
A world of wondrous worlds within itself;
A globule in the blood of space without.

I

PSAPPHA.[1]

Presumptuous! preposterous! Thou canst, my friend, no more
Sing Psappha into flesh and blood, as in the days of yore,
Than thou canst resurrect the dead, and give to them the glow,
With which their joyous faces shone, two thousand years ago!

Perhaps, I cannot — But, methinks, that, as the shades of night
From black to grey transfuse and fade, and then from gray to white,
I can discern a woman's form emerge from out the gloom,
And feel her warm breath in the wind the morning flowers perfume.

Her hair, the hour before the dawn, when the o'erspreading rack
Deepens the darkness of the night into the densest black;
A chaos of incarnate night, within whose sable folds,
Jehovah moves in silence and a new creation holds!

Her brow, the first gleams of the dawn that in the east appear,
After the rain and wind have rinsed and wrung the atmosphere;
A radiant front of purity, — the lustrous aureole
Of Nature's masterpiece, a maid, with an unsullied soul!

PSAPPHA.

Her eyes, the azure overhead, with a faint gleam of light,
Like the pale stars evanishing with the receding night;
A light alluring to the gaze,— the spark to woman given
Inflaming man to wield for her the thunderbolts of heaven!

Her lips, the red horizon where the sky and ocean glow;
The upper curt, as if, by chance, her pearly teeth to show;
The nether full and quivering, as if about to mutter
The secret of a throbbing heart too rapturous to utter!

Her voice, the round uprising sun, the glorious orb of day,
Infusing light and life and love into the coldest clay;
Aye, though it cease in sudden death, its tone for untold years,
Continuing like light through space, the music of the spheres!

Her being, all the beauty — all the rapture of the world,
Compounded in an eon, and voluptuously whirled
Into the fairest form of earth the rays of life illumine,
A love-impassioned, song-endowed, incomparable woman!

---

[1] Commonly written SAPPHO; but since the poet, in the Æolic dialect in which she wrote, called herself PSAPPHA, she is called so with especial propriety in a personal portraiture. She is believed to have been at the zenith of her fame about the year 610 B. C.

DIE DEUTSCHER'S FADERLAND.[1]

Loquitur.— An American citizen of German origin.

Vat vas die Deutscher's Faderland? I tells you dooble kvick,
(Zwei lager, Hans!) Gesundheit!— Ah, dot brewer vas a brick!—
Vell, after supper in mein house, I puts a keg on tap,
Und drinks, until I close mein eyes to take von leedle nap.

Sometime, den, kleine Gretchen — Ah, she vas a daisy girl,
Mit himmel-blauen in her eyes und sunshine in her curl!—
She takes die tom-cat in her arms, yoost like a baby — so!
Und sings to him von leedle song vas made long time ago.

Ah, vat shweet moosic fills mein ears, ven I begins to dream
I vas again in an old house, beside a mountain shtream —
I sees mein fader's big round vatch — I hears mein mutter's vord,
Und sheares mein leedle sister mit mein brudder's army sword.

Und den I goes to school again, und sees somebody dere,
Dot looks yoost like dot leedle girl, dot daisy I haves here;

Und after vile, ven she vas big as effer she vas got,
I shmacks her lips a hunnert times und neffer vonce vas caught.

Und den I goes to part mit her, und hears a someding say,
Deep in her bosom, Shtay! Oh, shtay! Meine Geliebte, shtay!
Or take me mit you ven you sails across die shtormy sea,
For ven you goes mit my poor heart, you takes all Germany!

(Zwei lager, Hans!) Gesundheit — so! Now, you can unnerstand
Vat vas die meaning of die vord, Die Deutscher's Faderland —
It vas dot someding in mein breast vom vich I neffer part —
It vas dot Germany I got mit Gretchen's mutter's heart!

Ah, yaw, mein freund! Dot big tom-cat — Prince Bismarck vas his name —
Since Gretchen loves dot blue Maltée, I loves him yoost die same —
I hangs a bell about his neck, upon a band of silk,
Und I will giff up beer before dot cat vill vant for milk!

---

[1] Edited by Mr. T. C. Zimmerman, the accomplished German scholar, and published first in the *Times and Dispatch*, Reading, Pa., 21st February, 1884.

THE SEA.

The soot and cinder of a world's combustion.

COREA, OR CHOSEN.[1]

Corea is a kingdom in the East —
The far Far East of Asia — and among
The smallest into which the continent
Has been divided by the shears of time.

It is the last of the exclusive realms
And isolated of the Orient:
And, in comparison with the adjunct
And neighb'ring China and Japan, it is
A sealèd casket to the outer world.
In consequence of which it is nicknamed
The Hermit Nation, the Forbidden Land,
And the Mysterious Peninsula.

Unto the man of science of the age —
The Darwin, Hæckel, Worsaae, Marsh, or Baird —
It is invested with the interest
And fascination that attaches to.
The indeterminable fauna of
A geologic period, of which
An inappreciable half a score
Of genera are known, between two ages,
The fossilized remains of which have been
Amassed in great museums and subject
To careful study and comparison.
To him, the merest observation is
A theme for contemplation; a detail,
A subject for comparison, belike,
From one realm to another, in a ring
Around the globe; and every fact established,
A link in countless scientific chains.

---

[1] The several names by which the last of the exclusive countries of the Orient is known are as follows: CORÉA, from

GAOGOWLI, the name of a northern province, reduced and corrupted to GAOLI, whence GORI, KORAI, and *The* CORÉA, as the English commonly say, absurdly conforming to the idiom of the French; CHOSEN,—the name in general use in Corea, China, and Japan, and pronounced like the past participle of the English verb *to choose*,—from CHAO-SIEN, the name of a northwestern province, and signifying the Country in the East—the Dawn, the Morning Calm, or Morning Serenity—being such, relatively considered, to the name-giving people of China; SILA,—a name given by Khordadbeh, an Arab geographer, of the 9th century,—from SINLO, a predominant province of the time; TCHUNG-QUO, a Chinese name, signifying, the Eastern Country; and SOL-HO, a Manchu Tatar name, of unknown meaning to the writer. The several sobriquets of the country, as given in the poem, have lost their applicability since the visit of the writer, (nominally, as the surgeon of a Japanese steamer, the *Tsuruga Maru*, belonging to the Mitsu Bishi Company,) in the early part of 1881, by the opening of the country to foreigners under treaties with the United States of America, Great Britain, Germany, France, and others of the treaty-bound nations and fraternizing peoples of the earth.

COREA — IN BRIEF.

Imagine, first, a huge, four-footed beast,
Unwieldy, wallowing within the mud
Of the Far Eastern Shores of Middle Asia.
The body, now, misshapen as it lies,
And grotesque in the shadows which it casts,
Is the enormous realm of China; and
The tail, defined with greater clearness and
A little cleaner, hanging over in
The great Pacific ocean, is Corea.
By dubbing now the beast, The Dragon of
The Orient, the picture is complete,
And the mysterious peninsula,
Corea, comprehended in the mind
As well as — well, the Sphinx of Asia, China!

This is facetious, you exclaim. So be it;
Yet, ne'ertheless, the picture I have drawn
Contains a rare approximation to
The truth, and is not only applicable
To the relations which exist between
The two realms, as contiguous domains,
But also and as well to those of a
Subjective subtile character which may
Supposably subsist between them as
Associated states and allied peoples.
Indeed, were I to cudgel my poor brains
A fortnight longer, I believe, I could
Convey no greater truth in fewer words
Than is involved within the imaged Dragon.

To be, now, more explicit, I may say,
(Reversing in review the monster,) that,
As the Coreans are to the Chinese,
In race, in language, and in history,
In manners, customs, morals, government,
Religion, thought — in, haply, every way
I can consider them as kindred peoples;
And as Corea is to China-land,
In size and shape and situation, so
The tail is to the body of a beast —
In this especial instance, a huge monster,
Conformed, compounded, and yclept, as I
Have said, The Dragon of the Orient.

Familiar hence, dear reader, with the beast
In its entirety, when, haply, you
Dissect the tail dissevered from the body
In some specific treatise on Corea —
In parting bone and ligament and muscle,
And artery and vein, (dissimilar,
By differentiation, in detail,
As they must necessarily all be,

But only in degree, from the like parts
In other regions of the beast,) you may
Appreciate, at every cut, the life,
Peculiar to the Chinese hulk, that has
Pervaded the appendage from afar,
And every part affected, even to
The ultimate of epithelial scales
Attached to the depending, sea-washed tip.[1]

---

[1] Having carefully considered the ethnologic affinities of the Coreans, I cannot conceive why the French Missionaries have reported them as resembling the Japanese much more than the Chinese, unless it be, that, never having traveled or lived among the Japanese, they knew no difference between them and the Coreans, and accordingly believed them to be very similar. The differences between the Coreans and the Chinese at first sight are great, but they are only superficial; while those between them and the Japanese are greater and penetrating to the core.

ON GETTING DRUNK — IN PARENTHESIS.

But why does the Corean drink and get
As drunk as whiskey made of rice can make him?
Or, rather, to survey mankind, like Johnson,
From China to Peru, why do all men,
Coreans, Hottentots, and you and I
Get drunk? *Sub rosa*, I will tell you. List.

When a Corean drinks — or you or I —
An alcohol-intoxicating liquor,
Primarily, it makes him more a man,
A higher evolution than before:
The struggle of the organism being,
You know, to be that which it never was,

And is not. In the sinking, soggy earth
Of his embodied being, it excites
A pleasurable feeling of expansion
And elevation; and, within the dark
And murky sky of his imagination
It kindles fiery thoughts, within the flash
And flame of which, albeit for an instant,
A glimpse is seen of an exalted life,
A higher, happier, and holier
Existence than e'er felt or feigned before.
The sinner thus becomes a saint; the fool,
A sage; the coward, a brave soldier; and
A beggar in his tatters in a ditch,
A king, in silk and velvet, on a throne!
This is the reason the Corean drinks —
Or you or I — a reason founded in
The meat and marrow of his very being.
He wants what liquor gives primarily,
Though secondarily — aye, there's the rub!
The evil of intoxicating liquor
Is not in getting drunk, but getting sober!
For, just in the proportion whiskey makes,
Primarily, a drinker more a man,
So, secondarily, a sob'rer less —
Reducing him, from the tiptopmost peak
Of manhood and of purity, down through
The several descending stages of
The semi-civilized and of the savage,
Unto the lowest wallow of the beast
In nameless, unimaginable filth!

In saying which — in confidence, remember —
You will observe, and make a note of it,
That, while I have descanted with one tongue,
I have not had one eye upon the subject,
But looked with my two eyes, as it behooves
A man, in order to attain the truth —
In strict accordance with the wisdom of

His ancestors in their entirety
Transmitted to him and expressed within
The severed senses of his organism.

EXCLUSIVE CHOSEN.

The ultimatum of the glyptodon:
Encompassed in a hard and compact case;
Incapable of further evolution;
Impenetrable to the world without;
An extinct monster still among the living.

THE FUNGHWANG, THE DRAGON, AND THE FENG-SHUI.

Chosen! where the gallant game-cock,—
Combed and spurred and flecked and painted
Gaudily from head to tail-tip,
Crowing loudly in the morning,
Rousing the Coreans from their
Slumbers to behold the sun rise
From the great Pacific ocean,—
Has, in the imagination
Of the roused and wond'ring people,
Passed into a bird of fancy—
Passed into a bird of fiction—
Passed into the fabled Funghwang!
Feathered with the rarest jewels,
Rubies, sapphires, pearls, and diamonds;
Speaking with a voice prophetic
Unto those who seek to know their
Fate within the coming morrow—
Warriors, before the battle—

Ministers, with secret plottings —
Kings, with horrible misgivings!
Aye, evolved into the Funghwang,
The prophetic Bird of Morning,
Nesting in the land of Chosen,
Rising in a blaze of beauty —
Rising in the gold and glitter
Of the oriental sunrise!
Winging thence its wand'ring westward,
Till behold it reäppearing
In the Phœnix of Arabia,
And the Sphinx of the Ægyptians![2]
Beauteous, jeweled, wondrous Funghwang!
Stripped of its ideal plumage,
But a gaudy, gallant game-cock —
But a spangled, strutting dunghill —
But a common, crowing chicken!
Like the proud bird of the fable,
Posing in a peacock's plumage,
Found on plucking but a jackdaw!

Chosen! where the stripèd tiger,
Haunting mountain, haunting valley,
From the far east to the far west,
From the far south to the far north,
Killing horses, dogs, and cattle,
Killing bold men in the day time,
Killing bolder in the night time,
Striking terror to the marrow
Of the boldest and the bravest!
Till, in the imagination
Of the people of Corea,
What the word, the most terrific
In the ears of all the people,
But the title of the tiger?
What the form, the most appalling
In the eyes of all the people,
But the picture of the tiger?

Till, at length, the wily chieftain,
To impress upon the people
His assumed or actual power,
Dubs himself, not Cæsar,[3] from the
Massive elephantine monster,
But an ear-appalling Tiger?[4]
And, as well, the cunning soldier,
To impress upon his foemen,
His assumed or actual valor,
Paints upon his flaunting banner,
Not the Cross, the sign of manhood,
Not the Crescent, sign of woman,
But an eye-appalling symbol
Of the tiger, called the Dragon![5]
Aye, the Dragon of the standards
Of the oriental nations,
China, Nipon, and Corea,
Is none other than the tiger,
Ranging from the earth's equator
Half way to the polar circle,[6]
And abounding in Corea,—
Of all savage beasts, the fiercest,
Of all savage beasts, the fellest,
The ferocious banded tiger
The terrific Béngal Tiger,
Like a special incarnation
Of a storm-cloud streaked with lightning!

Chosen! where the trader coming
From the northern wilds of Asia,
Telling of the wondrous wild beast,
Of the most stupendous bigness,
Of the most prodigious likeness,
Found imbedded in the glaciers
And the frozen sand and mud banks,
Perfect, even to the lustre
Of the eyes beneath the eyelids,
As if closed upon the coming

Of the beast into the sunshine,
Causing death unto it, haply;
And, in proof of his strange story,
Showing to the wond'ring people —
Selling to the wond'ring people —
The enormous iv'ry tushes
Of the mighty wool-clad monster!
Till, in the imagination
Of the people of Corea,
Lo! a mighty mole-like monster
Burrowing beneath the surface
Of the country of Corea —
Of the countries of the whole earth;
Living in the earth and darkness,
Dying in the air and sunshine;
Causing the prodigious earthquake
By the shaking of its body;
Causing the volcano also
In its awful rage and fury;
Causing all the strange and awful
Evils in the earth and on it —
All the floods and drouths and tempests —
All the fevers, wars, and famines —
All the woes innumerable
That afflict the helpless people
Of Corea and the whole earth!
An o'erwhelming mundane monster,
All-involving and controlling,
The protéan, many headed,
Mythic, mystic, Mongol monster,
The illimitable Feng-Shui! —
The symbolic Wind-and-Water! —
Of all Mongol myths, the strongest
Factor in impeding progress
In the little world of Chosen,
And the mighty world of China! —
Aye, the Feng-Shui of Corea
And the wondrous world of China,

Is none other than the mummy
Of the elephantine Mammoth
Found imbedded in the glaciers
And the frozen sand and mud banks
Of the northern wilds of Asia —
An inert and senseless mummy,
Not alone of a departed
Mammoth, but the Age of Mammoths![7]

---

[1] For further information about this wonderful bird, the curious reader is referred to *The History of Corea*, by the Rev. JAMES ROSS, pp. 189-195; and *The Hermit Nation*, by WM. E. GRIFFIS, p. 304; but the fact that the Funghwang is a mythic or fabulous evolution from the chicken-cock interblended with the blaze of the rising sun, as outlined in the poem, is found in neither. The Chinese, however, have not lost sight of the ideal bird's original in nature; and from their pictorial representations, noted by the writer during his travels in the northern provinces of China in the spring of 1881, it became known to him and led in due time to the conclusions stated.

[2] This, at first sight, may appear as improbable as far-fetched, even to those who have made the evolution and dispersion of myths and fables a study, but, it is believed by the writer, that a critical examination of all the circumstances involved in the Funghwang of the Coreans, the Phœnix of Herodotus, and the Sphinx — S-phœn-'x — of Œdipus and in general, will confirm their common origin — the prophetic chanticleer compounded with the glorious fulfillment of his prophesy in the fiery splendors of the rising sun.

[3] The word *Cæsar*, signifying elephant, is Punic, or Phœnician. It was borrowed from the Carthaginians as a regal title by the Romans before they had become acquainted with either the African or the Asiatic species save by report, and presumably without knowing its primary meaning; for when they beheld the huge mammal in objective reality, they applied to it the Grecian name among them of the vaguely known stag, *Elephas*. The latter word, however, never became a regal title, nor associated with the pride and pomp of state, except in the title of the little known and less important Order of the Elephant, instituted by Christian I., of Denmark, revived, after lapsing into desuetude, by Frederik II., and continued by his

successors, and in the family name Oliphant, derived either from a heraldic blazon or a tavern-sign, the well-known Elephant and Castle, which, in the vagarious realm of art, by lessening the beast and elongating its burden, has become the colloquial Pig and Whistle. The word *Cæsar*, having been the first to enter the field of honor and empire in Europe, has excluded all synonymous rivals.

[4] Several instances may be found in Ross's *History*, pp., 59, 241, and 249. In Japan, the Hawaiian Islands, New Zealand, and other islands of the Pacific, where the elephant, the lion, and the tiger are unknown, the name of the Shark is assumed by great warriors in the stead of Cæsar, Leo or Louis, and Woo or Yenban, and their equivalents.

[5] Generally, the Bengal tiger is ignored by the outside barbarian and foreign devil, but not by the Chinaman and his neighbors, as the father in fact of the so-called Dragon of oriental fancy; and vaguely by some, the object in nature from which the ideal monster has sprung, is conjectured to be the puny parachute-lizard of Asia, *Draco volans*; and very vaguely by others, a hypothetic dragon of the Tertiary Age, still flapping about and striking terror in the minds of the descendants of a hypothetic Miocene Man; and very, very vaguely by others still, the frightful flying-crocodile, Pterodactyle, of an earlier geologic age! By the way, several of the tricks of the Chinese artists, in imparting a seeming rapidity of movement to their motionless images of the tiger in paint, wood, ivory, stone, and bronze — notably, in the superb ornamental adjuncts to the astronomical instruments of the observatory of Peking, — are among their ultimate and most admirable achievements.

"The fauna of the Tertiary age from the Miocene down, which there is some reason to believe passed before the eyes of primæval man, would afford ample material for gorgons, dragons, sylphs, and satyrs, leviathan and behemoth, and the whole list of ancient and fabulous monsters. The birds with teeth, and the winged lizard of the Secondary age, (the Pterodactyle,) known very well by its fossil remains, if clothed with flesh and provided with limbs and wings, would make a creature in some respects like the dragon of fairy tales."— SAMUEL KNEELAND.

The living Bengal tiger, however, is all-sufficient for the Dragon of the Orient; the living chicken-cock, for the Funghwang and Phœnix; and the ice-encased mammoth in its entirety for the awful earth-emboweled Feng-shui.

⁶ But howsoever great this geographic range north and south of the Bengal tiger, it is doubled by that of the allied cougar or panther of America, (*Felis concolor,*) — from ice to ice across the equator!

⸱ ⁷ Cf., in confirmation, the following, from the Encyclopædia of KANGHI, in which the mammoth, (*Euelephas primigenius,*) alone is referred to : —

"The cold is extreme and almost continual on the coast of the Northern Sea, beyond the Tai-tong-Kiang. On this coast is found the animal Fen-shu, which resembles a rat in shape, but is as big as an elephant. It dwells in dark caverns, and ever shuns the light. There is obtained from it an ivory as white as that of the elephant, but easier to work, and not liable to split. Its flesh is very cold, and excellent for refreshing the blood."

Also, the following, from an ancient book, called the SHIN-Y-KING, in which the larger beast spoken of is the mammoth, and the smaller, the woolly rhinoceros, (*R. tichorrhinus* and a new species, *R. Merkii,* connecting the former with the living species,) —

"There is in the extreme north, among the snows and ice which cover this region, a *shu* which weighs up to a thousand pounds. Its flesh is very good for those who are heated. The TSE-SHU calls it Fen-shu, and speaks of another kind which is of less size, or about as large as a buffalo, according to this authority. It burrows like the moles, shuns the light, and almost always stays in its underground caves. It is said that it would die if it saw the light of the sun, or even of the moon."

THE MEDITERRANEAN.

The grandest water-way upon the globe!
The march of Man from an enlightened East
To an o'ershadowed West, and back again,
From an illumined West to a dark East.
As if the one half only of the world
Should be awake the while the other slept.

K

LA BELLE FRANCE.

Loquitur — A wretched wanderer, a Frenchman, between Baalbec and Damascus, Syria.

La Belle France! — Ah, there was a time, those words within me stirred
The spirit of a son of France, whenever they were heard!
A son of France, with heart to do, what other men have done;
A son of France, with hope to win, what other men have won!

When, in the vision of my youth, the great Napoleon's form
Rose with the awful grandeur of an overwhelming storm,
And sank into the secret self, I fancied, with a start,
That I could feel imprisoned in the donjon of my heart!

When, with a love enchanting life, I clasped the fair Lisette;
When, with a hate enchanting death, I spurned the false coquette;
Henceforth to go from bad to worse, and then from worse to worst, —
A weary, wasted wanderer, — this ghastly thing accursed!

O woman! what a world to man art thou to make or mar!
To ope the doors to wealth and fame, or close them with a bar;

To place a crown upon a head, or noose about a neck;
To make a man a demigod, or — this abandoned
    wreck!

La Belle France! God forgive me, No! A whited
    sepulchre,
As long as it entombs Lisette and what is foul in
    her;
Or till these shrunken, shivering limbs lie mould'ring
    in the earth,
And Lethe leaves one thought alone — the dear land
    of my birth!

THE PLAIN OF TROY.

Stop! Poet, in thy pilgrimage! and rest thee from
    thy toil,
For here thy weary footfalls press upon thy sacred
    soil!
This is the Plain of Ilium! these wide and wistful
    views,
The Palestine of Poesy! — the Mecca of the Muse!

This is the grand environment of gods and godlike
    men —
The seas, the sands, the sunlit skies, the very same as
    when
The Blind Bard sang, as blind bards see, the earth and
    heaven human,
And the great world revolving round the fair form of a
    woman!

The air is inspiration, breathe! the things are thoughts, behold!
The wind and wave are music, list! and sing anew the old!
Aye, let thy soul expand into the spirit of this shrine,
And make its immortality indissolubly thine!

What! sing of Zeus in Saxon song! and, in vicarious verse,
The direful consequences of Achilles' wrath rehearse?
As well wake up the Wooden Horse, of Sinon's wily scheme,
To work for us the wonders of the steed of steel and steam!

The world has long outgrown the Greek: the classic siege of Troy
Belongs not to the bearded man, but to the bookish boy,
Whose folios, filled with the forms of the Homeric hosts,
Are but the fossil-bearing shales of buried mental coasts.

Aye, aye, as well inveigle the primæval trilobite
To join the jeweled humming-bird in its aërial flight,
As summon Hector with his sword and buckler to repel
The soldier now advancing in a storm of shot and shell!

It is the Poet's function to embody in his song
The spirit of the age and clime to which he may belong;
To feel, with comprehensive heart, think, with constructive mind,
And voice the vital universe in numbers for mankind.

It is —— God help the sorry bard, that, ere his numbers swell,
Ensconces, like a hermit-crab, his bare breech in the shell
Of a departed whelk of worth, its shelter to enjoy —
God help the sorry bard to-day that sings the siege of Troy!

VALHALLA.

Hast ever seen at even, through the sun-illumined mist
That veils and yet reveals in a diffusive amethyst,
A mountain mass of bowlders, crags, and snow-capped peaks arise
In grim, chaotic grandeur and weird beauty in the skies?

So, in the purple glamour of a vision of the past,
Valhalla rises in review, inviting, vair, and vast!
Its rude and rugged features in the foreground lightly limned,
And all that's foul and frightful in the distance deftly dimmed.

In mortal guise, grim Odin sits, within the spacious hall,
At the great groaning table's head, the sovran lord of all;
Ruling the world, not by the right involved in wisdom's word,
But by the right wrought by the might that wields the strongest sword!

Perched on his brawny shoulders, see!— in sable hue
    to mark
The thoughts and memories that move mysterious in
    the dark,—
The ravens twain, which o'er the world take their di-
    urnal flight,
And whisper what they've seen and heard in Odin's
    ears at night.

And at his feet, two monstrous wolves,— symbolic of
    the greed
With which a greater god than man must obviously
    feed,—
Two monstrous wolves that eat his meat, in lieu of the
    divine,
The while the god regales himself with far-fetched
    precious wine.

While, to the right and to the left, within his royal
    sight,
An untold throng of heroes eat and drink throughout
    the night;
Their hunger never satisfied, their thirst, too, never
    quenched,
Albeit gorged from dusk to dawn, and copiously
    drenched!

The meat that steams upon the board, the flesh of a
    wild boar,
That's killed and cooked and served about, a hundred
    times and more;
But though dismembered and devoured, in every
    night-long feast,
It reäppears next morning an unscathed, unsodden
    beast!

The mead that foams within the horns the happy he-
    roes hold,
The milk that flows from a she goat within Valhalla's
    fold,—
Browsing upon a wondrous tree, of which the sages
    tell,
And dripping daily from her dugs a stoop of hydro-
    mel!

The maids that serve with supple limbs, the same that
    seek the plain
Strewn with the battle's gory dead, and, from among
    the slain,
Select the bravest of the brave, who fought, nor feared
    to fall,
To meet the warrior's reward in Odin's sumptuous
    hall!

Anon, an hour before the dawn, at Odin's stern com-
    mand,
The bard of bards, great Bragi,[1] takes his harp within
    his hand,
And, as the tuneful strings resound amid the joyous
    jar,
Sings loud and long the matchless song that stirs the
    heart to war!

And lo! at the first peep of day, as the wild music
    dies,
The heroes cast their horns aside, and, loudly cheering,
    rise;
And seizing each his sword and shield, that hang upon
    the wall,
Rush, with the surging ocean's roar, from out the
    ringing hall!

And from the dawn to dusk, behold! upon a mighty plain,
The untold throng of heroes fight their battles o'er again;
Till, falling as they fell on earth, with many a gaping wound,
They lie in ghastly, gory heaps upon the reeking ground!

Until the night sets in, when lo! the dead leap into life,
As when at dawn they sallied forth and met in warlike strife;
And taking each his weapon, like the hero's self restored,
Repair to eat and drink again at Odin's sumptuous board!

So hath the warfare of the world and grim organic greed
Evolved in the Berserker's [2] brain, the fallen warrior's meed;
A fight by day, a feast by night, in his ecstatic vision,
Above all other happiness, or felt or feigned, elysian!

---

[1] With the exception of the part performed by Bragi, the god of eloquence and poetry, (Cf., English *lard* and *brag*,) the description here given of Valhalla follows the authoritative Eddas of Father Sæmund Sigfusson and Snorri Sturlason.

[2] Commonly the word *Berserker* is said by etymologists to be the Norse for English *bare-shirter*. Then, contrary to the idiom of both languages, this *bare-shirter* is said to mean a warrior who goes into battle without a coat of mail! Then the fabulist and the myth-maker take up the Scandinavian *sans-culotte*, and — no matter, here. The word is simply a compound of *ber*, the sea, and *serker*, a searcher or seeker; meaning, accordingly, sea-searcher, sea-rover, or *pirate*. *B-R,* and their equivalents, signifying the sea, occur in scores of words and should be known to all linguists.

THE CRYSTAL PALACE OF THE CZAR.[1]

The czar commands. — And lo! as if he'd waved a magic wand,
Upon the winter's crystal bridge, the Neva's waters spanned,
Uprose a wondrous structure, decked with many a strange device,
From base to crucial pinnacle, a palace of pure ice!

The czar commands.— Throughout the realm, north, south, and east and west,
The minions speed across the snows in keen and eager quest,
Until, among the ragged serfs that throng the Volga's wharfs,
Are found a wretched man and maid, two hideous, hunchbacked dwarfs!

The czar commands.— The wretches doff their ragged garbs, and don
The richest robes of silk and gold; and, seated on a throne
Of ice, beneath the crystal dome, on Neva's frozen tide,
Await the czar to wed them thus, a bridegroom and a bride!

The czar commands.— A thousand lords and ladies of the land
Assemble in St. Petersburg, and long in waiting stand,
Until the merry monarch shall precede them on the ice,
To greet the dwarfs in mockery, and wed them in a trice!

L

The czar commands.— A trumpet sounds — a hundred
    cannons roar! —
The ice, responsive to the shock, upheaves from shore
    to shore,
Then gently swells, as if with pride, beneath the gilded
    car,
In which the mighty monarch rides, the merry-making
    czar!

The czar commands.— But, Christ behold! the bride-
    groom and the bride,
Immovable in gaudy state, sit speechless side by side!
Within the palace walls of ice, upon their crystal
    thrones,
The life-blood frozen in their hearts, the marrow in
    their bones!

The czar commands.— But from that day until his
    latest breath,
A spectre haunts his wretchedness, the hideous dwarfs
    in death!
Anticipating every joy, and chilling, in a trice,
His blood, as when he stepped within the palace built
    of ice!

---

[1] Whether or not this story is founded in fact, is unknown to the writer. It was suggested to him by a large painting on exhibition in the Academy of Arts at the time of his visit to the Paris of the North. The picture represents the horrifying discovery of the czar.

THE TITLE OF THE CZAR.

The lion and the elephant — how proud
The beasts should be, that their great conqueror, Man,
Should take their names to indicate his greatness!
Louis le Grand is simply the big lion;
And *Cæsar, Kaiser, Czar*, the elephant!

A CAPTIVE IN SWEDEN.

On seeing a stunted stalk of American Maize in the centre of a bed of flowers in a public garden of Stockholm.

Wretched, wretched fellow mortal,
From the world beyond the ocean,
Rooted here, a stunted starv'ling
In the country of the fir-tree —
In the country of the reindeer —
In the country of the Snow King,
Ruling, with a rod of iron,
All created, from the Baltic
To the Arctic Ocean, Sweden!

Wasted, in this cold and damp soil,
Withered, in this chill and wet wind,
Doomed to death, a helpless stranger
Cast upon a savage sea-coast —
Doomed to death, ere thou hast yielded
Of the bounty of thy being —
Of the golden, golden bounty
Of thy being unto others
Of thy fellow mortal creatures.

Aye, like Franklin, the explorer,
Doomed to perish in his manhood
Chained amid the polar ice-bergs;
Or the Russian noble, severed
From his family and kindred,
And, amid Siberian snow-fields,
Stinted both in food and raiment,
Stunted both in mind and body,
Till, at last, at three and thirty,
Cast into a drift, a carcase,

Shrivel'd, shrunken, scarce a maw-full
To the prowling wolf of winter!

Yet, methinks, among the herbage
That surrounds thee in this garden,
Like a guard of petty jailors, —
Thou, brave plant, erect and stately,
Plumed and decked with silken honors,
Bearest thy misfortune nobly!
Like the great imperial captive,
Bonaparte, at St. Heléna,
Undismayed among the minions
Of the Mistress of the Ocean —
Still the manifest commander!
Still the proud and haughty victor,
Whose achievements had enrolled him
First among the world's great soldiers!
E'en as thou art here a captive,
Still the chief among the grasses —
Still the king among the corn-plants —
Still the victor of the valley
Of the mighty Mississippi —
First and greatest of the New World's
Golden gifts unto the Old World —
Mighty Maize, imperial Zea!

Aye, methinks, brave plant, thou meetest
Thy destruction in the Old World,
With a calm, heroic firmness
Worthy of thy native New World —
Worthy of thy noble New World;
Where thy kinsman, Guatemozin,
Bound, above the blazing fagots,
By his cruel Spanish captors,
Smiled, as smiles a happy father
When he bends to kiss his first-born
Sleeping on its mother's bosom! —
Smiled, and spake, to ease the anguish

Of his friend and fellow victim
Writhing on the grill beside him,
" Rest I on a bed of roses! "

Now, farewell! thou noble captive!
Wheresoever I may wander
Over land or over water,
Thy heroic form and features,
In the hour of thy destruction,
Shall, in my imagination,
Take the semblance of a brother,
Giving solace in my sorrow,
Giving firmness in my faintness,
Giving virtue in my vileness,—
Saying to me kindly, calmly,
" Native of the noble New World,
Be thou worthy of the New World,
Free to wander with the wild wind,
Or devoted to destruction,
Still uphold thee like a victor,
Unto death, thy life triumphant! "

THE ALHAMRA.

There is a secret charm about the place.
I cannot see it, but I feel its spell —
As if Caligorant had cast his net
Upon me here and bound me to the spot.

THE GERMAN EMPIRE.

The grandeur of the German Empire grows,
The longer I remain within its borders;
As I have known the might and majesty
Of thundering Niagara to swell
From a big waterfall at first unto
An overwhelming wonder on acquaintance!

IN THE CATACOMBS OF PALERMO.

While half the ever-whirling globe's aglow in the sun's light,
The other's in the shadow of itself in blackest night;
Hence mortal man, the microcosm, the world incorporate,
Between extremes in everything doth likewise alternate.

What's snow-white to one person is as soot-black to another;
What's lovely to the sister is as loathesome to the brother;
What's at one time the greatest good is at another evil;
What's worshiped this year as a God, next year's the very devil!

So weal and woe, and love and hate, are ever changing faces;
And wealth and want, and life and death, are ever changing places;
As if the world — according to our philosophic survey —
Were constant only in one thing, in turning topsy-turvy!

And what more striking proof than this, here, in Palermo's tomb —
The aisles and cells and corridors of this vast catacomb, —
The ghastly skulls and mouldering bones and flesh-dust of the dead
Appareled in the garments of the living overhead!

For every beggar in the streets, in ragged wretchedness,
Here is a mummied mockery in an imperial dress;
For every meagre starveling, in want and woe abjéct,
Here is a pile of bones and dust in pearls and diamonds deckt!

Haste, haste the day Time's turn-about will melt old Ætna's snow,
And send a mighty lava-flood into the vale below,
That the survivors of the great catastrophe may learn
The use of the volcanic verbs, to bury and to burn!

———

But this is now nor time nor place for philosophic dreams;
For why, the cicerone talks, and list'ning us beseems;
While on we go from cell to cell, pursued by scores of cats
Imprisoned in the sepulchre to kill marauding rats.

———

A soldier this — As brave a man as e'er faced unseen ball;
Ever the foremost with a heart no danger could appal;
The hero of a dozen wars; bedizened o'er with brass;
And, in an hour of triumph, killed — kicked by a pedler's ass!

And this a bride — Of forty-four; if not just in her prime,
At least, as woman's nature is, just in the nick of time;
Who, turning to her wedded lord to give the nuptial kiss,
Sank to the floor a pallid corpse, and then decayed to this!

A statesman this — Aye, when he lived, the Isle of
    Sicily
Was an imprisoned lion's cage to such a man as he!
Indeed a hemisphere could not contain his mighty
    schemes,
And yet this little cell now holds both him and all his
    dreams!

An actress this — Upon the stage, arrayed in silk and
    gold,
Cleópatra, Zenobia, or other queen of old;
Behind the scenes, a fiddler's wife, suckling a child be-
    got
Of dissipation and excess, a helpless idiot!

A doctor this — A wretched man, to gain a livelihood,
Hobnobbing with Disease and Death and dabbling in
    foul blood;
Until by chance his scalpel slipped and pricked him in
    the thigh,
And people stared that such a wound should make a
    doctor die!

A beauty this — In Sicily, perhaps, without a peer;
Her hand in matrimony sought, by nobles far and
    near;
And yet she wed a low buffoon, not worth a pod of
    pepper;
Danced on a wire in spangled tights, and died — a
    loathesome leper!

A poet this — No; not a youth with youthful passion
    fired,
But an old man, of lore profound, by purest love in-
    spired,
Who wrote a mighty epic of imperishable fame;
A native of Palermo, but — I have forgot his name!

And this the mother of twelve sons — A woman, too,
    as blest
As ever suckled hungry babe upon a bounteous breast;
For none of them before her death died either poor
    or young,
Except the first to warn the rest, and he was early
    hung!

A sculptor this — The same that cut the gross, indecent
    group
That damns Palermo's central fount — a nude encir-
    cling troop
Of wanton water-gods and nymphs — a monstrous
    personage array
Amid the mangled heads of a decapitate menagerie!

And this a boy — A prodigy — a miracle of lore;
Acquainted with all history and human art before
He reached his sixteenth summer; and, before he
    reached his next, —
"Those whom the gods love, perish young," I think's
    the old Greek text.

A beggar this — A mendicant, most miserably poor,
Limping along for sixty years, or more, from door to
    door;
Found dead at last in a damp cell, amid a mass of
    mold,
His wasted, wretched carcase prone on thrice its
    weight of gold!

A painter this — A drunken sot and maddened debau-
    chee —
A beastly bacchanalian of the very worst degree;
And yet evolving from his vice his work the most ap-
    proved,
A Mary, the Immaculate, by God himself beloved!

M

And this a priest — A holy man, fasting for years alone,
His weight exceeding never once as much as sixteen
    stone;
And drinking only water fresh and pure from flowing
    river;
And yet the doctors all agreed he died of hob-nailed
    liver!

A harlot this — Cleansing herself, at least, of patch
    and paint,
Became at sixty-five a nun and died next year a saint;
Her wealth bequeathed in charities unto a motley
    crowd,
A nunnery established, and a hospital endowed.

And this a fool — A happy dog, laughing the livelong
    day,
Turning to mirth the cares of earth, and soaking well
    his clay;
The father of some sixteen boys, and eighteen girls,
    or more,
And dying at the good old age of fourteen and four
    score!

A lawyer this — An honest man as ever drew a brief;
And yet considered commonly a trickster and a thief;
But such, in fine, 's the moral of the stories I rehearse,
The fact and its attendant fame are often the reverse.

And so the cicerone went, satirical and witty,
From skeleton to skeleton, in the sepulchral city,
Making the ugly mockery of Death like Life arrayed,
A still more ghastly spectacle, a mirthful masquerade!

THE CRUSADES IN SONG.

In contemplating the Crusades in Song,
It is incumbent on the philosophic
To note as well the singer as the subject.

A poem being the result of a
Relation 'twixt the poet and his theme;
And no two bards being identical
In aught essential to a son of song,
It follows that the poems which involve
In their construction the Crusades, diverge
As widely as the several poets, in
Whose variable brains the Holy Wars
Have been idealized, and in whose art,
As variable as their brains, their thoughts
Have found expression in poetic form.

To the poetic youth, that, haply, finds,
In the exuberance of health and vigor,
A pleasure in the exercise of the
Increasing powers of his mind and body,
The Middle Ages seem a holiday;
The sands of Syria, a sunny mead;
The wars of the Crusades, a game of ball;
The lion-hearted Richard, captain of
The Nine distinguished by the Cross of Christ,
And Saladin, the captain of their rivals,
Distinguished by the Crescent of Muhammad;
The Holy Sepulchre, the gilded ball,
Or tinseled belt, the trophy of the winners;
The very distance of the scene of action
Lending the charm of freedom from restraint,
In which the bounding and ambitious boy
Fancies achieved the end of his existence,
His independence founded firmly, and

His individuality maintained
Among mankind, a factor, like his sire,
In the formation of society,
Religion, law, and government, e'en as
So many merry games to suit himself!
O happy, hopeful, head- and heart-strong boy!
Blind-folded to misfortune, woe, and death;
Sailing the seas in self-manned cockle-shells,
And riding out with ease the storm in which
The strongest ship would be o'erwhelmed and wrecked;
Coasting on self-wrought jumpers down Mont Blanc
A length before a thund'ring avalanche,
And leaping, with a thrill of wild delight,
A precipice of a sheer thousand feet,
As safely as a breaker on the hillside;
And so encompassing the Holy Wars,
Extending o'er two centuries, in time,
Enacted on three continents, in space,
And, in a myriad of forms, involving
The slaughter of as many human beings
As would suffice to stock the planet Mars! —
Encompassing, in fine, all this within
The merry, merry metes and bounds of base-ball!

So, to another poet, a fair maid,
Expanding into womanhood, in whom
Feeling and fancy bear full sway by turns,
The Middle Ages seem the midnight hour;
The plains of Palestine, the gilded hall;
The Christians and Muhammadans in arms,
Her rival lovers at her side in mask —
The red blood of the vanquished Saracen
And the red-cross of the victorious Frank,
From rose-buds haply indistinguishable;
The flashing of the sword and scimetar,
The glances of her jealous rivals from

The east and from the west within her sight;
The battle-cry, the curse, the rush and roar
Of armies in defeat and victory,
The hurried whispers in her ears at parting;
And the world's prize for which the hosts contended,
The Holy Sepulchre of Christ, her heart!
O beauteous bubble in the sunshine, maid!
Unconscious of the world of woe and wrack
Beneath the pressure of her earth-fixed feet,
E'en while her head and heart are high in heaven;
Looking across the burning sands of life
And living in expectant ecstasy
In the fair Paradise of the mirage;
Hanging above the dizzy precipice
To cull the flowers that bloom upon the brink,
That, for a single hour, they may commingle
Their beauty with her own in others' eyes;
Bridging, amid the tempest's roar and rack,
The sea with the resplendent arch of heaven;
Resolving the Crusades into a heart-beat!

So, to the bard, a man, in middle life,
In whom destruction as a principle
Swirls in a vast and all-involving vortex,—
In whom the struggle for existence is
Intensified, and every impulse shaped
And sharpened to an instrument of death,—
The wars of the Crusades are wars in fact,
In which, from first to last, the direst scenes,
Of rapine, pillage, strife, and slaughter, that
Occurred in horrible reality,
Are reënacted in ideal forms.
Again, the voice of the crazed hermit, Peter,
In thunder tones calls him to arms and action;
Again, the locust-hordes of unrestrained,
Undisiplined, and headstrong soldiery
Are massacred in mobs in Hungary;

Again, Constantinople, Marra, Nice,
Are girt about, besieged, and sacked;
Again, gaunt famine gnaws at Antioch;
Again, the field of Doryléum is
Concealed beneath the bodies of the slain;
Again, Edessa, Sidon, Ascalon,
Tyre, Acre, Jaffa, Damietta, and
The leprous Ramleh are inscribed in blood
Within the tome of immortality;
Again, Jerusalem is stormed and sacked,
And,— horror of all horrors of the wars!—
The Tomb of Christ, the sacred symbol of
Goodwill to all mankind, and peace on earth,
Submerged within a sea of human blood;
And so on to the end, until above
The Cross, the Crescent of Muhammad gleams
Within the Holy City as to-day!
O mighty, murderous, and monstrous man!
Forgetting father, mother, wife, and child,—
Dissevering himself from all mankind,
And, ranging with the savage beasts of prey,
Exceeding them in greed and wanton slaughter!
Exultant only as the life-blood flows,
And the o'erthrown are heaped up in his sight;
His pride increased and gratified in a
Crude calculation that assumes to tell
The time the blood shed in the Holy Wars
Would feed the torrent of Niagara;
And his self immortality assured
In an appalling pile of human heads
Rising above the Pyramids of Egypt!

So, to the poet, a good wife and mother,
In whom the principle of preservation
Engrosses every function of the body,—
In whom — as in the symbol myth of old —
The Ark of Life rides out the Flood of Death,—
The Middle Ages represent the plague

Prevailing in her home and vicinage;
The Holy Land, a silent, curtained room,
In which she comes and goes and has her being,
A ministering angel in disguise;
The Franks and Turks, the hosts of life and death
Antagonistic on the bed before her;
And the redemption of the Holy Tomb,
The restoration of the sick to health.
A ministering angel, aye, in fact!
Oblivious to the producing cause
To the effect before her, in her charge;
Blind to all sights, save sorrow and its soothing;
Deaf to all sounds, save suff'ring and salvation;
Encompassing the Holy Wars within
The sleepless nights she watched upon her knees
Beside a cot on which a sick son lay
In an uncertain light — O Holy Mother!
Is it the dawning of the day of life,
Or the dusk deep'ning of the night of death?

So, to the bard, an old and feeble man,
Casting a backward look o'er his long life,
And, setting side by side the ends achieved
In manhood, and the hopes and dreams of youth,
Contrasting them in maudlin misery,—
The Middle Ages are his middle life;
The Holy Land, the field in which he ploughed;
The Franks and Turks, successes and reverses;
The Holy Tomb, the whited sepulchre,
Himself, in the extremities of age!
It is the palsied grandsire, looking back
O'er the long line of little grassy mounds
That mark the graves of buried hopes, until,
At last, behold! he sees himself aghast
Upon the very crumbling brink-edge of
A fathomless abyss oped to receive him —
The Holy Wars and all the world contains,
A miserable mask and mockery!

While, to the bard, an old and feeble woman,
Sitting within the warmest chimney-nook,
Rocking a sleeping babe within a cradle,
And crooning o'er the while a simple song
She learned in childhood from her own great
    grandame —
Perchance, while slumb'ring as the babe before
    her, —
The Middle Ages are her children and
Her children's children thrice removed from her;
The soldiers of the Cross and of the Crescent,
The sons and daughters of her blood and issue
And those of alien intermarried with them;
And, happily, the Holy Sepulchre,
The cradle with the blessèd image of
The Infant Jesus at her feet — the Hope
Of an Eternal Life in flesh and blood!

And so to poets, in whom age and sex
Are made subordinate, in whole or part,
To an engrossing vice or virtue, or
To an absorbing love or loathing, or
To any all-involving want or aim, —
The Holy Wars become a vehicle
As variable as the sentiments
To be conveyed — a song-chamæleon
Assuming its surrounding hues and colors,
Till indistinguishable from the leaves
And twigs it lives among a mimic life.

Take Tasso, Ariosto, and Bajardo,
Among Italian poets, for example:
Cringing and fawning at the feet of power,
Vain-glorious in their patriotic strains,
Lax in their morals, in religion light,
And, howsoe'er mellifluous in song,
As false as false can be in fiction when
It is not formulated first by fact, —

The Holy Wars in their poetic tomes
Are an eversion of their several selves
Of infinitely greater accuracy
Than an exhibit of their seeming subject.

In fine and fact, the Holy Wars in Song
Are but the mask before the poet's face.

THE CAMEL DRIVER AT CARTHAGE.

Loquitur — An Arab Camel Driver, from Timbuctoo.

Aye, Carthage stood here where I stand; and when I'm dead and gone,
How much the better's Carthage than poor Hassan Ali's son? —
Life shall have been the same to both, a certain, troubled span,
And death a mouldering back to earth, where both of us began!

For what is this unsightly waste of shards and broken stones,
But Carthage rotting in the sun, and bared unto the bones? —
And these poor Arabs in their caves, — dark, damp, low-arched, and narrow,
Beneath Queen Dido's palace walls, — but maggots in the marrow?

But, as for that, what is the great, revolving globe beneath,
But a still greater Carthage in a deeper dust of death! —

Whereon the greatest wealth of life at any time
        amassed
Were but a camel's taste of grass within Sahara's
        waste!

Or rich or poor, or great or small, or ancient Hannibal,
Or modern Hassan Ali's son, this is the end of all!—
I thank thee, ruined Carthage, for the lesson I have
        got,
To be content with—aye, to bless the camel driver's
        lot!

Come! come! companion of my life upon Sahara's
        sand,
Earth knows no happier home than ours, in her most
        favored land;
With the dear dust beneath our feet, a cloudless sky
        o'erhead,
We are the world of life alone, and all besides, the
        dead!

Come! come! the rarer water flows, the dearer every
        drop;
Come! come! the wearier the way, the sweeter every
        stop;
Come! come! without the trials that forever us pur-
        sue,
There were no diamonds in the dust 'twixt here and
        Timbuctoo!

Ah, Timbuctoo! how quick thy name, to make my
        heart rejoice!
As if I heard in it afar the fond, familiar voice
Of her, the loadstar of my life, by Allah's mercy given,
To lead me o'er Sahara's sands, as if I were in
        Heaven!

JOHN CHINAMAN.

Loquitur — A Chinese Washerman, in California, contemplating the civilizations of the Eastern and Western Worlds, and contrasting the achievements of JOHN CHINAMAN with those of JOHN BULL and BROTHER JONATHAN.

Four hundred millions of mankind — one-third of all
    the souls,
Embodied in the human form, between the planet's
    poles! —
I aggregate; and yet, in the great universal plan,
Beyond my bourne, what am I but a pig-tailed wash-
    erman!

Strung on a string, like beads, my heads, bestowed by
    the Creator,
Would put a girdle round about the globe at the equa-
    tor;
And yet from out this world of brains, a thought has
    never been
Evolved and wrought into a good and practical ma-
    chine!

My aggregated height extends beyond the midnight
    moon;
And yet I've never gone aloft a foot in a balloon;
And with eight hundred million eyes — up-squinting
    eyes at that —
I've never seen in space, perhaps, as much as a tom-
    cat!

My aggregated blood would make a sea within my
    bones,
In which the largest ship could sail, or sink to Davy
    Jones,
And yet I've never built a boat more useful than a
    junk —
A sort of sloop stove-up astern — a schooner on a
    drunk!

My aggregated heart would hold the great symbolic
    dome
That rises like a mighty moon above the walls of
    Rome;
And yet I've never sung a song the world repeats for-
    ever,
Nor made a creed to civilize a savage unbeliever!

My aggregated breath would make about as big a bliz-
    zard
As that foretold by Wiggins, the Canadian weather-
    wizard;
And yet with all my strength of lungs, I do not blow
    a bubble
To aid the progress of the world, or save mankind
    from trouble.

I am a mighty multitude — of tadpoles in a puddle,
With the tadpolean tendency about the rim to huddle;
Four hundred million half-evolved or stunted polli-
    wogs
That can't exchange their gills for lungs and turn to
    toads and frogs!

Aye, aye, the tadpole, with its tail and undeveloped
    nature,
Well typifies John Chinaman in every striking feature;

As if, on a gigantic scale, in his prolonged submersion,
To prove the truth of Darwin's law about the type's
    reversion.

Four hundred million tadpoles, in an oriental bog,
Kowtowing to the Tatar, like a fossilized King Log;
Or, wriggling from the crowded pool, to 'Frisco or New
    York,
To find a tyrant in the Times as fatal as King Stork!

True, I've invented powder; but I've never had the
    knack, or
Appreciation of its worth, to make more than a
    cracker;
Which, when contrasted with the work with it by
    others wrought,
Is as a herring on a hook to all the rest uncaught!

And so, I've practised printing, in a crude way, for an
    age,
And never have advanced beyond the simplest stamp-
    ing stage;
Which, when contrasted with the work with it by
    others done,
Is as a burning tallow-dip unto the noonday sun!

So, I have known the needle for a thousand years or
    more,
And never used it save in sight of a familiar shore!—
For all the good it's been to me, or others of mankind,
I might as well have trusted to a kite-tail in the wind!

And so, before all others, I discovered, it would seem,
That water super-heated is converted into steam;
And yet I've never gone beyond my childhood's bath-
    tub splashing,
To use hot water anyway except to do my washing!

In fine, in this electric age, I am so far behind
The foremost of the fighters in the battle of mankind,
I must pronounce myself, in truth, a most stupendous
    sham —
Not worth, in the grand march of Man, a continental
    damn!

IN NORWAY.

The conscious brain conceiving only one
Thing at a time, it follows necessar'ly
A little thing may take precedence of
And occupy the mind to the exclusion
Of all the known and unknown world besides.
"The grand old ballad of Sir Patrick Spens,"
(As Coleridge styles the questionable poem,)
With an affrontery the most provoking,
Unbidden comes into the private chamber
Of my imagination, locks the door,
And takes a cozy chair before the fire,
And croaks, " To Noroway!" " To Noroway!"
With the persistency of Poe's weird raven,
When I would fain admit into my sanctum
The mighty Myth-men of the North, whose names
Send a courageous quiver through my veins,
And heave my breast with a heroic sigh!

LONDON.

Among the cities of the present age,
As the Atlantosaurus of the past
Among the monsters of the airy earth,
Preëminent, predominant, prodigious!

THE CANNIBAL ISLANDS.[1]

As, in the goodly body of a man,
There is a part peculiarly exempt
From the destructive wear and tear of work,
And the inevitable waste of passion;
And yet, in which corruption of the flesh
Is most engendered and most active in
Developing disease, decay, and death;
Albeit, in the midst of other parts
The most important in preserving life —
The heart, belike, the vital pendulum,
Or the bone-boxed cerébrum, wisdom's seat.

So, in the towns and cities of mankind,
There is a part peculiarly exempt
From the destructive wear and tear of work,
And the inevitable waste of war;
And yet, in which corruption of the mind
Is most engendered and most active in
Developing disorder, lawlessness,
And crime, in each and every of its forms,
From an assault upon a single man
To an o'erturning of a settled state;
Albeit, haply, in the shadow of
A hospital, endowed with untold wealth,
To minister unto the sick and sore,
And save the wreckage of mankind in body;
Or a cathedral, founded in the earth
And spired in heaven, to minister, as well,
Unto the hopeless, faint, and broken-hearted,
And save the wreckage of mankind in spirit.

And so, in the four quarters of the globe,
As in the goodly body of a man,

And in the towns and cities of mankind,
There is a part — the thousand isles between
The Indian and the Pacific oceans,
Malayan stocked — peculiarly exempt
From the destructive wear and tear of work
In order to maintain a livelihood —
A feast provided for the meanest man,
And set within his reach, the like of which,
With all his wealth, a Roman emperor
Ne'er placed upon the board before his guests —
The durian, belike, and mangosteen;
And equally exempt from the typhoons
That swirl o'erwhelming in the seas surrounding;
And yet, in which the forces of destruction,
Involved within the body and the mind,
Are most intense, engrossing, and o'erwhelming:
It is the land of lands, of robbery;
It is the sea of seas, of piracy;
It is the land and sea of butchery;
The savage greed of the inhabitants
Appeased not till the bodies of the slain
Are torn and mangled in their beastly jaws,
And mingled with their monstrous flesh and blood!
Albeit, in the sight of the fair flag
Of England, Holland, the United States,
Or other of the great enlightened league,
Combined for the protection of mankind
Against the very evils here engendered
As an inherent and eternal right!
And in the sound, as well, of the sweet bell
Of a society of holy men,
Who, in the name of Buddha or of Christ,
Seek to attain entire the end through love,
Which, only in a measure, the strong hand
Of government can bring about through war.

Methinks, in fine, that as to man, the part
Most prone in him to breed disease and death,—

And as to the great city of New York,
The dread Five Points, or to the greater London,
The Seven Dials, so, unto the world
At large, the Malay Archipelago,
The Islands of the South Sea Cannibals!

---

[1] "The Malayo-Polynesian races are possessed of an almost incredible degree of savagery and bloodthirstiness. They are the cannibals par eminence, not through want of food but through the peculiar hardness of their character. Cannibalism is practised not only among the inhabitants of the South Sea islands, but even among several of the civilized races of the west, such as the Bataks of Sumatra, who have produced a written literature, and who have cannibal rites in certain cases even prescribed by law." — G. A. F. VAN RHYN.

GREECE.

An epoch in the evolution of
The most evolved organic form of earth —
The ultimate attained by mortal man
Within the compass of the human hide:
In beauty, valor, virtue, wisdom, worth,—
In oratory, wit, philosophy,—
In sculpture, music, painting, poesy,—
Ere metamorphosing, by change and chance,
Into a super-self of steel and steam —
A super-human monster — a Machine!

VANDAL AND ANDALUSIA.

What mumbling masks of meaning are our words!
The Vandal is the hurricane incarnate
That leaves the world in chaos in its track;
While [V] Andalusia is — this Paradise!

A PRINCESS OF THE ORIENT.

Loquitur — The Princess . . . . , of . . . .

A princess! How I loathe the word! as if, within
    the sound,
A serpent, with constricting folds, my limbs and body
    bound,
Chilling the blood within my heart, envenoming my
    sighs,
While hissing hate and darting death within my ears
    and eyes!

A princess! Aye, a pyramid, like the stupendous pile
That symbolizes fire in stone, upon the banks of
    Nile,—
An apex in the social sky, with diamonds all aglow,
A base, as wide as woman, built upon a world of woe!

My father was of royal blood, but one step from the
    throne,
Till found in a depleted ditch, beneath a murderous
    stone;
And she that bare me in her womb, a Georgian slave
    by birth,
Ennobled by the nuptial knot — to curse with me the
    earth!

A babe — Not like the infant bee, destined to be a
    queen,
Fed full and fondly with the sweets ten thousand min-
    ions glean;

But stinted by a Nubian nurse, with lank and flabby dugs,
And stunted by a Mino maid, with hemp and poppy drugs.

A child — Within the harem's walls, a prisoner confined, —
The latitude allowed my limbs, the measure of my mind;
A whitened weed within a cave, amassing mould and smut;
A worm within the hardened shell of a decaying nut!

A bride — Did ever mottled moth emerge from its coccoon
To meet its mate in the soft light of the refulgent moon,
With greater change and greater joy, than I to greet my lord —
To find myself the bestial slave of one my soul abhorred!

A wife — Is there among the woes that human life beset —
Is there a scab, a scar, or sore, that crime and chance begot,
More overwhelming in its weight, and no escape allows,
Than to a woman the embrace of a disgusting spouse!

A mother — Aye, the mother of a babe I hoped to be
The recompense for all the woes the world had heaped on me;
But like his sire —— Oh, God forgive the heart I cannot hide!
I never felt a greater joy than when my baby died!

A widow — Aye, there is but one conclusion to a life
Of riotous debauchery, in unremitting strife
With Nature's laws, no monarch's moan or mandate
    can suspend,—
Decay, disease, a maddened brain, and an untimely
    end!

A woman — Not yet twenty-two, and yet, within that
    span,
Tortured with all that ever tried the woman-half of
    man,
From the most menial Æthiop, that groveled in the
    ground,
To the most noble princess — whom the social serpent
    bound!

A woman — One whom Time and Space have organized
    for naught:
To waste away from day to day, henceforth, and then
    to rot —
Without a future in the flesh in any other form
Than in the bloated segments of the blind sepulchral
    worm![1]

O Allah! I would rather be the basest of the base,
So be it I might live and love incarnate with a race,
Than gleam another instant in this artificial glare,
A Princess of the Orient, incorporate Despair!

---

[1] Cf., the sentiment of Antigone, on dying without issue.

THE EASTERN HEMISPHERE.

The Old World — Nay, to me, at least, the New:
So all things vary from a selfish view.

THE WANDERING JEW.

LOQUITUR—A Jewish Rabbi on Mount Olivet.

I stand upon Mount Olivet, to feel, as ne'er before,
Jehovah's curse on Israel in its appalling power!—
The curse that drave my fathers hence and ceased not
    to pursue,
Until each outcast felt himself, as I — The Wandering
    Jew.

For what behold I from this height? The fields my
    fathers tilled,
And to transmit them to their sons, their dearest
    heart's-blood spilled,—
This weather-washed and worn-out waste! this stretch
    of ghastly stones!—
Like a wolf-haunted graveyard strewn with dead men's
    bleaching bones!

And there, the City of the Jews, where, from a moun-
    tain base,
The Temple of Jehovah rose to sanctify the place;—
Where, now, the Garden Serpent lives within the fanes
    of foes,
And Israel is driven forth with banished Adam's woes!

Where, now, at the closed gate, on guard, the Angel of
    the Lord
Stands with the baleful blade of old, a double-edgèd
    sword—
The Christian and the Saracen in an incessant jar,
Changing with strife the Place of Peace into the Place
    of War!

O mockery of mockeries, of this illusive earth!
The sacred city of my sires, the womb-land of my
    birth,—
This donjon-keep upon a rock, where self-imprisoned
    hosts,
In earnest of eternal life, make one another ghosts!

I turn in anguish from the scene; and lo! within my
    gaze,
The waters of the Jordan flow, as in the olden days!
O symbol stream of Israel! descended from the skies,
And flowing ever thus unto the gates of Paradise!....

Ah, no! I see the shimmer of a shrinking, sunken sea,
As well as Jordan's pearly flood, a symbol unto me!—
It is the end of Israel! It is—I gasp for breath!—
It is the end of Israel in bitterness and death!

O woe! to see my fathers' fields, a waste in foemen's
    hands!
O woe! to see my fathers' shrines, the spoils of war-
    ring bands!
O woe! to see the Stream of Life its course accursed
    pursue
Into the bitter Sea of Death! O woe! the Wandering
    Jew!

THE GERMAN.

A mongrel cross between the Hun and Goth:
The Hun, the mother, captive ta'en in war,
Out-cropping in her dark-skinned, lozenge-headed,
Up-squinting eyed, and music-loving daughters;
The Goth, the father, grim at work and war,
Transmitting to his sons his language, laws,
Lore, love of arms, round head, and mystic brain.

THE RIDDLE OF THE SPHINX.

Loquitur — A Donkey-Driver, from Cairo.

I am a donkey-driver, Sphinx.   Now, tell me, what art
    thou? —
The Watch-dog of the Pyramids? — Or, lacking a
    bow-wow,
The Demon of the Desert, with a sullen flow of bile,
Contémplating the conquest of the Valley of the
    Nile?

Or, haply, good old Mother Earth, time-touched and
    weather-worn,
With still the special vanity in every woman born,
Craning as high as possible thy wrinkled neck forever,
To see thyself reflected in the mirror of the river?

I mock thee, Sphinx! — And pause, in awe, to stare
    into the eyes,
That, silently and steadily, like planets in the skies,
Have seen the sultans of the earth, the sages, and the
    saints,
The sculptor with his chisel, and the limner with his
    paints, —

Come and depart in little clouds of dust within the
    track
Of a stupendous caravan, extending back, back, back,
Into the dusk and darkness of the world's primæval
    waste,
The lampless and unlettered, the illimitable past!

The eyes of stone, that with the self-same calm com-
    placency,
Now look out and behold, among the sons of Ægypt,
    me!—
In the brief instant of my life, the well- or ill-spent
    span,
In which this cloud of desert dust assumes the shape
    of Man!

And yet since thou, that art, like me, made of the
    desert dust,
Canst live through all the ages an insensible stone bust,
Why may not I immortal be, and never come to
    naught,
As sentient shape and substance, or as subtler, skull-
    less Thought?

As subtler, skull-less Thought, like that imparted unto
    thee,
That makes thee an Ægyptian and an image unto
    me—
A second self in solid stone—a souvenir through time,
To show me—and my donkey—what I was when in
    my prime!

Come, come, my donkey! swell thyself! until thy
    sweenied hide
Conform to the proportions of the Sphinx that will
    thee ride,
When I —— What! wilt begin to bray, when I before
    thee pass?
Thou indurated ingrate! thou impenetrable ass!

MILITARY GERMANY.

A porcupine — bristling with bayonets.

DOWN THE ANDES IN A HAND-CAR.

The descent was made on Wednesday, the 7th day of January, 1885, on the standard-gauge trans-Andean railroad of Peru, (called El Ferro Caril del Callao, Lima y Oroya,) from its present mountain terminus, Chicla, at an elevation of 12,220 feet above the level of the sea, to San Bartolome, at an elevation of 4049 feet — a distance of 39 English miles, at an average gradient of 186½ feet to the mile: the minimum being zero for a few rods at the nine V's, or switchbacks, and the maximum 264 feet to the mile. The summit tunnel of this railroad, already cut for the passage of the workmen, is at an elevation of 15,722 feet, which, I believe, is the highest point attained by any railroad on the globe. The construction of the road so far has cost the great sum of twenty-eight millions of American money; and according to the reported contract, recently [1885] awarded by the government of Peru to Grace & Company, of New York and Lima, a further sum of thirty millions will be expended for its completion over the great mountain chain to one of the navigable tributaries of the Amazon in the heavily wooded and marvelously productive valley beyond.

From Chicla to San Bartolome, the railroad is constructed along the precipitous walls of the great quebrada, barranca, break, or cañon of the river Rimac; and among the noteworthy features of the line are tunnels connected by bridges; in two places, two parallel tunnels, one directly over the other; in several places, three and four lines above one another; the highest railway bridge in the world, (unless the Kinzua bridge in Pennsylvania exceeds it;) and the marvel of all marvels in the world of railroad engineering, a stone arch bridge within a tunnel over a cavernous abyss found in the heart of one of the largest masses of rock pierced in that part of the cañon called El Infiernillo, or the Little Hell.

Compared with a similar hand-car descent of the foot-hills of the Himalayas, from Darjiling, at an elevation of approximately 8000 feet, to Guyabára, at an elevation of 4000, the descent of the Andes is infinitely more thrilling and pleasurable on account of the extreme narrowness and ruggedness of the cañon traversed, the myriad of weird and ghastly scenes presented, and the bewildering beauty of a rushing, roaring, milk-

P

white river passing from rapid to cataract and from cataract to seething caldron without intermission for 39 miles! — to say nothing of the greater danger, whirrring and whizzing ever, except in the tunnels and a few cuttings and fillings, on the brink of a precipice, over which the breaking of a wheel, a little stone on the track, or the unexpected factor of the thousand and one every-day accidents, would hurl the rider into eternity.

Clear and cold the ambient æther,
In the first hours of the morning,
In the cheerless town of Chicla,
Near the snow-line of the Andes,
In the country of the Incas,
Conquered by the steel-clad Spaniards
Headed by the bold Pizarro.

Sharp the clink and clear the clangor
Of the wheels and tracks impinging,
As the roadmen, raw-hide sandaled,
Take the hand-car from a terrace
And adjust it on the twin rails
Of the wonder way of iron
Winding up and down the Andes,
In the grim and ghastly cañon
Cut and fashioned by the Rimac[1]
In its rushing from the snow-line
Of the mighty Cordilléras
To the shore-line of the ocean,
The Pacific, or the South Sea.

Oiled the axles, laid the cushions,
"Ready!" cries the sturdy master,[2]
Gloved and muffled in a great coat,
With his right hand on the brake-bar,
And his left to me extended.
Seated by the burly master —
Oh, will not my head cease aching!
And my heart its hurried beating!

And my breast its panting, panting,
Like a wounded pigeon taken
'Twixt the sportsman's thumb and finger!
No; it is not fear affects me,
But the Demon of Surroche,[3]
In the rare and radiant æther,
Near the snow-line of the Andes —
On the confines of the kingdom
Mortal beast nor bird ne'er enters,
Nor approaches, save the llama,
Half and half a goat and camel,
Clinging to the cañon's brink-edge,
And the condor, king of vultures,
Soaring o'er the lagging llama,
Waiting for the first of missteps
To provide him with a mawfull
In the dark depth of the cañon.

Round the wheels go, fast and faster!
Cold the blast comes, strong and stronger!
O'er my shoulders bending forward,
Parted streams my grizzled whiskers;
From my lashes, half-closed, quiv'ring,
Flit in spray diffusive tear-drops.
Ho! was ever race more rapid!
On the swiftest of toboggans —
On the fleetest of the ice-boats!
Or more thrilling, weird, and eldritch!
On the back of phantom charger —
On the shoulders of the devil,
By the short-cut of a crater,
Dashing from the world of sunshine
Into that of sin and sulphur!

Round the wheels go, fast and faster!
Rattling, roaring, rumbling, rasping,
Scirring, scouring, skimming, scorching —
Circled now and then with fire-streaks

Streaming from the closing brake-blocks!
Over bridges, light and airy;
Thorough tunnels, dark as dungeons;
Now, within a ragged cutting;
Now, adown a land-slide filling;
Now, along a dizzy brink-edge,
Swinging, swaying, reeling, rocking,
As if vacillating, whether
To continue on the twin tracks,
Or forsake them — God have mercy!

Glancing eagerly around me —
Gneiss and porphyry and greenstone,
Shale and marble, coal and granite,
Yellow streaks of lead and silver,
Passing quickly in succession,
Interblending form and color
In a vast and vague mosaic —
In a vision to a dreamer
Lapped and folded in a silken
Quilt of divers hues and shapings.

Glancing eagerly above me —
Cliffs and crags and peaks confounding
In their vastness and confusion
Metaphoric nomenclature —
Castles, battlemented towers,
Steeples, cyclopéan ruins, —
Baalbec, Stonehenge, Karnak, Memphis,
In a circumvolving chaos!
Snowy patches in the sunshine
Dazzling in their lustrous whiteness;
And above them in the blue sky,
Lo! the moon, 'twixt half and gibbous,
Like a jelly-fish careening
In the azure of the ocean!

Glancing eagerly beneath me —
Gulch, ravine, barranca, cañon,

Gorge, quebrada, gap, and crevice,
In whose darkened depths descending,
Lo! the snow-born river Rimac!
Ha! the rushing, roaring Rimac,
Like a herd of milk-white horses
Plunging madly down the cañon —
Manes and tails and forelocks streaming,
Hoofs against the rocks resounding,
Nostrils streaming, eyeballs gleaming,
Flakes of froth around them flying!
Ha! a herd of maddened horses
Racing with the whirring hand-car —
With the whizzing, whistling hand-car,
From the snow-line of the Andes
To the shore-line of the ocean!

Stop! Responsive to the brake-bar
In the right hand of the master,
Lo! the wheels have ceased their motion
Just midway 'twixt hell and heaven!
Where the mountain walls contracting
Form a narrow gorge compounding
The sublime, the weird, and awful;
Where the railroad robs the river
Of the right of way for ages
And diverts it through a tunnel
And adown a rugged stairway
To a dark, profound quebrada,
Over which an iron cobweb
Stretches from opposing tunnels,
Whence the steaming locomotive
Issues on the airy fabric
And retreats into the darkness,
Like a monstrous hairy spider
In a corner of the Andes,
In pursuit of moths and millers
In the flitting clouds and shadows;
Where a sheer stupendous column

With abutting curving strata
Seem a pier and arch in ruin
Of a viaduct constructed
By the Titans of the old tales,
By the Brobdingnags of modern.

Seated once more in the hand-car;
Round the wheels go, fast and faster;
Cold the blast comes, strong and stronger;
Whirling, whirring, whizzing, whistling,
From the shadow into sunlight,
From the sunlight into shadow,
Racing with the river Rimac! —
What a wondrous thing of beauty
Falling water in the chaos
Of a myriad of motions —
Interchanging form and color —
Interblending light and shadow —
Intermingling the observer
With the falling in the compound,
Till behold! the twain a union —
Falling water and observer —
Like long-severed man and woman
In the gloaming come together.

This, the town of San Matéo
Sacked and burned by the Chilénos —
What a ghastly exposition,
In this cañon of the Andes,
Of the woe and waste of warfare !
That, upon yon granite boulder —
That the skull of a Chiléno
Slaughtered by a Cholo woman
Fleeing frenzied with her first-born
Snatched from out a burning cottage,
Blackened, charred, a child of ashes !

Those, yon dangling frayed-out rope-ends —
Those, the means by which suspended

O'er the precipice, the workmen
Cut a foot-hold in the sheer wall —
Cut a foot-hold, then a platform,
For the tunnels, slopes, and sidings
Of this wondrous mountain railway! —
Heroes they, those workmen swinging
In the air a hundred fathoms
From the ragged cliff above them
And the surging sea beneath them,—
Aye, as well as those ennobled
In the warring of the nations
And the storming of the oceans!

This, the bridge of Chaupicháca;
This, the town of Matucána;
This, the great bridge of Verrúgas —
Highest of the bridges spanning
Gorge and river in the whole world! —
Every rivet representing
One that died here in its building —
Died of the Oróya fever,
Deadliest of intermittents,
Or the plague of warts, verrúgas —
Whence the name of bridge and river.

Bridge and tunnel, cut and filling,
Cut and filling, bridge and tunnel —
See the flashing rays of sunlight,
In the midnight of the mountain,
Upward borne along the bright tracks,
Upward borne along the curved tracks,
From the world beyond the cavern;
Like the glances from the great eyes
Of the demon of a nightmare,
Faint at first, then growing brighter,
As the fiend comes nearer, nearer,
Till upon the sleeper's waking,

Lo! they pass into the sunshine
Streaming through the parted curtains!

That commotion in the village —
Those in mask and garb fantastic,
Dancing to the piper's music,
Celebrate an ancient festa —
Festa of the Kings, they call it.
See the aprons of the women,
Worn upon the left side only
From the shoulder to the ankle —
Worn, they say, as a memento
Of the empire of the Incas —
Of their dead and buried fathers —
They that built the terrace gardens
Now in dreary waste and ruin
On the mountain steeps above us,
On the mountain steeps below us,
Like the steps of the stone courses
Of the Pyramids of Ghizeh —
They that cut the water-channels
In the granite, gneiss, and greenstone,
From the snow-line of the Andes,
To the level of their gardens,
Changing, as if by enchantment,
These bald wastes of mountain desert
Into oases of plenty
Teeming with a happy people —
Oases of fruits and flowers
Rivaling the hanging gardens
Of the City of the Chaldee,
Babylon, the old world's London —
Rivaling the floating gardens
Of the City of the Aztecs,
Mexico, the new world's Venice —
Realizing unto millions
All the wonders, wealth, and beauty
Of the gardens feigned by fancy,

From the Eden of the Hebrews
To the Garden of Alcina.

On, from one depth to another,
Deeper, deeper, deeper, deeper,
Down the cañon of the Rimac;
Curving now within a cutting
Round the face of sheer headland
With the ease and grace of motion
Of the albatross exulting
In the fury of a tempest,
Pirouetting on a wing-tip
In the spind-drift of a wave-crest!
Ha! was ever speed compounded
With such grace and joy of motion
On the brink-edge of destruction!
Now zigzagging, like a dolphin,
Swiftest of the ocean swimmers,
Coursing with an iron steamer,
Darting hither, darting thither,
Disappearing, reäppearing,
As if teasing the great monster
To forsake its life of labor
And pursue it in its gambols!
Doubling now and passing thorough
Tunnels one above the other;
Like a cunning rabbit, feeling
On its flanks the greyhound's hot breath,
Darting under first one fence-rail
Then aback beneath another,
Leaving its pursuer baffled!
Ha! as I have left behind me
The fell Demon of Surróche,
The dread monster of the Andes,
In the guise of a grim savant,
With a bell-glass and an air-pump,
Sitting on the Cordilléras —

Q

He that clapped o'er me his bell-glass,
Then with a spasmodic action,
Pumped out half the air around me;
Ogling me through double lenses,
And with scrutinizing tortions,
While I panted, puffed, and stifled,
While I passed from pain to torture,
Bleeding from my ears and nostrils,
Temples bursting like a bombshell,
All the Andes on my breast-bone! —
Till I took the whirring hand-car —
Took the whizzing, whistling hand-car,
And my leave of the grim savant,
With his bell-glass and his air-pump,
Sitting on the Cordilléras!

Five and thirty bridges passed o'er,
Ten and thirty tunnels raced through,
Nine and thirty miles of railroad
Traversed in the whirring hand-car —
Stop! Responsive to the brake-bar
In the right hand of the master,
Lo! the wheels have ceased their motion
At San Bártol'me, a station,
In the valley of the Rimac
'Mong the foot-hills of the Andes,
And my mad-cap ride is ended —
In the sound of mirth and laughter,
In the sight of pears and melons,
In the scent of steaming dishes,
In the touch of plate and platter,
In the taste of a rare breakfast —
Earth unto the earthy, after
The celestial spirit's rapture
In its flight adown the Andes,
Like —— How opportune the object
In my sight the while I want it! —
Like yon meteor descending

In the sunshine and the shadow
From the æther of the zenith
To the earth of the horizon![4]

---

[1] The accent of the name of this mountain river is not on the final syllable, as placed by some, according to the Spanish rule of pronunciation with respect to words terminating in a consonant, but on the penultimate, as in its transmuted form *Lima*, by dropping the unaccented *c*, and making the usual change of *r* into *l*. The word is not Spanish, but Quichua; and signifying *He that speaks*, or *has spoken*, was originally the name of a famous oracular deity enshrined in the ancient city whose extensive ruins are found to-day on the banks of the river near the village of La Magdalena. From the oracle, the name passed to the river; and from the river, in the form of *Lima*, to the city founded by Pizarro and called by him La Ciudad de los Reyes, or the City of the Kings.

[2] Mr. WILLIAM ELLIS, a native of Cleveland, Ohio, to whom the writer takes great pleasure in acknowledging his obligations for one of the most pleasurable experiences of his varied life.

[3] The word *soroche*, *surroche*, or *sirochi*, (as it is spelled variously,) applied in Peru to the distress or disease produced by breathing the rarified air of great altitudes, is a corrupted form of the word *sirocco*, applied to an intensely oppressive and smothering wind in the North of Africa and the South of Europe — the *brickfielder* of the Mediterranean, as an Australian would say. So agonizing are the tortures of the Demon of the Andes to many persons, that the only enjoyment and memorable experience they have in making the ascent of the mountain is (paradoxically, or after the manner of the Milesians of popular belief,) in making the descent, and that as quickly as possible. Mr. GALEGA, the English journalist, tells the story of a man who suffered so much on his arrival at Chicla that he paid the railroad company $1,500.00, to take him down on the locomotive immediately to a point at which he could breathe in comfort.

[4] The appearance of this fire-ball, shooting-star, aërolite, or whatsoever meteor it was in the shape and semblance of a globe of gleaming silver, occurred at one of the several stops made in the descent, and passed from the outer into the inner vision of the writer as a most felicitous symbol of speech to express his rapid flight in a perfect glow of enthusiasm from the rare and radiant environment of Chicla to the every-day earthies of the earth of San Bartolome.

HUMOR IN HOLLAND.

No, no, my dear, because the Dutch live forty feet or more
Beneath the surface of the sea, along a sunken shore,
The Dutch girls are not mermaids, those anomalously odd fish
Depicted by the poets as half woman and half codfish!

And since they are amphibious, in habitat at least,
They're not web-footed and duck-billed, like the Australian beast —
Or-nith-o-rhyn-chus — Catch your breath, now, — *par-a-dox-us,* — so! —
That puzzled the zoölogists some forty years ago!

And never having seen a hill save in reverse — a hole,
I take it, a true Hollander, to save his very soul,
Cannot imagine mountain peaks, of which he's heard and read,
Without inverting all the world, or standing on his head!

And never having seen the sea except above the plain,
He can't conceive of cataracts descending to the main! —
And, for the very life of him, he can't become the wiser,
And see a waterfall but in an upward spouting geyser!

And looking ever down into the hollow of his land,
It is not very difficult for us to understand,

How he should leave to all besides the love of flow'rs
    and fruit,
And fall enraptured on his knees before a tulip root!

Indeed, my dear, since mortal mind, no matter what
    its bent,
Is but a sentient photograph of its environment,
We should not be surprised to find this truth down in
    the well,
The Dutchman thinks he's going to Heaven, when on
    his way to hell!

Hence, what appears the best to us must seem to him
    the worst,
And every blessèd town he has, in consequence, ac-
    cursed; —
In truth, from infancy, without the least compunctious
    qualm,
He never mentions one without a most emphatic dam!

THE WORLD.

The world — a little love, success, or weal,
Converts into an orb so beautiful,
The savage sun looks down on it aglow
With admiration and enthusiasm;
The timid moon creeps up at dusky eve
To gaze on it in wonder and delight;
And all the shrinking, fearful stars afar
Come out together to behold its splendor!
The world — a little hate, defeat, or woe,
Converts into a putrifying carcase —
A sick'ning stench unto the very snails,
Withdrawing in their solitary cells,
In soul-sequestered, stone-encased seclusion!

AT WATERLOO.

I do not say there were in fact, but that, to me, at
 least,
It seems there were two Bonapartes — a man and
 monstrous beast!
The man, of woman born, to die, as you and I must
 do;
The beast, ripped from the womb of war, to rot at
 Waterloo!

The man, in form, a Puss-in-Boots, to ladies in the hall,
And to the soldiers in the field, the Little Corporal;
The beast, in form —— men stood aghast, and stared,
 with bated breath,
And saw not till the beast had passed, it bore the
 shape of Death!

The man, upon his little legs, scarce walking half a
 league,
Without perspiring freely and complaining of fatigue;
The monster here, there, everywhere, coming or having
 passed,
Indifferent to time and space as a cyclonic blast!

The man, perhaps, a day or two, at Madrid, Brussels,
 Rome,
Vienna, Moscow, Jaffa, or Great Alexander's tomb;
The beast, for years, a pestilence, as fearful and as fell,
Extending o'er three continents the horrors of a hell!

The man, perhaps, like you and I, partaking, thrice
 a day,
Of meat and drink, and getting full, in a familiar way;

The monster ravaging the earth, to pity deaf and
    blind,
Devouring with insatiate greed two millions of man-
    kind!

The man reposing now in dust, beneath a marble mass,
As indistinguishable from a man as from an ass;
The monster rotting in this mound, a stench unto the
    sky —
As terrible a dragon as e'er feigned in fantasy!

Baugh! baugh! the British Lion, on this monumental
    mound,
When a far better symbol of Old England could be
    found!
Instead of this, the King of Beasts, how came she not
    to forge
The figure of her patron saint, The Dragon-slaying
    George!

CHINA.

A pterodactyle with extended wings,
O'ershadowing the mud of Middle Asia.

In worshiping the dead and buried past,
Bearing a world upon its brawny shoulders,
An Atlas ever bowed down to the earth.

THE HUN.

A strange and eldritch figure jutting out
From mediæval murkiness, like a
Grim gargoyle from a ruined abbey wall.

THE GOTH AND THE HUN.

To me, in contemplation — when the outer world has sped,
And that within is peopled with the spectres of the dead, —
The mediæval Goth and Hun, of the historic page,
Assume strange shapes within the gloom of a departed age.

Betimes, the Goth, of massive mould, with shaggy beard and hair,
Comes in the monstrous semblance of the huge spelæan bear;
And the fierce Hun, fur-clad to face the northern winter's rigor,
In the appalling guise of the ferocious sword-toothed tiger!

Anon, the rival monsters, in their savage search of food,
Meet in terrific conflict in the wild primæval wood;
The grim, gigantic Gothic bear, erect with short-sword claws,
The Hunnic tiger in the air, with sabres in his jaws!

And lo! just as they join in fight, by some phantasmal trick,
The bear assumes the likeness of the mighty Álaric!
And the fierce tiger in the air, as lithe as willow-rod,
Dread Attila, upon his steed, the savage Scourge of God!

IN THE CITY OF MEXICO.

It was the morning after I arrived
In Mexico, (a refuge in a marsh
To savages some centuries ago,
And now a city to their Christian sons
Among a motley mob from every part
Of Christendom,) I wandered out alone
And came, by chance, before the great Cathedral:
A monstrous pile, embracing every style
Of architecture known to Romans, Greeks,
And Goths, and their barbaric ancestors
Back to the troglodytes inhabiting,
By turns with bears and wolves, the mountain
    caves, —
A massive and misshapen pile, — among
The tabernacles of God's foot-stool, as
The megatherium among the beasts!

Caramba! said I, (as a trav'ler must
Begin his sentences in Mexico,
If he would have the flavor in his speech
Of pulque, Popocatepetl, and
The Lord alone knows what besides within
The limits of the Country of the Cactus!)
If, from the shrine, the worshiped god within
May be inferred, God help the monstrous god
That's here compounded of all climes and times! —
When, tripping on the curb, as I approached,
My eyes descended to a garden group
Of broken columns, capitals, and plinths,
Belonging to an ancient temple of
The aborigines of Anahuac —
Or Aztec, Toltec, or — no matter, here —

R

Which stood upon the site of the Cathedral
Till rased for its successor's building by
Th' invading Christian Vandals from Old Spain;
And rested on a coiled and feathered snake
Of sculptured stone, the Aztec Serpent-God,
Upon the head of which a garland lay
Of flowers freshly plucked, in token of
This fact, that, though the temple be in ruin,
And the religion of the savages
Supplanted by the Christian for at least
Three hundred years, still in the hearts
Of the descendants of the savages,
The worship lives that wrought in love and faith
The Serpent-God and built for it the shrine!

I passed the idol every day for weeks;
And every day, I saw the withered crown
Of yesterday replaced by one of fresh
And fragrant flowers culled within the night;
And every day, I worshiped at that shrine —
That simple, savage, sub-Cathedral shrine;
For in it I beheld a symbol of
My secret self and that of all mankind:
Expressive of the fact of facts, inwrought
Within our very bones and flesh and blood,
That, kneel by day before what gods we will,
And prate with pride of present purposes,
And future aims achieved of fame and fortune,
Still, in the night, when all is dark and still,
And we are isolated from the world,
We cull the fairest flowers of the mind
And weave them into crowns, and with a sigh
Of sadness from the bottom of the heart,
Before the sun alarms us with its light,
We lay them on our idols of the past.

And from the savage shrine, I went into
The civilized, and worshiped there as well,

And with a new-found comprehension of
The idols crowned with flowers in my sight,
That made the great Cathedral a Panthéon,
The holiest of shrines, amassing in
Its monstrous and misshapen elements,
The shrines of all the idols of mankind,
In their ascent from savage troglodytes,
Barbaric hordes, Jews, Romans, Greeks, and Goths,
To the Last Man, the Crown of God on All!

CAMOENS.

Camóëns! Aye, it is enough, that, for all time, his name
Has been inscribed among the first upon the roll of Fame;
Albeit, in the span between the cradle and the grave,
He suffered all that may befall the worthy and the brave.

Camóëns! Aye, it is enough his graven form should stand
Upon a marble monument, the fairest in the land;
Albeit, in Lisbón's bounds, and in the very street,
Where, wandering in want and woe, he walked with weary feet.

It is enough his glory, in the skies of Portugal,
Should shine a sun among the stars, its light involving all;
Albeit, while upon the earth, within a dungeon's gloom,
He saw no more the sunshine than a maggot in a tomb.

It is enough the stranger, from a far and alien strand,
"The Country of Camõëns!" hails the poet's native
    land;
Albeit, while the poet lived, he had of earth no more
Than the poor wretch swept from a wreck to die upon
    the shore.

There is a brazen balance in the universe of man,
That, in the light or in the dark, do what he may or
    can,
Gives weight for weight of weal and woe, of worth and
    its reward,
To jeweled king and tinseled clown, to robed and rag-
    ged bard.

AT ILIUM.

Methinks, a bard should be both old and blind —
An incarnation of experience
And sight-subordinate imagination.
Old Homer, Ossian, and the like, to me
Are simply symbols of this secret sense —
Avátars of the God of Poesy,
Or Aretéas' periodic visits.

AT CYPRUS.

The Isle of Venus? No! The Isle of Love
Is compassed only by the boundless sea
That whirls and tosses in its viewless waves
This whelk, the mites upon it call the world.

ON THE PACIFIC.

Hast ever wished to be above the world and worldlings base,
A solitary, sentient star in circumambient space,
That, like an eye and heart conjoined, thou mightest in midsky
Survey the whole and swell in soul throughout infinity!

Ah, many a time and oft thou hast; and wert thou now with me,
A thousand miles or more from shore, upon the great South Sea,
Thou'dst find, belike, as I have found, thy wish in fact fulfilled,
As if a god, with gracious nod, had in thy wishing willed.

Thou'dst see the very universe resolved into a hue,
The sky above, the sea below, an interblending blue,
And feel thyself above the earth and from the flesh apart,
A sentient star, a conscious sphere, an interstellar heart!

Thou'dst know not north, south, east and west; thou'dst know not day and night;
For space and time would cease to be in thy supernal sight;
Thou'dst know not mother, wife, and child, from any of mankind,
For all must merge as they converge within a single mind.

Thou'dst be the very ultimate by contemplation
    wrought,
The soul, dissevered from its cell, subsisting as a
    thought —
A subtile, special mode of force, words can no more
    define,
Than plummet sound this sea profound — the Energy
    Divine!

Thou'dst be, in short, that thing of thought, an insola-
    ted god
From aught organic or evolved from out a common
    clod;
A thing of thought, whose only thought, I dare to say,
    a man,
Would be to turn again and burn within a human
    brain!

Thou'dst be this god, this thing of thought, or sentient
    star no more,
But rather, twice ten thousand times, a mortal man on
    shore,
Among the vilest of the vile, so be it, thou might'st
    find
Thy mortal mud in flesh and blood commingled with
    mankind!

And so, in solemn, sober truth, it seems to me the
    course
Of Nature is a shifting 'twixt its matter and its force;
Earth would be heaven, heaven earth — the universal
    plan —
The Man of Mud becoming God, and God becoming
    Man!

JAPAN AND THE JAPANESE.

       Japan,
The fairest of the lands of the Far East!
As if a section of the coast of Asia
Had been submerged in the Pacific Ocean
Till cleansed of all its continental filth;
Then shattered by successive earthquakes, and
Upheaved by submarine volcanoes, till,
Behold! a thousand isles of wondrous beauty!
Lapped in the loam of decomposing lava,
Moist in the mist of the encircling sea,
Bright in the sunshine of a genial clime,
A thousand islands of as many shapes,
A thousand islands of as many hues,
A thousand gems in the Pacific Ocean!—
The British Isles of the Pacific Ocean;
In size and number in accordance with
The greater sea contrasted with the less!

       The Japanese,
The noblest of mankind in the Far East!
As if the Mongol horde of Middle Asia
Had been submerged, as well, in the great sea,
Till cleansed of all their continental filth;
Then shaken by the earthquakes into action,
And lifted by the submarine volcanoes
Into a higher and a nobler sphere;
And lo! a wonder wrought, the like of which
Has never yet been seen upon the earth!
A drop of Aryan blood, somehow conveyed
Into the Mongol horde in Middle Asia,
And saved in their submergence in the sea,
Acts, like the little leaven in the lump,
Of which the scriptures tell, and, in due time,
Converts the Mongols of the continent

Into the Mongol-Aryans of Japan,
The modern Japanese, the French of Asia! —
In stature, short; belike, as much below
The standard of their neighbors, the Coreans,
As are the Gauls below that of the Germans;
As quick to quarrel on a point of honor,
And as courageous to avenge a wrong,
As, man for man, their numbers in brave France;
As courteous, polite, and affable,
As their Parisian parallels; and so,
In all the arts of war and peace, as apt;
In fine, so like the French, that, whilom, when
Their guarded gates were opened to the world,
And all the peoples who saw fit to enter,
The English, Russians, Germans, Portuguese,
Americans, Danes, Swedes, — it was the French
With whom they mingled as their next of kin,
And fashioned them in all the outward forms
Of their new worldly life! Aye, blood will tell!

And so, in brief, Japan may be defined,
The British Isles of the Pacific Ocean,
Stocked and ennobled by the French of Asia.[1]

---

[1] Since penning the above, the writer has made his second tour of the world, and, from his special study of the races of mankind, has changed his opinion with respect to the ethnologic affinities of the Japanese, and accounts for the affiliation of this remarkable people with the French on a different hypothesis; but lest he change his mind again on the exceedingly complicated problem, before the publication of his thesis on the races of mankind, he will not venture to express a possible third opinion now. The high estimation, however, in which he holds the Japanese as an enlightened, indomitable, and progressive people, is not subject to like variations.

TUNISIA.

A begging Bedouin in Frankish stocks.

FUJIYAMA.

Fuji, Fujiyama, or Fusiyama, is the highest mountain of Japan; a volcanic cone — or extinct volcano, if you will — rising 12,365 feet above the level of the sea. It is a very symmetric snow-capped peak, with slightly concave flanks, and as picturesque, perhaps, as any single mountain of the globe. By the Japanese, who are a nation of artists as well as artisans, it is held in such estimation as to approximate veneration and worship. It appears in almost every ideal landscape; and miniatures of it in party-colored stones are favorite household and garden ornaments.

Hail! Fujiyama, peerless peak of picturesque Japan! —
These richly robed and happy isles! — this Paradise to Man! —
I marvel not the islanders regard thee as divine,
For all that moves the heart of man to worship aught is thine!

Aye, all that moves the human heart to swell and rise above
Earth's sweat and blood commingled mass into a heaven of love;
As thy fair form uprises, from a base of earth below,
Into an apex in the skies of purest ice and snow!

O symbol mountain of Japan! Long may thy snows receive
The sun's warm welcome in the morn, and fond farewell at eve;
The first and last fair object in the over-arching sky,
The first and last fair image in the all-involving eye!

An image in a myriad minds, to reäppear in dreams,
Surrounded with a halo of illuminating gleams;
An inwrought aspiration to the greatest good in man —
A national incentive to the glory of Japan!

Aye, Fujiyama, peerless peak, enshrined thus in the
    heart,
Long may thy hallowed form engross the sphere of
    native art;
That, multiplied a million-fold, on plate and fan and
    robe,
Thou mayest prove an impulse to the glory of the
    globe!

AT RHODES.

Now, Rhodes and Chares and the great Colossus,
Holding aloft a lamp to symbolize
The Sun illuminating all the world;
Anon, New York, Bartholdi, and the Statue
Of Liberty enlightening the world!
So, up and down the mundane see-saw goes;
And who can say the next two thousand years
Will not behold the former on his legs
A seventh wonder of the world again,
And the gigantic goddess of great Gotham
Transported to the Mountains of the Moon,
And set up in the stead of Mumbo Jumbo?

PORTUGAL.

A relic of a great and glorious past:
The foot or femur of the extinct dodo —
A recollection of the giant auk.

WHAT IS POESY?

Suggested by the exquisitely beautiful waterfall of Nant d' Arpenaz, seen on the way from Chamouni to Geneva, and written at the latter place, 1st September, 1880.

Aye, what is Poesy? A question to
Be answered ere I pen another line.

It is the icy pinnacle of Thought,
That, melting in the sunshine of Good Feeling,
Descends the isolated mount of Self
To circle in and swell the Social Sea:

Here, prattling over pebbles, in a rill;
There, babbling under bridges, in a brook;
Now, oping eyes of wonder, in a pool;
Anon, with laughter, playing hide-and-seek
Among the ruins of a castled crag;
At length, in fond fear, quiv'ring on a brink;
Then leaping boldly into unknown depths,—
A veil of spray, that wavers in the wind,
And, fast as feeling comes and goes, reveals
The beauty of the rainbow in its being,
And shapes itself insensibly into
A perfect, pure, beloved and loving woman—

A thing of thought, of beauty, and of love,
Ennobling earth, and making heaven human!

ATHENS.

The Purple Crowned — Aye, with the purple blood
That flushed the brain of Socrates in thought.

IN A SILVER SHAFT OF NEVADA.

Loquitur — An English Miner.

Five hundred fathoms under ground! — in an eternal night,
With only this small miner's lamp to shed a ray of light! —
And full two thousand leagues from home! — from my beloved wife,—
My boys, — and my poor crippled girl, I love more than my life!

Shine, shine, O lamp! thou art the sun, within my lowly cot,
That cheers the heart of Margaret, above the porridge pot, —
That doubles in their shadows, Tom and Dick upon the floor,
That crippled Peggie looking down, may play with them as four!

And thou, my pick! be sharp of point to pierce these rocky walls,
And quick of stroke to widen out these hot and humid halls, —
Thou art the ship before the wind upon the stormy sea,
To take me back to England or bring England here to me!

And thou, my heart! be full of faith, that in this world of strife,
There is a recompense for all the miseries of life, —

There is bright sunshine for this night, — a heaven for
    this hell, —
Where heart to heart, we can thank God, that all at
    last is well!

And thou, O God! I pray to thee, to whom our lives
    belong,
Since she is weak, my faithful wife, let me be hale and
    strong;
Since they should play, my bounding boys, let me not
    labor shirk;
And since poor Peggie's crushed — for her, Oh, save
    me at my work!

MOUNT ÆTNA.

A Satyr 'mong the mountains of the world;
A monster made of man and goat and fire.

A white-veiled nun, consumed with passion, till
The energy of earth o'erwhelming all,
The vow is broken with a heated breath,
The vestment rent with shameless frenzy,
And virtue left irreparable ruin!

COAL IN SITU.

The sunshine of a world asleep in stone.

A secret cell of treasured light, in night;
A reservoir of strength, in solid stone;
A cavern of concentred storms, at rest;
A wondrous womb of giant life, in death.

THE TIDES.

The earth rotates in atmospheric loops
(Ellipses like the orbit of the earth)
Affected by the light of sun and moon;
And following, responsive to these rings,
The waters of the ocean rise and fall
At the same time at points antipodal—
An universal sympathetic heart!—

The key, or open-sesame, unto
The secret chambers of the universe,
Is not a quality of matter, Weight,
But rather one of force, to wit, Rotation.
The theory of Gravitation does
Not solve the problem of opposing tides.
Matter and Force are not convertible;
While Forms of Matter interchange, it seems,
And Modes of Force, or Motion, correlate.

SEA SICKNESS.

From Folkestone to Boulogne, three hours in hell!

Monstrous! the stomach of a man cannot
Incorporate a geyser, and much less
Involve Vesuvius — and yet —— and yet ——
I think I've turned the whole world inside out!

THE SEA.

The Sea, a second sympathetic Self:
The tides, the throbbing of a greater heart;
The storm, the raging of a stronger passion;
The shadows flitting o'er the mirroring sheen,
The vague reflections of a cosmic mind.

THE GOLDEN CHERSONESUS.

The time has been, when, to the wisest man,
The *soil* was that he pressed beneath his *sole;*
The *land* was that which *lay* beneath and 'round
    him;
The *sky*, all that within his vision's *scope;*
The *sea*, the wat'ry waste o'er which he *saw;*
The *earth*, that which he sometime *eared*, or
    ploughed;
And *heaven*, that which *heaved* around and o'er
    him;
The *world* that which was *whirled* above his head;
And *God*, the *good* to him within the world:
Himself the centre of the universe,
His vision's circle, its circumference!

Then was the world a little world indeed;
And man, involving all within his brain,
Proportionately of so big a bulk,
He shaped the great Creator of the world
Into the likeness of himself, a man!—
Belike, a potter making images
In mud of those around him like himself,
As the Jehovah of the Jew made Adam.

But, haply, from the neighb'ring hill-top's height,
The vision of the first philosopher
Was stretched o'er lands and seas ne'er seen be-
    fore;
And from the farthest mount to which he ven-
    tured,
With still the same world-aggrandizing end!
And as the world increased in size and lost
Its finite metes and bounds, the man decreased,

And his Creator than himself was greater,
But still a man — upon his hinder parts,
If not his face, he still could look and live;
As Moses saw Jehovah on Mt. Sinai.

Anon, a ship came sailing from the east,
Another from the north, and south, and west,
And the philosopher learned that the world
Was spread indefinitely 'round him 'twixt
Two regions in the north and south, of cold
And heat, and two lands in the west and east, —
The farthest Thule in the setting sun
And Golden Chersonesus in the rising:
The Iceland of to-day, belike, and the
Peninsula of south and eastern Asia.
And as the world waxed as before, the man
Waned, till behold! in contrast with his God —
The world idealized and deified —
He saw himself a puppet in the power
Of one, the form and functions of a man
No longer served to compass in his mind,
And the indefinite, diversified,
And double-dealing sign must stand in stead!
Woe worth the day, in his development,
The Jew beheld Jehovah in the Ark
In one form, and the Serpent in another —
In other words, the God, that, as a man,
Made Adam and revealed himself to Moses,
Divided into twain, a man and woman,
And compassable only by sex symbols!

Anon, a ship came sailing 'round the earth,
And lo! there was nor north, nor south, nor east,
Nor west, save as conventionally fixed —
The earth being a great rotating ball,
Nor here nor there, nor up nor down, but turning
Itself and all things topsy-turvy, till,
Bewildered, dizzy, the philosopher

Beheld the earth in its complex relations
With the fair moon, the glowing sun, the stars,
The Milky Way and nebulæ beyond!
And as the world expanded into space,
As infinite unto the telescope
As formerly unto the naked eye,
The man shrank to a miserable worm
No greater in the comprehension of
The Infinite Incomprehensible,
Than unto him, a microscopic mite!

Oh, for a moment of the long ago,
The infancy of man upon the earth,
When the great world and all that it contains
Was made for man, and God was like himself,
To meet him face to face, and talk to him,
As Adam to Jehovah in the Garden!

Or, for a moment of the later age,
The boyhood of mankind, when the great world
Was still his heritage, and God, still man,
Heard, if not seen, within the burning bush!

Or, for a moment of the later age,
The youth of man, when the great world had still
A limit in the west and in the east, —
The farthest Thule in the setting sun,
And Golden Chersonesus in the rising, —
And God was somewhere in the Ark and Serpent!

For, in the science of this latest age,
The manhood of mankind upon the earth,
The last fixed point has vanished from the world;
The finite God become the Infinite;
And man, the inverse of his thought of God,
A speck in the infinity of space,

T

A tick in the infinity of time,
A something-nothing, nothing-something what?

That man is blest, that, going through the world
If not around it, as the earth revolves,
Ne'er goes beyond the Golden Chersonesus!

BOUJIE.

Boujie — a name the Frenchman has applied
To that compound of wax and wick, a candle,
Which, next, perhaps, to "tips" and "pour boires,"
Has caused the unsophisticated tourist
From Yankeeland, to stare, and knit his brows,
And utter maledictions deep and dire
Against mine itemizing host and hostess!
Enter the D'Angleterre at noon, and dine,
And call then for your bill, and ten to one,
Somewhere among your wines and meats, you'll
    find
That little word stuck in, as if, in fact,
You had been dining a la Eskimo!

PHILIPPEVILLE.

The hope of the consumptive — Philippeville!
God grant it be not 'neath this azure dome,
Where all is light and life, the mockery
It proved in the great cavern of Kentucky!
Into the depth of which, with buoyant spirits,
A score of flushed and heated invalids
Descended, as into a Paradise,
Albeit dark as death, and never came
Into the sunshine of the world again!
O Hope! how often art thou but the path
That leadest to the pitfall of destruction!

HOME ON THE HIMÁLAYAS.

LOQUITUR— A Buddhist Thibetan, at Tunglu, one of the minor heights of the Himálaya Mountains, about a mile and a half above the level of the Valley of the Ganges, and nearly four miles beneath the icy summit in sight of Deodonga, or Mt. Everest, the highest measured mountain of the globe,— 29,002 feet above the level of the sea.

Mine is the home of Frost and Fire in an eternal strife;
Mine is the borderland between opposing Death and
    Life;
Mine is the half-way house between the Poles and the
    Equator;
Mine is the Mountain King of Earth, ice-crowned by
    the Creator!

I know no North, I know no South, but up and down
    alone;
And as the seasons come and go, in this inverted zone,
Keeping the grass beneath my feet, the ice above my
    head,
I rise and fall — the gauge between the Living and the
    Dead!

The yak and sheep my all in all, as up and down I
    pass,
Descending with the snow and ice, ascending with the
    grass;
The big beast bearing house and home as its accustom-
    ed pack,
The little, with life's precious salt well strapped upon
    its back.

It's mine from infancy to find a fellow in the storm,
And be familiar with its force and most appalling form;
To have in sight the world of shapes of clime succeeding clime,
And formulate my fancies from the awful and sublime!

It's mine, at midday, to look down upon the peopled plain,
Where the gigantic Ganges rolls its waters to the main, —
To moralize upon the depth to which a man may sink,
Down, down into the mud of vice — to putrify and stink!

Again, at midnight, to look up into the crystal dome,
Where, like a thousand lamps, the stars illume a heavenly home, —
To meditate upon the height to which a man may rise,
Up, up the mount of virtue to an acme in the skies!

Perhaps to see, as I have oft, before the day-gleams glance, —
Above the darkness of the vale — of childhood's ignorance, —
Above the roaring of the storm — of manhood's crime and vice, —
Above the world — of age's woes, — a sunlit point of ice!

The grandest mountain of the globe — five miles or more in height —
Burst, sun-illumined, from the black and all-involving night! —
To symbolize unto my mind the ultimate of good
Achieved by mortal man on earth — the end attained by Buddh!

O awful apparition of the night and day combined,
Of Earth and Heaven — Man and God — in glorious
 grandeur joined! —
To give a foresight to the soul of what above may be
Of infinite effulgence and eternal ecstasy!

With head and heart and hand conjoined, in happy
 harmony,
I turn the sacred symbol wheel, in worship unto
 Thee, —
Thou, Light of Asia woman-born, through Brahma's[1]
 mercy given,
To lead Man from the Ganges up Himál'ya's height to
 Heaven!

---

[1] While Buddhism in its purity is atheistic, it involves a variety of ideas of Divinity in the corrupted forms in which it is found among the millions of South-eastern Asia.

CARTHAGE.

The hide-bound citadel of Queen Elissa.

THE SWEDES.

The Swedes — the healthiest, the handsomest,
The happiest, and honestest of all
The people I have met with yet in Europe.

OFF THE COAST OF ABYSSINIA.

Behold! the sun is setting on my right,
Behind the hills of Abyssinia! —
Ah, me! I am indeed far, far from home,
When the whole width of the Dark Continent
And the Atlantic Ocean lie between!

THE PORPOISE, OR DOLPHIN.

Like ponies in a circus leaping hurdles.

Like wethers bounding o'er the barnyard bars.

THE SPHINX.

An effigy of Ægypt is the Sphinx:
A marred and mutilated human face
Uplifted in the sunlight of to-day
Above the body of a buried beast
In the o'erwhelming desert of the past.

THE ICE-BERG.

A Flying Dutchman of the Cronian Sea.

THE FLYING FISH.

Ambitious fish that would be butterflies.

An infant reaching out to catch the moon.

Like hawkmoths heavy with the evening dew.

Impassioned and impulsive impotence —
An effort to emerge from out a sea
Of sorrow into sunshine, but in vain.

ARABIA.

The aromatic egg-land of the Phœnix.

A barren, barren looking coast indeed,
To breed so many fantasies afar!
But, after all, the beautiful and good
Are never close at hand, but far away.

THE TAJ MAHÁL.

As to the mass of man, his beating heart,
So to the world, the throbbing realm of Ind;
And as to man, his heart of hearts, or soul,
So to the world, in Ind, the Taj Mahál!

Describe it? Nay! impossible, in words;
Depict it? Nay! impossible, in paint;
As well attempt a storm at sea in song,
Or the resplendent crown of the Creator,
The jeweled rainbow, on a yard of canvas!

And yet, since naught avails more potent than
The pen and pencil to poor mortals, I
Must fain make use of one or both, fair lady,
Or lay me mute and palsied at your feet.
So, by your gracious leave, I will take up
The pen and pencil as it best beseems
The subject. Look without, but see within.

Within this beautiful and wondrous world,
The fairest and the fertilest of lands,
Boned by the Ghauts and the sublime Himál'yas,
Veined by the holiest of streams, the Ganges,
And fleshed with an alluvium producing
The grandest growths of plants and animals, —
The sacred soil of the divine Rig-Veda, —
The classic scene of the Mahábharáta,
The Rámayána, and Sakúntala, —
The motherland of history and art, —
The fatherland of wisdom and religion, —
The lotus-land of love and luxury, —
The cradle, haply, of humanity, —
The koh-in-oor of England's crown, fair Ind.

Within this beautiful and wondrous land,
A city of surpassing loveliness,
Upon the sacred Jumna's beauteous banks, —
The city whilom of the kings of Lodi, —
The city afterward of their successors,
The mighty monarchs of the Chagtai Turks, —
The city known to fame throughout the world
For its unrivaled palace, mosques, and tombs, —
The city of the Great Mughál, fair Agra.

Within this beautiful and wondrous city,
Of fine red sandstone, hewn and laid with skill,
Four lofty walls, joined deftly at right angles
To form a perfect parallelogram,
A third and over of an English mile
In length, by a full fifth, or more, in width;
With a fair turret at each corner, and
A grand gate in the middle of the front,
And each of the side walls, as well — the front,
The grandest of the three, surmounted with
A score of marble domes ranged in two rows;
And from the parapet above, and through
The doorway of the vaulted room beneath,
Affording to the eye the fairest views.

Within these beautiful and wondrous walls,
In the eternal summer of the South,
A garden of delight, as fair in fact
As ever feigned in oriental fancy;
Unto the eye, filled with the forms of ferns
And palms, in filmy, feathery arcades,
And cypresses in dark contrasting spires,
And spangled with the rarest flowers that bloom;
Unto the ear, filled with the hum of bees, —
Winging their honied way from flower to flower,
And thence to the suspended hive within
The sheltered apex of a gateway arch, —
And the sweet melody of countless birds, —

Among the myriad, the love-sick bulbul
Outpouring to the rose its soul, as sweetly
As sung within the poesy of Persia;
Unto the nostril, filled, as well, with the
Sweet perfumes of a myriad of flowers
Compounded and distilled into a breath,
As sweet belike as that which passed from God
Into the red-earth of the first of men;
In fine, unto the all-involving senses,
A beautiful and blissful Paradise!

Within this beautiful and wondrous garden,
A marble basin parting it in twain,—
A fountain studded with a hundred jets,
Which, when in action, add the grace and beauty
Of cataracts of gems unto the scene;
And when at rest, leaving the fount a mirror,
In which, to the observer from the gateway,
The foliage and flow'rs upon the sides,
The birds and butterflies flitting above,
Are, one and all, reflected, and, as well,
The Taj set in the soft blue sky, beyond,—
The marble of its domes and minarets
Transformed, as by enchantment, into pearl!

Beyond this beautiful and wondrous tank,
Extending the full width of the fair garden,
Upon the river's brink, a mural base,
With marble faced, and forming a broad platform,
A fathom, scant a third, above the garden.
Upon this platform, on the left, approaching,
A mosque of sandstone with three marble domes;
And on the right, a counterpart in all
Save the essential fronting of a mosque;
Twin structures of exceeding grace, opposing
As a fair face its image in a mirror.

U

Between these beautiful and wondrous mosques,
A marble plinth, rising above the base
Three fathoms — in effect, a second platform,
In shape, a square of two and fifty fathoms.
And, at each corner of the square, uprising
A minaret of marble, tapering,
Cylindric, and surmounted with a railed
And roofed pavillion of the same fair substance —
A tower in height full twenty-seven fathoms!

Among these beautiful and wondrous towers,
Uprising from the centre of the plinth,
The ultimate of the grand garden tombs
Peculiar to the Mughál emperors
Of Upper India, or Hindostan —
The mausoleum proper of the Taj!
In shape, a cube — the corners, opposite
The minarets cut off, and occupying
A space of one and thirty fathoms square;
Surmounted with a cluster of fair domes,
As graceful as if turned upon a lathe;
The central of them, in diameter,
Eight fathoms and a third, and thirteen high;
The crecent of Muhammad on the top,
Full forty fathoms and a half above
The level of the garden — higher than
The summit of the great Kutúb Minár,
The peerless Asiatic shaft, at Delhi!
And more than half the height of the world's
    wonder
That towers above the valley of the Nile!
The whole of white and polished marble, cut
And fit with nicest skill, with, here and there,
Relieving to the lustre of the walls,
Inscriptions from the text of the Qurán,
In Persian characters, inlaid in jet.

In one grand view, upon a single plinth,
The monument of Trajan, of old Rome,

THE TAJ MAHÁL.

The shaft of the Vendôme, of modern Paris,
The Alexander shaft, of Petersburgh,
And the Albert Memorial, of London,
With half of great St. Peter's in their midst!

Within this beautiful and wondrous pile,
A series of communicating chambers.
Within the central and the chief, beneath
An echoing dome, a marble fence or screen,
So finely chiseled in an open pattern
That it can be compared alone to lace,
And so inlaid with precious stones, in floral,
And other apt designs, that it can be
Compared alone to what hath ne'er been seen
Save in the fancy of the covetous —
In caverns, in the depths untold of earth,
Illumined with a galaxy of gems
Set in a sapphire sky instead of stars;
Or gardens, wrought by an enchanter's wand,
In which the verdant leaves are emeralds,
The ruddy roses, rubies, and the dew
Bespangling all, the scattered dust of diamonds!

Within this beautiful and wondrous screen,
Two monumental slabs, or cenotaphs,
Of marble of the finest mold and finish,
Transmitting to all time the names of those
Who rest beneath, in two sarcophagi, —
The empress, Mumtaz, in whose memory,
And Sháh Jehán, the emp'ror, at whose word.
The peerless and incomparable tomb
Was built — employing twenty thousand men
For twenty years! at an expenditure
Of gold enough to make a casket of
The precious metal to contain itself!

But oh, how feeble and imperfect fact
And figure to convey an image of

The Taj as a sublime, seraphic whole,
And its effect upon the wanderer
Responsive to the beautiful and pure!

One cries aloud, "There is no mystery,
No sense of partial failure, in the Taj.
A thing of perfect beauty in detail,
It might pass for the work of genii, who
Knew nothing of the weaknesses and ills
With which mankind incarnate are beset!" —
(BAYARD TAYLOR.)

Another says, "The Taj is more a vision
Of beauty than a firm reality —
A dream in palpable and solid marble —
A thought, a sentiment of tenderness,
A sigh of an engrossing mortal love,
Caught and imbued with such eternity
As the foundations of the earth can give!" —
(ANONYMOUS.)

A third exclaims, "Until the day I die,
Mid mountain streams and moonlit forest strolls,
Wherever and whenever the mood comes,
When all that is most sacred and sublime
Recur to shed their radiance upon
The tranquil mind, there will be found among
My treasures a rare gem of priceless worth,
The mem'ry of that lovely charm, the Taj!"
(ANDREW CARNEGIE.)

A fourth declares, "The Taj Mahal! it is
Too pure to be the work of human hands.
The angels must have brought it from high heaven,
And a glass case should be placed over it
To shield it from the faintest breath of air!" —
(ZOFFANY, A RUSSIAN.)

A fifth exclaims, "The Taj! the sight of it
Marks a new era in a mortal's life!" —
                (BHOLANAUTH CHUNDER, A HINDOO.)

A sixth, "It stands, in beauty, purity,
And lustre, as unrivaled on the earth,
As the effulgent full moon in high heaven!" —
                            (ANONYMOUS.)

A seventh sees in it, "Of wedded love,
The most sublime romance!" —
                            (ANONYMOUS.)

                        An eighth, as well,
"The last triumphant wonder of the world!" —
                            (LADY NUGENT.)

To add to or to supplement all which,
What can I say? But this alone, in truth,
That, having viewed in a succession the
Most beautiful of all the buildings of
The continental quarters of the globe,
And while their images were still distinct
And lustrous in my memory, the Taj
Surpassed, not only all I had beheld,
But also the extravagant conceptions
I had compounded with rapt vision from
The glowing pages of my predecessors.

When, standing in the grandest of the gateways,
I, from that vantage point, beheld it first,
I stood in a suspense of ecstasy;
Until my senses, sunk within the sea
Of wild emotion welling from my heart,
I staggered in a strange bewilderment,
And sank exhausted in a flood of tears!

I do not feign a feeling I have not.
It hath been writ of yore, that strong men oft,

Beholding, the first time, the peerless Taj,
So wondrously effective in itself,
In its surroundings, and in sentiment,
Have wept, as children weep; and when the strong
Give way to tears, why may not, too, the weak?

HELIOPOLIS.

Of Heliopolis, an obelisk,
Its glyphs bedaubed by wasps, alone remains:
Like a projecting rib of a great carcase
Now indistinguishable from Nile mud.

THE RED SEA.

An arm of the Arabian Sea out-reached
To show the way and lend a hand to Lesseps.

IVAN IVANOVITCH.

When placed beside Ivan Ivanovitch,
Striding from continent to continent,
The Rhodian Colossus were a pygmy.

THE CLEPSYDRA.

Man being but an involution of
The world into an aping organism,
There cannot be a thought conceived within
The convolutions of the sage's brain,
That has not been prefigured and set up
In most stupendous shapes and characters,
Before the sentient mirror of his mind.
The water-clock — what is the ocean, with
Its regular recurrent tides, but an
Enormous and eternal clepsydra?

A STORM AT SEA.

On the 23rd of October, 1880, in order to traverse the watery way between London, England, and Oporto, Portugal, I embarked on an English merchant-ship, of 720 tons burden, called the BENBOW, after the gallant English admiral of that name.

The little vessel, built exclusively for the transportation of goods, was so meagre in its accommodations even for a single passenger, that the captain was obliged to give me my choice between the chart-room amidships and his stateroom in the cabin in the stern. I chose the stateroom, a cramped and close recess which may be compared, without exaggeration, to a closet containing a bureau and a bunk on top, to which access was obtained only by making a ladder of the knobs of the bureau drawers.

The greater part of the weight of the cargo comprised sugar, cement, and iron; while the greater part of the bulk consisted of empty wine casks: bunged, as I was happy to observe when I embarked: each and every of them forming, as I conceived, a water-tight compartment, and guaranteeing the vessel's keeping afloat until parted in twain and the barrels liberated.

The weather for the preceding ten days had been stormy; and in the lull at London, I looked forward to a smooth and pleasant voyage across the Bay of Biscay, which is noted for the frequency and severity of its tempests.

In crossing the Margate Sands, at the mouth of the Thames, however, my expectations were abandoned suddenly in such a battering, bumping, thumping, pitching, tossing—sky-toading one minute, and plunging into unfathomable depths the next, as I had never experienced before; and, I may add, too, in such agony as I had never realized before the human body was capable of enduring for more than a few minutes; albeit, wretchedly sea-sick in every vessel, large and small, in which I had ever ventured upon the ocean.

With the first rolling and pitching of the little vessel in the ground-swell of the Channel, I ascended the ladder of drawer-knobs, and lay down on the bunk; which happily was protected by a guard-rail high enough to prevent me from rolling out in any movement of the vessel less than overturning bottom-upward.

And there I lay, aching, wretching, straining, writhing, smothering, moaning, groaning, and gasping, for four days!

Until, my stomach, retaining neither food nor drink during this long period, and my body worn out with the ceaseless rocking and rolling and beating about in my bunk combined with the exhausting effects of sea-sickness, I became insensible to pain, and sank into a sleep that seemed to others to be my last; in my delirious dreams constantly slaking my thirst at the purling fountains and rippling rills among the hills and valleys of my native land, rapidly receding from my memory and forever!

When, alarmed at my condition, the good captain directed the sailors to carry me out of the feverish atmosphere of the little cabin, and place me in the open air in a sheltered place on the bridge, above the engine-house and chart-room amidships.

Accordingly, I was carried up the narrow companion-way, down which the splash of the waves descended by tubfuls whenever the turtle-back shield which protected its entrance was removed; thence, along a fore-and-aft gang-way that connected the cabin in the stern with the chart-room; and thence, up a ladder to the bridge; where, seated on a camp-stool, and lashed to a stancheon behind a screen of canvas, I was left to revive.

In a short time, reänimated by the cool fresh air entering and abating the fever in my lungs, and the splash and spray of the troubled waters ever and anon bathing my heated head,—encouraged by the kindly care of my companions,—and invigorated by the excitement of the elemental war in the midst of which I was bound, hand and foot, a helpless prisoner, I found relief, and, in a measure, recovered my health and spirits; and, in the course of the storm's continuance, from the moment of my reänimation, I became a studious observer of the tempest, in its all-involving grandeur and sublimity.

The wind blew from the south-west a terrific gale: so strangely solid in its viewless might, it seemed to be an avalanche of atmospheric ice.

The ship, belittled in the midst of the immensities of wind and wave, projected from the ocean like a half-submerged, seesawing, tree-trunk snag: in its opposing prow, a pointed tap-root cleaving both

A STORM AT SEA.   169

the ocean flood and airy avalanche; and in its masts and rigging, spreading branches ripping, tearing, riving, rasping through the seeming ice-crevásse, no sooner oped than closed.

The iron cordage rang in weird harmonic tones: tempest-twanged, resounding like the strings of a gigantic harp when struck with fury to incite to war.

A tattered top-sail flapped against the quivering mast; then, streaming in the wind, it cracked like an ox-driver's whip; till, having parted from its broken spar, it swirled and fluttered like an albatross wing-crippled by a gun-shot in midsky.

The billows came in a succession of majestic ridges from the waste of the Atlantic; on! on! on! from crest to crest, the length from stem to stern of the included vessel; on! on! on! from crest to trough, the height from bridge to keelson; on! on! on! as rhythmically as pulsations from an oceanic heart.

Anon, the line of ridge-like billows broke into a chaos of stupendous waves.

The vessel quivered as it pitched and rolled, like an organic sentient thing strained in a struggle for existence: fore and aft, its joined and mortised timbers creaking as if wrenched within a point of parting in a general dismemberment; and every part less fixed, and parcel movable, in its encompassing, or rubbing; scraping, flapping, striking, crashing, or the like, — compounding an incessant and portentous din: betimes alarming, like an earthquake to a dweller in a cave.

The ship descending a receding sea, the flanged propelling screw, raised from the water by the heaving stern, whirled in the less resisting air with rapidly

V

increased velocity: the shaft transmitting this unto the world of wheels within: the wheels unto the engine, till it fluttered in its puffing like a swallow on the wing.

And lo! before the sinking aft and rising forward of the vessel came, to mount aright the flank of the succeeding wave, the bow plunged into an enormous water-wall: on-coming seemingly in overwhelming magnitude and might.

The water shipped poured in a broad sheet from the forec's'le to the sunken deck, and swept and swashed along it — seemingly, with baffled rage, like a ferocious beast entrapped.

The crest of the great wave, cut off, caught up, and carried by the wind, came bounding over and against the bridge — a tiger leap combined with a cascade.

The captain bowed his head below the canvas bulwark and escaped the flying flood; but the old sailor at the wheel, behind him without shelter, vanished for a moment in the deluge that came down upon his head and beat against his face and breast.

The rapidly revolving screw reëntered the resisting water, jarring the belabored ship from truck to keelson: its expanded convoluted flanges striking the sea-surface, like the tail of a deep-wounded whale, in its descent impelled by fright and pain.

But howsoc'er chaotic the sea-surface at first view, the rhythmical pulsations still pervaded the unfathomable depths: appearing only to the vision of experience, like the successive formative upheavals in the intricacies of the Alps to eyes familiar with the mountain-maze of Appalachia.

On! on! on! they came, like periodic paroxysms; on! on! on! unnumbered times — for numbers were invented to count pence and pounds, not kisses and convulsions; on! on! on! in agonizing iteration: till the pulses passed into the pendulum of an enormous clock, — the snail-paced finger on the dial féscuing, not finite time, but infinite eternity.

Anon, cross seas appeared: pulsations coming at the same time from the south-west and the west: creating at the points of intersection most colossal single seas: upheaving, seething water-domes: half geyser and half whirlpool: monsters born untimely and short-lived.

The captain spake — his accents startling like the shock of a galvanic battery.

The wheel went round and round.

I looked along the fixed line of the captain's vision, and behold! a water-mountain seemingly uprising from the bottom of the ocean, off the vessel's starboard bow, and, deviating from the general direction of the tempest's course, a-sidling tow'rd the ship in sinistral obliquity: a black and grizzled monster of malignity!

A moment later and the good ship met the moving mountain at its base, and steadily and buoyantly ascended its forbidding flank, until, the summit almost reached, it wavered, wabbled, and, departing for an instant from its course, went adrift — the rudder being smaller than the broadside of the ship!

And going with the tempest, not against it as before, — the hurricane seemed suddenly to hold its breath: as I did mine: awaiting the engulfing of the vessel which the strange lull seemed to augur, as the sick-bed's light'ning, death!

The ship was at the mercy of the wind and wave.

But for an awful moment, happily.

Till righted in the only line allowed it for resistance; and presenting in its prow again, a cleaving wedge unto the forces of the ocean and the air, it shivered, pitched, and rolled — it ripped, and rasped, and rang, — it struggled, groaned, and panted, as before.

And the gigantic ocean-clock, not having struck the hour of doom, continued, in the periodic throes, to tick eternity.

Anon, the waves were capped with white, as far as I could see; then churned into a sea of foam; then streaked and mottled strangely to vast depths; then whisked up into such a spray of flying water, whitened and solidified, they seemed to be converted into driven snow.

And lo! the snow-storm having passed, the spind-drift, in the swirling gusts that followed, spread out o'er the sable mantle of the ocean like a shawl of lustrous white and deftly woven lace.

But what is that — and that — and that, that breaks the surface with a shape not soluble? A bed! a trunk! a spar! O shuddering sight! we are among the drifting wreckage of a foundered ship!

My eyes, bedimmed and smarting with the spray and water whisked and driven into them betimes, ached in my fate-forseeing apprehension to discern the semblance of a human being clinging to the wreckage to prolong the agony of his existence in the vortex of inevitable death; but happily my eyes were spared that awful spectacle!

Anon, the storm-rack veiled the light of day: condensing, dipping low, and deep'ning in lividity; on-bringing an unnatural night: increasing in forbidding gloom like a descent into a panther-haunted cave: and filled with dread uncertainty, like an adventuring alone into an unexplored recess.

The lightning darted with increasing frequency and blinding brilliancy: zigzagging purple-tinted in the overarching sky, like cracks appearing in the bottom of a ladle dipped in molten steel.

The thunder rattled, crashed, and rolled: subordinating ever and anon the sense of sight to that of hearing, and transporting me in fancy from the elemental war at sea to an engagement 'twixt embattled hosts on land.

The rain came on apace.

I caught the spluttering drops of the prelusive sprinkle in my open mouth, and found in their diffusion on my tongue the first relief to my delirious thirst.

Succeeding showers descended like great curtains: waving in the wind, and sensibly abating its velocity and violence.

And the infinity of water pellets pattered on the heads of the gigantic waves, till they were humbled and deprived of their defiant crests.

But what! hath this most inconsiderable globule that alights upon my tongue and weighs not down the tip — hath this minutest water-sphere the power in its descent to hobble the tornado in its air-congealing course, and shackle the Atlantic in its mountain-moving might? Yea, even so! as softest accents fall into the ears of the enraged and furious, and calm the storm of passion in a monster's breast.

Anon, the darkness of the cloud-eclipse decreased.

The solid sky broke into fragments in confusion: driving here, dividing there, and massing yonder, like the mud and blood begrimed survivors of the French at Waterloo, impetuously fleeing, wildly scatt'ring, and fortuitously gath'ring in bewildered groups.

At length, a patch of blue appeared in the chaotic sky.

The slanting beams of the descending sun came through the breach in the dividing and dissolving rack with dazzling brilliancy.

And lo! the arch of a resplendent rainbow spanned the eastern sky!

And the surrounding world of waters, but a moment since as black and sheenless as the fabled floods of Acheron, was changed into an ocean of commingling gems: transparent, sparkling, interblending: ruby, sapphire, emerald, and diamond!

Were ever the opposing eyes of man filled with a more enchanting spectacle!

Most pitifully weak from the combined effects of my prolonged sea-sickness and privation from both food and drink, I, ne'ertheless, incited by the beauty of the scene, had strength enough to get upon my feet, and, clinging to the canvas-shield and iron stancheons of the bridge, to scan, with the most comprehensive scope of vision, the bejeweled sea and sky — the all-involving world, a flashing iridescent gem!

An d then, in my responsive rapture, wonderment, and awe, to close my eyes unto the might and splendor of the storm: forever after, willing to be blind; and bow my head: resigned to any fate.

I had involved a power and a glory not transcended on the earth.

Earth had no more to give; Life had no more to take.

I was content to die.

I had beheld the face of God, and felt His hand.

The captain of the BENBOW had headed the vessel toward the Spanish harbor of Vigo for shelter; but when, in the evening of the fifth day out from London, the storm had abated somewhat, he turned its bow again to the storm and the open sea.

In the morning of the sixth day, we approached the harbor of Oporto, but were warned by cannons fired on the shore not to attempt to cross the dangerous bar at its mouth.

The bow of the BENBOW was turned again to the storm and the open sea; and it was not until the following morning, seven full days lacking two hours from the time we set sail, that we crossed the bar in safety and anchored in the snug little harbor of the port which has given name to Portugal.

It remains now, only to be told that in the storm which the BENBOW survived, as many as *one hundred and sixty* vessels, according to THE ILLUSTRATED LONDON NEWS, for the following week, were wrecked on the shores of the British Isles alone!

ASIA.

Metempsychosis to Americans —
A visual transmigration back into
The bodies of an immature existence.

THE SUEZ CANAL.

"A canal is impossible — the thing would be a ditch." —
ROBERT STEPHENSON.

A ditch. So be it; but a ditch that makes
An island of the Ebon Continent,
And buckles up the girdle of the world
A hole or two, the better for its business.

THE HELL OF HÁLEMÁUMAU.[1]

Hawáii[2] is the most southerly and easterly, the largest, and the most recently formed of the cluster of eleven islets in the North Pacific Ocean which constitute the domain of the kingdom of Hawáii, the Hawáiian, or Sandwich Islands. It is a pile of volcanic mountain cones, or essentially a vast volcano, which, rising from the abyss of the Pacific Ocean and attaining an altitude of nearly 14,000 feet above its surface, equals, in altitude above the bottom of the sea, the highest of the Himálayas above the level of the valley of the Ganges; and as such, it presents an exposition of the volcano as a factor in the formation of the solid earth, which for grandeur and sublimity as a spectacle and at the same time for completeness and convenience of study, is without a parallel on the globe.

Kilauéa[3] is the most persistently active of the superficial volcanoes of Hawáii; and as an individual, aside from its associates, it is among the largest of the active volcanoes of the world. It is the fifth and most recently developed of the culminating points of the volcanic activity of the island, and is situated on its southeastern aspect, or strictly in accordance with the formula of the formative forces of Hawáii and the group to which it belongs, from the northwest to the southeast, and in accordance with the intersecting lines of fracture in the crust of the earth as delineated by Mr. William Lowthian Green, assuming that the globe in cooling from a molten spherical mass has collapsed into a wavering compromise or uncertain equipoise between a spheroid and a hexa-tetrahedron — the constant activity of Kilauéa attesting it an ultimate, or a terminal point of earth-formation which, in its relation to the Hawáiian Islands, may be likened to the purple flower-bud of the banana in advance of the cluster of its fruit. The rim of its crater-pit, compound crater, or cálderon, is about 4,000 feet above the level of the sea; the circumference of the same 8.6865 miles, or nearly nine; and the depth from 500 to 1,800 feet, as the liquid lava rises and falls in it — at present (28th February, 1885,) it is supposed to be about 600 feet to the general level of the floor of the cálderon, and 500 to the level of the liquid lava in its several active centres, craters, or lakes. By the walls of the volcano giving way, the gradually accumulated lava is discharged by a lateral vent every eight or nine years; and only once in its history, in 1789, has there been an explosive eruption from the crater-mouth.

Hálemáumau is the older and the more active, picturesque, and remarkable in many ways of the two great craters containing lava in tumultuous ebullition at present in the cálderon of Kilauéa, and the most interesting of the infinity of phenomena which the volcano presents—in fine, the centre of the attractions of Hawáii. In its relation with the volcanoes of the earth at large, it (or Kilauéa as a whole) is perhaps the least evolved, and may be put at the foot of the list, with Vesuvius at the head; the one in one of the four great tetrahedral oceanic-areas of depression of the earth, emitting simple, basic, doleritic and anhydrous, or cosmical lavas, (identical mineralogically with a vast number of the solid meteorites which from time to time have fallen on the surface of the earth,) and the other in one of the four great tetrahedral continental-areas of elevation, emitting lavas of the most complex character; the one quietly and steadily active and the other explosively and spasmodically; the one, according to the conceptions of Mr. Green, (for which may the volcanic mountain-mass of Hawáii be an eternal monument!) a resultant at the intersection of the tetrahedral shrinkage-fractures of the earth, and the other in the line of the great telluric twist of the earth on its axis; or, regarding the earth as a hexa-tetrahedron, in the line of the shifting of its planes into a macled form of the crystalline figure.[4] It may be likened to a barometer on a stupendous scale; for as the liquid mercury rises in the tube of the barometer responsive to the pressure of the atmosphere upon the metal contained in the compressible and elastic bulb at the base of the instrument, so the liquid lava of Hálemáumau rises in its self-formed cylinder in accordance with the pressure upon the molten forms of matter contained in the shrinking sack, or the flexible frangible crust, of the cooling collapsing earth. The present cone of the crater called Hálemáumau has been developed since the year 1868. Its walls rise from eighty to one hundred and fifty feet above the level of the liquid interior; and albeit of the most chaotic character, they exhibit an interesting series of concave lines of stratification, showing their formation to have been made by successive outpourings and their apparent upheaval effected in part by an ascending central force, and in part by lateral (hydrostatic) pressure.

Péle[3] is a mental mythic monster of the Hawáiians, compounded of the phenomena of their grand volcanic environment and themselves—a malignant and destructive monster, half volcanic outburst and half savage; and curiously of the feminine gender, a she-divinity (to use the phraseology of one of England's poets,) or a goddess; as if in recognition of the fact, not beyond the comprehension of savages, that a woman has the might and means within herself to be a greater monster of destruction than a man, he being limited to the past and present, and she having the range of the past, the present, and the future. She was supposed to reside, by turns, in the several active volcanoes, but especially in Kilauéa, in Hálemáumau; and she was the recipient of a worship possibly more general among the Hawáiians than any other of their gods and goddesses—and which, by no means, has become extinct yet; as the sacrifice of the Princess Ruth as late as 1881, referred to in the poem, is a sufficient proof. A complete exposition of Péle, however, as a historical, religious, and social personage, albeit an ideal monster, would require, like any of the foregoing subjects, a volume rather than a paragraph.

I sit upon the good ship's quarter-deck,
In silent, self-secluded reverie:
A musing barnacle upon the back
Of a Pacific sulphur-bottom whale.
(I like a simile, especially
When it involves me in a grotesque guise;
As children love to look in wrinkled mirrors
And see themselves as mannikins and monsters.)
Now, noting, haply, in the sky astern,
The sooty albatross, with outspread wings,
Shaped like a scythe or the crescentic moon,
Sweep, swirl, and pirouette, as if it were
The curve of beauty avified upon
The palette of the painter of the sea;
Now, in the sea abeam, the shadow of
A roving shark — its pointed dorsal fin
Uprising from the rippling surface, like
The black-flag of a dreaded pirate-craft
On the horizon heaving into sight;
Anon, ahead, a startled flying-fish,
With glassy wing-like fins, rise from the sea

And wing a gleaming scintillating flight
In the bright sunshine for a moment, then
Sink in the all-concealing ocean, like
A fact that rises from the salt, salt sea
Of commonplace and flits a fancy in
The sunshine of my musing for a time, —
The length of the first kiss of lovelings, — then
Sinks in the ocean of oblivion.

Until, oho! the ship is anchored in
The bay of Hilo, and behold! the isle
Hawáii: a long-buried age and clime,
In miniature, of the revolving earth;
When the first cooling crag of its great mass
Of molten matter, whirling from the sun,
Appeared above the cinders of the sea
Within the fire-freed gases of the air,
And the first forms of vegetable life,
The lichen, moss, and fern, began to weave
A cincture for the new-born planet Eve.
Hawáii — Aye, a mimic infant Earth,
"Mewling and puking in the nurse's arms."

Well mounted on a sinewy, fresh-shod horse,
As sure of foot as a cliff-climbing goat,
I jog along a narrow, rugged path,
Worn in the lava by my predecessors,
And bringing back to mind the wheel-worn rut
Within the lava pavement of Pompéii.

Now, turning to the right to note the flood
That came from mighty Máuna Lóa's[6] mouth
Four years ago — a flood of molten lava,
In self-encasing arteries of slag,
Descending slope, ravine, and precipice —
A deluge of destruction pouring down
Resistless, a Niagara of fire!
And staying not, until, approaching Hilo,

Full forty miles from its volcanic source,
The Princess Ruth, of ancient faith, appeared,
And sacrificing raiment, meat and drink
Unto the goddess of her heathen sires,
The dreaded Péle — fire personified —
The flood of fire was turned to solid stone!
And so remains, in attestation of
The pow'r of Péle and the faith of Ruth,
To all the world unto the end of time,
In black, appalling, overwhelming waves,
Upon the edge of the uninjured town!

But out upon this shaping of the world
To fit our fancies, whims, conceits, and dreams,
Till self-deluded, we believe in them
As entities outside our simple selves
And worship them as gods of good and evil;
Instead of shaping our ideas, thoughts,
And fantasies to fit the world of fact —
The entities of our environment
Within the reach and rapture of our senses!

Now, turning to the left to note a fern [7]
Among the leafy wonders of the isle:
A circle of unbroken, arching fronds,
Full thirty feet from tip to tip, above
A drapery of drooping lifeless leaves
Around the trunk of their supporting tree:
A crown unto the forest chieftain's head,
And to his face a mummer's mask as well.

Now, holding a straight course amid a copse
Of such resplendent and luxuriant growth,
I seem to sit again in a canoe
And drift adown the mighty Amazon,
A speechless wonderer among its palms
Transformed into as vast and varied ferns —
A marvel here,[8] full forty feet in height,

And two in width across its tree-like trunk;
Another there, the feathers of the Roc
Of Sindbad metamorphosed into fronds!

Anon, within a scrubby wilderness,
In which the horse, the ass, the ox, the sheep,
The goat, the hog, the dog, the cat, and chicken
Have wandered back into their primal state
Of savag'ry before the wit of man
Subordinated them unto his will.

Until, at length, borne over thirty miles
Of lava in unnumbered curious forms —
Swirled, hummocked, pitted, caverned, creased,
 o'erlapped,
Cragged, fretted, bulged, rent, fluted, rolled, and
 crushed, —
And lifted up some forty hundred feet
Above the level of the circling sea,
I check my jaded horse upon the brink
Of an abyss a hundred fathoms deep,
And, in circumference, three leagues or more,
The compound cálderon of Kilauéa :
The counterfeit presentment, at my feet,
In planetary objectivity,
Of the volcanic moon, above my head,
In interstellar sheen and mysticism!
Was ever revelation unto man
More wonderful! As if I had, in fact,
The moon beneath a microscopic lens —
Its orb expanded twenty thousand times,
And every pockmark in its seeming face
Enlarged into an isle-engulfing pit;
The silver in the heavens dross on earth,
Black, broken, ragged, jagged furnace-slag!
Aye, looking into Kilauéa, I
Behold the moon, as Gulliver, among
The Brobdingnags, the charms of Glumdalclitch!

THE HELL OF HÁLEMÁUMAU.

Descensus facilis Averni; so
The way into the depths of Kilauéa.
From crag to crag, with alpine-stock in hand,
(And Virgil, as he traversed hell with Dante,
Beside me, in the guise of a Kanáka,[9])
I pass into the fire-formed, slag-walled chasm.
Now, noting on the brink of the abyss
A fringe of interwoven ferns and roses,
Recalling to my mind the floral wreaths
Around the bald skulls of Palermo's dead,
And the allurements of the limner's art
Upon the house-walls of Pompéii's vice.
Now, coming to the great crescentic plane
That forms the northern portion of the pit, —
What bushes hang their berries in my sight,[10]
As if, with Atalanta's art, to tempt
Me from my course — pink berries, tartly sweet,
Like pouting lips that cry and kiss at once;
But all in vain; I stoop and eat, but stay not.
Now, coming to a second level plane
That forms the floor of Kilauéa proper,
I leave the line of life and all is death —
I walk upon the surface of a sea,
As black and still, though broken into waves,
And swirling eddies, curling crests and surf,
As if it were the floods of Acheron
Tossed by a tempest to the highest notch,
And in that instant frozen into ice!
A Mer-de-Glace of glassy, glossy lava,
Bespangled with a dust of olivine
In golden points and iridescent hues,
As I have seen the sea at midnight starred
And streaming with prismatic living light —
That of the phosphorescent acalephs.
Anon, amid the fumes and gases from
A score of vents, and in the scorching heat
Emitted from two glowing, flaming chimneys
Yclept the Little Beggars — in their throats

Great diphtheritic clots depending, like
Stalactites in a limestone cave, — I pause,
Uncertain, hesitating, fearful, lest
The crust of lava break beneath my feet,
As haply it has done a thousand times,
And in the liquid fire, I perish, like
Empedocles within the flood of Ætna!
I pause, but for a moment, then proceed —
My fears henceforth dispelled in the delight
Of apprehended imminent destruction.

Until, at length, a league of lava traversed,
And a great ragged, rock-like, reeking rim,
(In the similitude of an immense
Cathedral pile in smoking, toppling ruin,)
Ascended and descended, I recoil
A step, and stand transfixed in awe and wonder:
I am within the trembling, steaming walls
Of Kilauéa's centre, and behold
The lake of liquid lava, Hálemáumau![11]
In shape elliptic, and in circuit half
A mile, in ragged lines obscured by steam;
The surface of the molten mass, a scum,
Like sable satin, ever setting from
The centre, and, in crinkling laps and folds
And crunching volutes, breaking on the shores;
Here, parting and revealing through a rent
The liquid fire beneath, in bands and seams
Of interblending pink and cherry-red;
There, heaving in elastic billows, and,
In vast concentric circles eddying,
Till parting in a swaying arc, an ooze
Of glowing lava, pink and orange hued,
Appears, and like a worm of unctious fire
Upon a deep black velvet leaflet, writhes,
Until, with fading colors, it expires;
Here, parting on the shore-surf's crinkling crest,
A myriad of jets of bluish flame

Leap from the sharp uplifted fracture, like
A fringe of blue upon a fun'ral pall;
There, cracking suddenly from shore to shore,
The liquid fire appears along the line
Like lurid lightning in a midnight sky —
And see! that jet of water-gas escape
And carry with it in the air a spurt
Of lava in the form of glassy floss [12]
As fine as ever spun by China's worm —
A lock belike from Péle's frizzled pow;
And here, the surface rocking, swirling, till
Dissolving, lo! within the circle formed,
A fount of fire! the solid central cones
Uprising twenty feet, the spluttering spurts
As many more, and falling with the sound
Of roof-snow passing into pavement-slush —
A fount of fire assuming various forms,
A trident now, and now a spreading tree,
A head-dress now, and now a devil-fish,
But ever of one hue, the rare compound
Of pink and orange found within the folds
Of the pomegranate's dainty, filmy bloom,
Or in the rounded lips of one among
Ten thousand fair-haired, blue-eyed girls —
A solid color without tint or shade,
And though composed of seeming lambent fire,
Emitting strangely no more light than sound —
A daub and splotch of a pomegranate-red
Upon a sable ground, and nothing more;
And there, against a vertically cut
Half-cone, upon the margin of the lake,
The surface setting in pulsating throbs,
Until behold! a miniature volcano
Combining the phenomena of both
Vesuvius and Hálemáumau: an
Eruptive show'r of lava falling on
The half-cone on the shore, and a cascade
Returning to the source from which it came.

And so the scene is ever varied and
Disjoined, until behold! the lava lake
Is all aglow and twenty fountains play
Within the wondrous circle of its shores!
Oh, for the word to compass in its sound
This seething, surging, spouting sea of fire!
It is a mighty maelstrom ladle-dipped
From out the ocean caldron of the Sun!
Aye, Hálemáumau is the orb of day
Within the circuit of a half a mile;
And in my journey hither — to this lake
Within the walls of Kilauéa and
The foam-fringed confines of Hawáii, — I,
In philosophic fact, have visited
The Earth, emerging from its primal floods,
The Moon, a-cold beyond Poor Tom's degree,
And the ensphered volcanic fire, the Sun!

O glorious age of glass — of lens and prism,
That purblind man, with comprehensive gaze,
May see the far anear, the near afar,
And poets and philosophers compound
Their facts and fancies in resultant truth![13]

Anon, the rubber of a cloudy night
Erases all the world save that within
The walls of Hálemáumau, in my sight
And hearing: lava-lighted crater-crags
In-arching like the petals of a great
Corolla, tinted yellow, pink, and blue;
Thin clouds of water-gas, obscurely white
And fumes of sulphur, as obscurely blue,
Ascending from the circle of the lake,
An incense from a thousand unseen censers;
And, in the surface of the lava lake,
The satin sable turned to velvet black,
And the pomegranate red transmuted to

The glowing yellow hue of molten gold;
A fitful light diffusing from the founts
Illuming weirdly the volcanic void
Without or shade or sheen: the only gleam
Upon the velvet scum a shimmering
Reflection from the vapor-clouds above;
Until, the periodic break-up come,
The surface for a moment is a glare —
A sunburst through a dark'ning tempest's rack,
And then a sunset in a golden glamour.

I sit upon a lava rock and watch
The varying phases of the wondrous lake,
Until the real passes from my sight
And the ideal enters in its stead:
The thing a thought within my musing mind;
The fact a fancy in my reverie;
The world of wonders of the fire-abyss
A filmy breath-blown bubble of the brain.

I pass into the being of Macbeth,
And lo! in looking into Hálemáumau,
I look into the witches' caldron — see
The eye of newt and toe of frog descend
Into the seething hell-broth to compound
The diabolic charm; the while I hear,
In the cascading of the fiery founts,
The "bubble, bubble, toil and trouble" of
The mystic mumbling of the midnight hags.

Anon, I creep up to a pitfall's brink,
Within the jungle of a Bengal vale,
And through the broken reeds across the chasm
Behold the livid black and yellow bands
And glaring eyes of an emprisoned tiger —
A beast that, startled at my coming, leaps
From wall to wall so swift and fiercely that
It seems, in my bewildered sight, to be

Expanded to the compass of the pit;
The while I hear a low deep growl that shakes
The mountain walls around me to their base.

Anon, I enter Rome — Imperial Rome —
And one among a hundred thousand press
Into the Coliseum, and conduct
Me to a seat, whence looking down I see,
In the arena eighty feet below,
A thousand Goth and Gallic warriors
With sword and shield engage in battle strife;
To know nor pause nor end, until I see
The flashing blades of steel ope founts of blood,
And then the battle-field a sea of gore;
And hear a dying moan hushed in the cheer
Of the encircling, surging, blood-crazed throng!

Anon, I listen to a murderer,
Repentant, in the throes and dread of death,
Recount the story of his awful deeds
At midnight done with an unfeeling blade;
Until I seem to see, betwixt his ribs,
The hell of Hálemáumau in his heart —
Its fires eternal to his sinful soul,
Consuming yet consuming not for aye.

Anon, I see the goddess Péle rise
Amid the fountains of the fiery lake,
A black-skinned, bloated, blood-shot, breastless hag!
Around her neck a lei [14] of leprous sores;
And in her hands a fire-charred newborn babe
Torn from a fruitful mother's dripping dug
And strangled in the hate of barrenness
Unto all things that mate and multiply;
A hag so horrible in form and feature,
A hag so terrible in aim and action,
A hag so hellish in her head and heart,

THE HELL OF HÁLEMÁUMAU.

No eye can see nor fantasy conceive
Save in the fire-formed Hell of Hálemáumau!

---

[1] Originally published in 1885, at Honolulu, in the form of an octavo pamphlet under the title of A VISIT IN VERSE TO HÁLEMÁUMAU, and dedicated to His Majesty, KALAKÁUA, King of the Hawáiian Islands.

[2] Hawáii is pronounced conventionally as if spelled Hah-wye-ee, with the accent on the second syllable; correctly Hah-wáh-ee-ee. It is identical with the Hawa-iki of the Maoris of New Zealand, and signifies Little Java.

[3] Kilauéa is pronounced as if spelled Kee-low-ay-ah, with a slight accent on the first syllable and a strong on the third. It means in Hawáiian the Big Smoking Pit.

Hálemáumau is pronounced as if spelled Hah-lay-mow-mow, with an accent on the first and third syllables. It signifies literally, House Everlasting, or figuratively, the Grave; from the fact that a similar crater in approximately the same place has been regarded by the Hawáiians from time immemorial as a fit burial place for the bodies in whole or in part of their dead, in their worship of Péle — not the House of Everlasting Fire or Burning, as rendered by some.

[4] Vestiges of the Molten Globe, as exhibited in the Figure of the Earth, Volcanic Action and Physiography. By WILLIAM LOWTHIAN GREEN, Minister of Foreign Affairs to the King of the Sandwich Islands. 8vo., pp. 59. London: Edward Stanford, 55 Charing Cross. 1875

A synopsis of MR. GREEN's theory is given also in La Symétrie sur le Globe Terrestre par A. DE LAPPARENT, Professeur à l' Institut Catholique de Paris. (Extrait de la Revue des Questions Scientifiques, Janvier, 1882.) Bruxelles: Alfred Vromant, Imprimeur-Éditeur, 3 Rue de la Chapelle. 8vo., pp. 35.

[5] Péle is pronounced as if spelled Pay-lay, with the stress on the first syllable. It signifies simply Fire. Compare the lingering worship of the terrible goddess, as exemplified in the recent sacrifice of the PRINCESS RUTH, with that among the Mexicans of to-day for the feathered Serpent-god of their Aztec ancestors, as set forth in the lines hereinbefore headed, IN THE CITY OF MEXICO.

[6] Máuna Lóa (pronounced as if spelled Mow-na Lo-a, accented on the first syllable of each word, and signifying the Long Mountain) is the largest in bulk of the volcanic cones of

Hawáii, its height being 13,650 feet above the level of the sea, or 155 less than that of Máuna Kéa (Kay-ah, signifying the White Mountain,) and its base being coëxtensive with a great part of the island. Its crater-pit or cálderon, called Mókuawéowéo, (Mo-koo-ah-way-o-way-o, accented on the first, fourth, and sixth syllables, and signifying the Red Island,) is elliptic in shape, its long diameter 13,000 feet and its short 8000, and its depth about 800 feet. Its eruptions, which occur at irregular intervals of three, four, seven, eight, and eleven years or so, are of the grandest proportions known, the volume of lava ejected, as estimated, ranging from seventeen to fifty billions of cubic feet. The last outburst occurred in 1880-1.

[7] The bird's-nest fern, *Asplenium nidus*. For the size of the specimen referred to, attest MR. CHARLES N. ARNOLD, of Hilo, who cut it into four sections and sent it to His Majesty, KING KALAKÁUA.

[8] The tree-ferns of Hawáii exceed in girth of trunk any I have ever seen in India and Brazil. I have seen higher, however, among the foothills of the Himálayas, and in Australia. Scrubby, though they be in comparison with their ancestors of the fern-age of the earth's history, they are none the less magnificent trees, and truly may be classed among the leafy wonders of the world.

[9] Kanáka, used as a noun, a Hawáiian man, and, used as an adjective, Hawáiian in general.

[10] A kind of cranberry, *Vaccinium reticulatum*. The fruit of this plant was considered sacred to Péle; and it was customary for the Hawáiians, before eating the same in the crater, to cast some of the berries into the molten lava as an offering to her.

[11] The description of the crater of Hálemáumau is given as I beheld it during the afternoon and night of Saturday, the 28th of February, 1885. Every phenomenon is given as it appeared to me, not, however, in the sequence as reported in the poem, but as isolated from the world of wonders before me at the time and carefully considered with a view to its accurate reproduction in speech. I observed with especial care, (seeking confirmation from a number of ladies and gentlemen at my side, before recording a conclusion,) the various colors presented in the ever-varying picture, since, it seemed to me, I had never seen exactly the same hues in any painting of the volcano I had inspected. While, accordingly, the usual allowance might be made for lack of accuracy in a poetic description, I should prefer that the metrical lines be considered prose and accepted as prosaic truth or subjected to the ordeal of the

same. The steam or water-gas noted as rising from the rim and fractured scum of the crater and forming the cloud above, which, like a frosted lamp-shade, served to reflect the light from the molten lava and diffuse it throughout the volcanic void, is believed to have come wholly from the atmosphere, either in the form of rain falling directly into and about the crater or that of moisture involved in the convection currents of the crater in the air and liquid lava, and not from the lava as a volcanic product. As it was raining at the time, and had been for several days previously, the amount of steam in the crater at the time I beheld it was doubtless in excess of that which usually is seen.

[12] This flossy product of the volcano is called Péle's hair. A similar substance is produced by turning a jet of steam on the molten slag of a furnace. It is called by some slag-wool; and it has been utilized to a small extent as a substitute for asbestos in the manufacture of a non-conducting covering for steam-pipes, etc.

[13] If the modern method of investigation known as spectrum analysis — the glorious invention of Dr. DAVID ALTER, of Freeport, Pennsylvania — has made one thing a positive fact in the realm of science that before was questionable, it is that the sun and other stars are revolving spheres of molten matter, as like the liquid lake of Kilauéa as a whole of infinite size may be to a finite part.

[14] Lei, (pronounced conventionally as if spelled lay,) a wreath or garland, one of the most common and characteristic ornaments of a Hawáiian woman.

THE ONE HUNDRED AND EIGHTIETH DEGREE OF LONGITUDE.

The line o'er which the earth looks east and west,
A two-faced Janus for a verity.

THE SHIP'S LANTERNS.

The lanterns of a ship at night look like
The glowing nose of Bardolph set against
The glaring orbit of the Green-eyed Monster.

THE TERRACES OF ROTOMÁHANA.[1]

Thursday, 10th June, 1886, — a twelvemonth after the visit of the writer to the Terraces of Rotomáhana and the publication in Auckland, New Zealand, of the following description, prefaced by an admirable paper on their formation and volcanic environment, by MR. JOSIAH MARTIN, F.G.S., etc., — the beautiful structures were involved in a superficial volcanic eruption and destroyed.

From the Hawáiian Islands, south and west,
Some twelve or thirteen hundred leagues,
By steamer, to New Zealand. Yea, but where
In space and what in substance is New Zealand?
A question to be asked by one and all,
And answered ere I go another step.

Conceive the surface of the sphere, the Earth,
Divided into hemispheres, the one
Encompassing the bulk of all the land,
The other that of all the sea. Then will
The centre of the hemisphere of land
Be England in the North — Old England, and
The centre of the hemisphere of water,
New Zealand in the South — the New Sea Land.
The New Sea Land, by some prophetic chance,
So called by its discoverers, the Dutch;
And Aotearóa[2] by the natives —
The Long White Land, another Albion!
The Britian of the South, in name and nature!

In size about the bigness of Great Britain;
In shape, an old and sole-less outcast boot:
A rent between the foot and leg, Cook's Strait,
Another 'twixt the leg and straps, Foveaux',
Dividing it into the Northern Isle,

The South or Middle Isle, and Stewart's Isle.
The relics, haply, of a vanished world,
As kinless as a meteoric crag
New fall'n from space among the continents.
The country of the earthquake[3] and volcano;[4]
The country of the sea-gorge[5] and the glacier;[6]
The country of the geyser[7] and the terrace;[8]
The country of the póunamu,[9] or greenstone;
The country of the wood-in-worm awháto;[10]
The country of the ponga[11] and the nikau;[12]
The country of the rata[13] and the kauri;[14]
The country of the toke[15] and tu'tára;[16]
The country of the kákapo[17] and kéa;[18]
The country of the kiwi[19] and the moa;[20]
The country of the kuri[21] and the Maori;[22]
The country of the moko[23] and the mere;[24]
The country of the Tiki[25] and the tapu;[26]
The Wonderland beneath the Southern Cross!

I enter a great cove, and go ashore
At Auckland, chief among the cities of
The present and the future of New Zealand.
Set strangely on a narrow neck of land
Betwixt two seas, among two score or more
Of dead volcano cones, about as big
Beside Vesuvius, as that by Ætna—
Two score or more of possibilities
Of making some day Auckland a Pompéii!

From Auckland, then, south, eight-and-fifty
    leagues,
By rail, coach, whale-boat, shanksmare, and canoe,
I jog on to the Terraces, the White
And Pink of Rotomáhana:[27] the chief
Of all the wonders of New Zealand: two
Compoundings and embodiments of the
Old elements, fire, water, earth, and air,
As similar and yet dissimilar,

And supplemental each unto the other
To form a perfect whole, as man and woman,
Their counterparts in an organic form:
Te Tárata,[29] the Maoris call the one:
The Ridges — ridge-on-ridge, or Terraces;
The other, Te Otúkapúarángi:[29]
The Fountain of the Evening Clouds of Heaven.

I visit first the White; and, book in hand,
As the phenomena of my environment
Become as many facts, and these same facts
Evolve into and interblend with fancies —
As in the compound art-productions of
The Japanese, the real and ideal —
I jot them down, in whatsoever words,
Signs, symbols, figures, and similitudes,
Come first as willing slaves to do my bidding —
Archaic imps and hyphen-joined hobgoblins,
Outlandish ogres and dissonant dwarfs,
Weird witch and warlock wordings, graveyard ghosts,
And eldritch elves of echoes from the wilds
Of Maori-land: Te Áoteáróa —
The Long White Land: the Island-fish of Máui.[30]

Conceive, a vast volcanic energy
Diffused and dissipated in a belt
Or network of telluric rents and fissures,
A hundred miles or so in width, across
The instep of the boot-shaped land, from sea
To sea: in its expression ranging from
A fire-volcano proper, Tongaríro,
Through seething lakes of sulphur, geyser-founts,
Steam hells and horns innumerable, down
To Maori boiling-pots and steaming-pits —
To Maori warming-pans and coddling-beds —[31]
To Maori morning, noon, and midnight baths —

Y

As in the towns of Whákaréwaréwa,
Ohínemútu, and elsewhere: the realm
Of the fire-goddess Máhuíka.[32] Now,
Within the centre of this wonder-world,
Conceive a mount, two hundred feet in height,
Beside a lakelet, half a mile in width;
The mountain of acidic rocks and earths,
Obsidian and rotten rhyolite —
Or laterite, as doctors of all kinds
Will differ; clad with scrubby mánuka —[33]
A kind of myrtle, heather-like in form,
And of a dark-green hue — club-moss and ferns;
And plumed with puffs of steam at many points:
The kites, belike, of mythic Whákatau;[34]
The lakelet fringed with raupo,[35] fern, and sedge,
And bristling with the tap'ring spears of rush;
O'erflown, o'erswam, and circled round with ducks,
Pink-legged stilts and dark-blue water-hens:
The Warm Lake, Rotomáhana.

Upon the westward aspect of the mount,
About a hundred feet above the lake,
A crater, thirty yards or more across,
Surrounded, on the north and east and south,
With wet and steaming walls of white and pink
And red acidic earths, with here and there
A bush of mánuka or bit of fern.
A crater whence afar is seen a cloud
Of steam arising half a mile or more:
The smoke, belike, that coming from the jar
Found and unsealed by the poor fisherman,
Became the genii of the Eastern tale —
Nay, rather, the soul-sighing of fond Papa
Made visible in its ascent to Rangi,
According to the myth of Earth and Heaven.[36]

A crater whence anear is seen a well
Of ever boiling water, heated by

Volcanic fires below: a fountain, now,
With scarce a ripple on its surface, and
Of such an exquisite and radiant blue,
That, changing with the varying light and shade,
Beneath its veil of bluish-tinted steam,
It seems to be the central gushing source
Of all the azures of the earth, between
The pale eyes of a Swedish newborn babe
And the dark plumage of the peacock's neck.
Anon, responsive to a southern gale,
A whirlpool, with a deep descending swirl,
Sucking itself into the earth below,
Full fathoms five, or haply, many more,
With a cavernous, self-engulfing growl —
A maelstrom nautilus withdrawn into
The inmost chamber of its pearly shell.
Revealing in the hollow of its bowl
A lining of the purest silica,
In crystal, sponge-like masses, soft and thick,
And white and lustrous as Andéan snow:
A pure precipitate, enveloping,
As with celestial garbs, the forms of moths
And dragonflies, caught in the steam and drowned,
And whatsoe'er falls into it by chance.
Revealing also in a little vale
A lakelet of transcendent loveliness:
A sapphire deliquescent into dew
Within a basin of the flowers of flint:
The eye of maidenhood, awaking from
The first of fond love dreams, dissolved in tears.
Anon (the boiling water of the well
Returning, with the veering of the wind,
And rising with a fierce, appalling roar,)
A geyser, casting up a spire of water
Two hundred feet above the crater rim,
Or twice the height of the surrounding mount:
A spire as it ascends, a spectacle,
An ultimatum of sublimity!

A dazzling point of light, above a grey,
Opaque columnar mass, enveloped in
A fast-pursuing, thick'ning cloud of steam
Of lustrous whiteness with prismatic hues;
Until, the acme of its action reached,
The point of dazzling light dissolves in the
Upcoming cloud of iridescent steam;
The column spreads into a sparkling spray
And shower, falling back into the well;
The while, the cloud above, as if upcast
Against a plate of glass, spreads far and wide,
Until transmuted into the unseen,
The circumambient empyrean!
This twice or thrice, until the weight of water
Within the crater balances the force
Impelling from the unknown depth below,
And then a seething sapphire fount again.

A wondrous well of water and as well
A well of wondrous water, holding in
Solution many earthy substances:
A lithic lymph: an inorganic ichor:
A min'ral magma, milk, or menstruum:
A cosmic chyme or chyle: a confluent
Conglomerate — Nay, nay, a water-womb,
Whence whatsoever issues from it in
The form of rock — a lithic progeny
Yclept among the wise silicious sinter,
Including geyserite and hydrophane
And hyalite, and others — is akin,
As cousins-german of the human race,
To many of the fairest gems of earth,
Jade, jasper, onyx, lapis lazuli,
Sard, catseye, agate, topaz, chrysoprase,
True emerald or beryl, tourmaline,
Rock-crystal, citrine, opal, amethyst,
Chalcedony, carnelian, rose-quartz,
Schoerl, cairngorm, siderite, and hyacinth;

As well, with the more homely and familiar
Quartz, quartzose, hornstone, touchstone, flint and
　　chert;
And so allied, in various degrees,
With the volcanic sept of sinters from
Basaltic to obsidian, or glass;
In fine, in an affinity in some
Degree with most of the mankind of min'rals —
The elemental silicon the blood
Of a telluric Shem uniting all.

The overflow escaping toward the west,
Within the gap in the encircling walls,
Some five-and-twenty yards in width, around
A central craggy islet — Lucy's Isle —[36]
Of black volcanic glass and laterite,
With fern and club-moss clad: in profile like
A couchant lion in a Turkish bath,
Or an Ægyptian sphinx in London fog.
Accessible betimes, I go upon this isle,
And lo! an aureole about my head —
My sinful head — in shadow on the steam
Above the sapphire caldron; and, above
The halo, overspreading half the pool,
A radiant arch of white — a rainbow blanched —
Or lunar brugh intensified in brightness.

And now, returning to the overflow —
This, in descending to the lake below,
Adown a slope two hundred yards or more,
Outspreading like a crushed and broken fan
And, in outspreading like a crumpled fan,
Decreasing in caloric from steam-hot,
Above the boiling-point,[38] to fish-blood cold;
And in decreasing thus in temper'ture,
Depositing by dissolution all
The earthy substances contained in it
In a composite rock-like mass of sinter,

Cream-white when dripping wet, snow-white when
    dry,
With tints of yellow, salmon, pink, and brown;
And in depositing its earthy matters thus,
O'erlaying and encrusting everything
Within its course, steep, shelf, log, limb and leaf;
And forming, with the change of circumstance,
Of wave, wind, angle, area and arc,
A series of the fairest earthy forms
Extending over acres, possibly
Without a parallel in the wide world.

Here, round the crater mouth, a beveled lip
Projecting inward as it has been formed
By deposition in the course of years;
Contracting the great outlet in a measure
And threatening in time to close it wholly —
And kill, of course, the geyser by a kind
Of eburnation or ossification.

Here, in the summit shallow steaming pools
(As seen from Lucy's Isle with best effect,)
A number of compressed spheroidal masses
All bristling with acicular accretions,
Like cushions made of hoar-frost: great sea-eggs
Converted into little isles of coral:
Fijian wigs well limed and crystallized:
Or misty moons submerged and petrified:
Or what you will — the fretful porcupine
Of Shakespeare that has suffered a sea-change
Into a something rich and strange, indeed!

Here (looking downward from a central point,)
A myriad of overflowing cups,
In shape, like bivalve shells — specifically
Tridacna gigas — set in rows around
About, and on successive scalloped shelves,
Down to the level of the rush-speared lake ;

In size, decreasing — generally — from
A central and extended, broken ridge,
Around its variable steeps and slopes,
From Caracalla's marble swimming-pools,
To Chinese porcelain tea and coffee cups;
And in their composition on inspection,
With laminated rims, composed of scales
Upturning like the petals of a rose
Unfolding into bloom, and set within
With dainty efflorescent increments,
Like granulated Afric ivory.
The color of the water in these cups,
A series of peculiar cloudy blues,
Extending from the opalescent tinge
Of the long-buried tear-tubes of Pompéii,
To the opaque hue of the turquoise-beads
Worn by the dusky natives of Nepaul.

Here, fretted, stalactitic underhangings,
Beneath the rounded rim of a great cup,
O'erlapping and depending full a fathom,
Like icicle on icicle o'erforming
In the alternate night-cold and day-warmth
Of lagging winter lapsing into spring;
Or like a white silk tasseled pall upon
A monarch's catafalque, fold after fold,
Compounding in a heavy swell and roll
And overhanging in a fleecy fringe —
And dripping with warm water drops in the
Similitude of a fond people's tears.
And under and behind this dripping fringe,
A wall thick set with sinter tubercles,
Ranging in size from millet-seed to cherries:
A windrow of new fallen summer hail:
A Turkish saddle studded o'er with cowries:
A shield embossed with opal-headed nails:
A girdle beaded round with precious pearls:
A fantasy of nacre and shagreen:

Or barracouta-teeth and barley-corn.
Here, lace-like intricacies, laps and folds,
Extending over half an acre, like
A wrinkled shawl as fine as ever knit
By Flemish dames for Spanish royalty;
Or — to a surgeon — the epiploön:
The superficial fascia of the muscles:
Or the arachnoid membrane of the brain;
Or like — how things of undefinable
Perfection fire the fancy to invention! —
The glass-sponge of Japan strewn o'er a hill;
The finest filamentous feathers of
The bird of Paradise commingled with
A cataract of cream-chalcedony;
The súmaúma's seed-silk [39] from Brazil
Wrought in the moonlight by the water-elves
And sprites into a bridal-veil for Undine;
The cobwebs of a Pennsylvania mead
At sunrise in September, white with dew,
Tenting the field for fairy warriors;
The dreams of Hindu metaphysicists
For ages turned into a maze of marble!

And here a yellow down: organic growth
Or inorganic stain, I know not what:
A filmy, fulvous fringe, as fine and fair
As that which clothes the new-born mullein-leaf.

Here, myrtle-branch and twig and leaf and fruit,
Fern-frond and club-moss spray o'erwhelmed,
Enshrouded and entombed in pearl and coral:
The fact evolved into a fantasy
As in a philosophic poet's dream.

Here, steep succeeding steep encrusted, like
As many frozen cataracts in winter:
The tepid water o'er the fretted mass
Descending in thin, lustrous, throbbing wavelets,

Like shimm'ring moonlight on a breeze-fanned
    billow:
Or, the remembrance in a morning dream
Of a fair palpitating bosom seen
With downcast eyes through filmy folds of lace
In the embracing of a midnight waltz.

Here, fungus-like concretions, bringing back
To mind the strange white filmy growths beheld
By lamplight in a Pennsylvania coal-pit.

Here, in a shallow pool, a seeming scum
Resolving, on inspection close at hand,
Into a dainty miniature atoll—
A mimic coral isle with central lake
As fair as ever fancied in the dream
Of boyhood on an old beach-comber's knee,
Nid-nodding o'er the oft-repeated tale
Of the fair islets of the great South Sea.

Here, mushroom-like concretions — seeming huts
For water-elves and fairies to inhabit.

Here, iron stains imparting to the sinter
The hue of human flesh — converting in
An instant all the rounded rims of the
Infinity of dripping cups into
As many rounded interlacing limbs—
Imparting to the sinter life and love,
As the environment of crimson velvet
To Dannecker's cold marble Ariadne.

Here, umber stains and chocolate, below
The grandest of the steaming bathing-pools.
And here, what sinter surgery is this?
A rupture in the rim of the great pool
Through which the water pours, is healing up

Around, about, within, without, as if endowed, in
    fact,
With an organic pow'r of reparation —
The life-blood that has built the wondrous fabric
Rebuilding and restoring it in ruin!

And here, a craggy rock, of mottled brown
And red and white, projecting from a ledge
Of sinter, like the head of a great monster,
Awaking and uprising in the midst
Of the world's wonder in bewilderment —
A craggy rock yclept the Wild Boar's Head.

And here, a wondrous series, shelf on shelf
Of conjugations of concretion, or,
Of demilunes of deposition, like
A fossil forest full of basking boas
In endless coils and curvings, limb on limb;
Or a dead sea of ammonites — Nay, like
An ancient Greek gymnasium in gypsum;
Or cycloid cornice of cathedral foils,
Tre-, quatre-, cinque-, and mille- compounding —
    Nay,
A chiliad of blessèd basin bracts
On temple walls — Nay, swallow-nests of sea-foam
Accrete to overhanging chalky cliffs;
Or a compounding of opossum-pouch
In ring and wrinkle round and round, in lay'r
And lapping up and down — in marble, a
Marsupiátal Ephesus-Diana! —
The limpid, opalescent levels of
These chalices of chert-precipitation,
A fantasy of isothermal lines!

Here, interaxial, isthmic buttresses
And bonds, between the bases of the bowls,
Striated, stalagmitic, ostracoid:
The whirligig of time, that, soon or late,

Turns all things topsy-turvy, here, inverting
The sage old saw about the constant drip.

Here, green and yellow stains: perhaps a mould
Upon the walls but seldom wet with water.
And here more catkined, bearded, rounded rims,
Projecting like the fleecy flanks of beasts
Caught in a mount or winter storm of sleet;
The llama and alpaca of the Andes;
The sheep and yak of the Himálayas;
The bighorn and the grizzly of the Rockies —
The largest masses in the likeness of
The wool-clad mammoth and rhinoceros
Encased in ice on Lena's frozen shore,
And under and behind the seeming flank
Of the enormous beast, another wall
Of tendon-white, adnascent mammillations;
Enameled nodes: like pearl-corn on the cob,

Here, isles of mánuka, club-moss, and fern,
Within the sea of sinter spreading wide
As it descends the hill-side to the lake.

And here, below the craggy Wild Boar's Head,
A series of cold water pools, apart
Somewhat from all above them and around;
Their rims decayed, streaked, mottled, smooth;
The water in them still, a turquoise blue,
In all save one; in the exception, pink —
As pink as an albino rabbit's eyes.
A series of cold water pools, perhaps
The product of a geyser-fount between
Them and the Wild Boar's Head, but now occluded.
Stripped for a bath, I step out into one
And sink into an ooze of silicates
Up to my waist — an ooze as soft and cold
As if composed of jelly-fish and frog-spawn:

A bath to be remembered with an ugh!
And then a shudder, to my dying day.

And here, upon the margin of the lake
(Where its warm water finds an outlet in
A breast-deep streamlet to the lake below —
Lake Tarawera, or the Hot Ridge Lake,)
The lowest level of the wonderful
Formation, overflown with tepid water,
Filled with a myriad of little larvæ —
Belike, the grub of the annoying sand-fly;
If so, long life and tapeworm appetites
Unto the birds that dine upon them daily! —
A plane of rotten, dirty, treach'rous sinter
Upon a spongy bog of unknown depth.
A pioneering staff within my hand
Descends an ell or more, as if in paste,
Soft-soap, or paper-pulp, and stays my steps.
A plane of sinter, when compared with that
Descending from the geyser crater-rim,
As a long train of silk, smirched in the mud
Of a street-crossing, to the cataract
Of flounces, furbelows, and lace, above,
In the perfection of their purity.
A plane, whence, turning back and looking up,
The whole formation, from the base to summit,
Is seen, encompassed in a single view:
The rims of the infinity of cups,
Uprising one above the other, like
The steps in ruin of a pyramid
Of water-dripping, creamy, dreamy, marble.

O thou sublimity of quartz and chert!
Thou, marvelous mirage in solid crystal!
Thou, morganatic fata fixed in flint!
Cellini's concepts in chalcedony!
The poetry of Petrarch in fire-opal!
Hold! hold! there is a world of wonders yet

To be involved before erupting into
Ideal and abstract extravagances.

Adjunct and accessory to the White,
Conceive, in the succession I behold them,
Three little boiling springs, surrounded each
With a low ring or crater-cone of sinter:
In size, three whelks beside a Greenland whale.
Next, two great boiling wells, the one some ten,
The other twenty feet in width and depth,
In dashing, splashing, lashing ebullition,
As if involving, one, within its hold,
A typic Washoe zephyr, and the other,
A T"erra-del-Fuego williewaw,
In rabid rage and ranc'rous rivalry!
Or one, the Maori god of storms, Tawhíri,[40]
The other, fearful Tínenúitépo,[41]
The goddess of destruction, Darkness, Death.

Between these walls, a narrow slippy path
Of white and pinkish slimy laterite —
A rotten bridge between two boiling hells
Sufficient to appal a sinner surely!
A few steps further on, a roaring steam-horn;
And then a geyser in incessant action,
Upcasting solid cones, explosive bombs,
Divergent plumes, and overarching tree-ferns
Of splashing, sputt'ring, steaming boiling water,
From ten to thirty feet in height, or more:
As if incorporating in itself
A score or more of spouting whales in sport!
The basin rim of this superb cascade
Encrusted with a dark brown flinty sinter,
Thickset with upright papillary points,
Suggesting tripe and land and water urchins.

A chain beyond, a score of boiling springs;
And then another terrace-forming caldron —

A caldron heart-shaped, fifteen feet in length,
By ten or twelve in width, the sinter rim
Projecting inward in symmetric knobs
Approximately of one size and shape,
Like little buttons turned on big, of horn,
Or garden-snails arranged in single file.

And further on, some forty feet or more
Above the level of the tepid lake,
The crater of a quondam boiling lake,
Now filled with ooze and mud, containing scores
Of simm'ring pools of milky unctuous mud;
The ripples forming wondrous arabesques
Of oily dark brown on a ground of grey;
And mimic miniatures in mud and mire
Of Kilauéa and Vesuvius.
In one, steam-bubbles of tenacious paste
Uprising, bursting, and collapsing in
A series of such shapes as to excite
To mirth and laughter rather than to wonder —
Cups, saucers, plates and bowls, in May-day sport;
Buns, pancakes, rolls, and waffles on a spree;
Wens, goitres, bumps, and mumps, in merry mask;
Swelled katzenjammer heads; and heaving hearts
That break and heal and heave and break again,
As if in satire of humanity;
And in another, a peculiar paste
The Maoris eat of, taking each his peck,
Prescribed to one and all by the old saw,
Without division or dilution boldly.
Touching my tongue-tip to a steaming stickful,
I taste a chalky, acid substance, and
My appetite is satisfied at once:
De gustibus non disputandum, truly!

And here, a lakelet of opaque green water —
A pool, belike, of melted greenstone méres,
The wondrous two-edged war-sword of the Maoris.

And see! uprising from the hills around,
A thousand jets of vapor: one and all,
Like Tangotango, the celestial maid,
With her first-born of earth upon her back,
Uprising from the ridge-pole of Tawháki,
Dissolving and evanishing in ether!⁴²

Proceeding, now, in a canoe across
The Warm Lake, Rotomáhana,
I visit and inspect the second of
The wondrous Terraces, the Pink: unto
The White, the man, the supplemental woman.

Conceive a similar causation and
Effect to those belonging to the White :
A mount beside a lake ; a geyser-crater
Upon the lake-side half-way up the steep ;
A cloud of steam uprising constantly ;
A sinter flange and lining to the caldron ;
A sapphire depth of transcendental beauty ;
The overflowing water holding in
Solution many earthy substances,
And losing them, on cooling, as it spreads
And trickles down the hillside to the lake ;
Upbuilding in succession, in its course,
Cups, saucers, basins, bowls, and bathing-pools,
Of various swallow-nest and chamoid shapes,
Containing such a spectral series of
Cerulean tints, as if they held in them
Decoctions and dilutions of the sum
Of all the azures of the sea and sky ;
The mounts of Moab seen at dawn across
The Dead Sea from the heights of Olivet ;
The ageratum fields of Mexico ;
The Morpho-butterflies of Amazon ;
The columns sheathed with lapis lazuli
Around the chapel altars of the Kremlin ;
The pottery of Old Japan and China ;

The tassel of the scarlet cap of Tunis;
The mantle of the Marys of Murillo;
The starlit field of Freedom's Flag — Enough,
The opal, turquoise, and forget-me-not
Pervading and predominant in all;
And shelves or terraces; and there an end,
The likeness ceasing with the general.

Conceive, now, to encompass the details
Of difference — conceive the whole reduced
In size a fourth: in summit caldron, height
Above the lake, and length and spread of flow;
The water in the caldron boiling gently;
The flange projecting farther to the centre;
The sinter in two forms; an under, old,
And crystalline deposit, like the white —
The record of the geyser's early action;
And over this a new precipitation,
Vitrescent and slow-forming, without crystals,
As smooth as cut and polished alabaster,
And in its color pink: a pearly pink,
Like that within the mouth of many shells —
The *Strombus pugilis*, especially;
Or that of coral from the Middle Sea;
Or that within the dew-bathed bosom of
An op'ning salmon-tinted tea-rose; or,
The lining of the lips of sucking babes —
A fantasy of ruby and enamel;
Unhappily, howe'er, with many stains
Of graphite in the names of idiots
And fools, imperishable underneath
The overforming and translucent sinter —
With stains as well, but less objectionable,
Of charcoal, from the burning bush around,
Of soil and sulphur: mottled, but not marred;
The rounded rims of the o'erflowing cups
More lip- and limb-like: giving to a bath
Within the steaming turquoise-colored pools

A sense of love and luxury beyond
The rapture of a Persian poet's dream:
A dip into the morning dew within
The ruby-tinted chalice of a rose
Were but the thousandth tithing of the bliss
Enjoyed within these wondrous warm and smooth,
Delicious — nay, delirious sinter pools!

Enough! The boat awaits! Come! come! I hear.
Oh, shall I kiss these love-lips never more?
Nor press this bosom to mine own again?
Nor feel this warm breath intergasp with mine?
Oh, must I leave the arms of this fond woman?
Oh, must I leave this land of life and love?
Adieu, thou rapture of my soul, for aye!
Thy fond forget-me-nots not voiced in vain!

The prow of the unfeeling log canoe
Divides the rushes in its course, returning,
Across the Warm Lake, to its sedge-fringed outlet.
On, on, until Te Tárata, the White,
Appears in startling splendor, rousing me
From the reaction of ecstatic bliss.

The foreground of the picture, a canoe,
Among the rushes in the shallow lake;
Uprising from the lake, six water-hens;
Along the shoreline, two pink-legged stilts;
The centre, the White Terrace: step on step:
Up, up, and round and round, from base to summit;
Above the summit and the upper steps,
Great clouds of vapor rising to the sky,
Commingling with a rain-cloud in the east —
A fitting background, dark, chaotic, cold;
Around the summit, glimpses of the mount
That girds the three-fourths of the boiling caldron:

Faint streaks of white and pink and purple earths,
And dark green spots of mánuka and fern;
Against the terrace, mount, and rising steam.
A cone of vivifying, gleaming light,
Projecting from a sinking sun behind me;
And over all, by the most happy chance,
A double rainbow of the rarest splendor:
The whole, a fancy of the elements!
A dream composed of fire, earth, air and water!
A dream within the cosmic brain of God!

Within the current of the outlet stream,
The boat glides swiftly on, and soon — too soon
The picture passes from my sight, but not —
Not from my mem'ry and imagination.
As man and woman are involved in Man,
The images of both the White and Pink,
The man and woman, interblend in one,
A terrace of ideal form and color
Combining the perfections of the twain
In a harmonious, beauteous, wondrous whole,
The Terrace of Enchantment of New Zealand.

The Terrace of Enchantment — Aye, that once
Conceived within the mind takes to itself
The myriads untold of things and thoughts
Within the worlds of fact and fancy, with
The waving of a wand, the scripture of
A circle, or the mouthing of a word —
Resolves, rebuilds, contracts, expands, amends;
Moulds space and time; and gives to things unseen,
Unheard, unfelt, the qualities of things
Around about us in the world of fact;
To airy musings and imaginings
A firm foundation, fixity, and form;
To desert dreams, an oasis of life;
To nothingness, length, breadth, and depth and
 thickness.

By chance, in reverie, I roam again
Among the Chagtai tombs of Hindustán,
And stand in an ecstatic awe before
The Taj Mahál, the Tomb of Mumtaz Begum.
And lo! wrought by the Terrace of Enchantment,
I see the wondrous mausoleum set
Upon a mountain-height; then melted in
The waters of its fountains, and adown
The mountain poured; and, strangely, in its ruin,
Retaining all the beauty of its being:
The creamy whiteness of its marble walls;
The curve of arch and dome and minaret;
The plane and parallel of floor and wall;
The chisled tracery and arabesque;
The inlaid ornamental Persian script;
The precious stones set in the lace-like screen;
The sheen and glamour of the polished slabs;
And over all the tint of all the roses
Of the embowered acres of the tomb:
The Taj dissolved indeed, but evermore
Indissoluble in its being with
The Terrace of Enchantment of New Zealand.

Anon, aboard the good ship "Patterson,"[43]
I pass again into Magellan's straits,
And see, within the glinting of the sun
Through parting rack above the northern heights,
A glacier coming o'er the mountains from
The cloud-swept south — a flood of lustrous white;
The while, the williewaws descending sweep
And swirl the surface of the swelling seas
Into a maze of lace-like foam and spindrift.
Anon, the sun descends and night sets in —
A night opaquely dark — until the clouds
Drift broken by, and lo! a crimson light,
Diffusing from the southern pole, o'erspreads
The sky, the mountains, and the storm-swept
    waves.

And presto! as I con these several scenes,
The Terrace of Enchantment takes them up,
The glacier-flood, the foam, and austral light,
And turns them in a trice into itself!

Anon, I sleep again beneath the sky —
The blue silk counterpane — of Italy,
And dream a dream of Michael Angelo:
Of marble simulating man and woman;
Of man and woman simulating marble;
Of great cathedral piles, plinth, column, dome,
And frieze with human forms in high relief —
All in confusion and obscurity,
Commingled with the waters of the Arno.
Till presto! in the twinkling of an eye,
Behold the chaos and the darkness gone,
And all the marble and the human forms,
The blue silk sky and waters of the Arno,
Combined within the Terrace of Enchantment!

Anon, within an arbor overgrown
With perfumed honeysuckle, painted rose,
And   pendant   fuchsia : moonlight streaming
    through
The meshes of the interlacing stems
And partings of the overlapping leaves:
A woman — one among the millions of
The earth in countless eons — in my arms:
I hear a symphony of Mendelssohn
Borne half a mile across a placid lake;
And as I hear, the sounds, the scents, the sweets
Of my surroundings, all becoming sights,
I see, before my tongue can tell the word,
The music, moonlight, flow'rs, and love combined
In the incomparable radiant Terrace!

Anon, I see Anacreon arise
From the entombment of the centuries,

And hear him sing his songs of wine and woman ;
And, quick as thought, in the similitude
Of the rare Terrace, lo! I see these songs
Descend from lip to lip, and cup to cup,
In a wide-spreading and divergent course,
Adown the mountain steep of ages to
The yielding ooze, the present, at its base.

Anon, I see a nameless man or god,
Involving man and woman in perfection,
Come into being, live a holy life,
And pass away: his face and form unlimned
By art: no work of his in brick or brass
Remaining: yet, behind him leaving in
The mem'ry of mankind a recollection,
In shapeless, vague, chaotic, dreamlike thought,
Of every instant of his years on earth —
Of every heart-beat of his holiness.
Oh, for the word to shape within the sight
This recollection of ten thousand parts
In a complete and perfect god-like whole!
Give spot and compass to ubiquity;
Create a universe anew from chaos;
And crystallize a limitless mirage
Into a mountain fixity, a pearl
And marble purity, a peerless form,
And, interfusing and pervading all,
The hue and heart-beat of humanity!
O blest interposition of the Terrace —
The Terrace of Enchantment of New Zealand!
Fulfilling in thy form and function all
The requisites of this composite symbol!
His blood, thy wondrous well of wondrous water,
Upgushing to a mountain height, and then
Descending to the world-encircling sea;
His brain and its pure thoughts, thy unskulled
    spheres
And sunlit labyrinths of seeming coral;

His lips and uttered words, thy myriad
Of overflowing cups of alabaster;
His arms, and their infolding to his breast
In universal sympathy and love,
Thy thousand interlocking rounded rims;
His influence, extending far and wide,
Involving all, the highest and the lowest,
For ages past and ages yet to come,
Thy flood in its outpouring and descent,
And sinter deposition over all,
Imparting purity to things impure,
The lustrous hues of gems to mud and mire,
The beauty of the living to the dead;
His very being, soul and body, thine,
Involving Earth, and yet reflecting Heaven!

Such are the Terraces, the White and Pink,
Of Rotomáhana, in fact and fancy:
Within the water-world, the monument
Of earth that marks for man its geyser-centre;
Within the world beneath the Cross in Heaven,
The sign and symbol of the Christ on Earth.

---

[1] Originally published in the form of an octavo pamphlet in 1885 at Auckland, New Zealand, under the title of FACT AND FANCY IN NEW ZEALAND. THE TERRACES OF ROTOMÁHANA: A Poem, by FRANK COWAN. To which is prefixed a Paper on GEYSER ERUPTIONS AND TERRACE FORMATIONS, by JOSIAH MARTIN, F.G.S. Subsequently, a second edition was published by MR. MARTIN, in quarto, interfoliated with photographic views of the Terraces and neighboring geysers, etc. Both editions were dedicated to SIR GEORGE GREY, K.C.B., "a soldier, statesman, and scholar, whose biography is part of the honorable history for half a century of the tri-partite division of the British Colonies of the Southern Hemisphere."

[2] AOTEAROA: Literally a-o, world, universe, or, a part for the whole, land; te-a, white; and ro-a, long. By the first of the Maoris to come to New Zealand from their traditional fatherland Hawaiki, a compound of the first two words was given to the Great Barrier Island, off the northeast coast of the North

Island, from its appearance, involved in white clouds, as they approached it; the compound of the three was afterward given to the mainland, or properly, to that part of New Zealand, which is called North Island. Curiously, too, while I record for the first time the correspondence in signification between Aotea and Albion, in its commonly accepted derivation, I may note here another iota of seeming happy prophecy in the native name of New Zealand to the fate it has found. The word *te-a* belongs to the sacerdotal vocabulary of the Maoris; and, signifying white especially in its relation to other human colors or complexions, was applied always with a mystic, special, sacred, symbolic, or double meaning. While, accordingly, Aotea is generally speaking a White Land, or a second Albion, it is especially and essentially a White Man's Land: and so may it be in the fullest sense of the words, is my earnest prayer.

[3] A noteworthy illustration of the involution of the seismic environment of New Zealand by the Maoris is found in the Legend of the Maiden of Rotorua. It occurs in the description of the agitation of the heroine, Hine-Moa on hearing the trumpet of her lover: as translated — and not interpolated, as he has averred to the writer — by SIR GEORGE GREY, in his *Polynesian Mythology*, p. 148, as follows: "And the young and beautiful chieftainess felt as if an earthquake shook her to make her go to the beloved of her heart."

[4] The volcano similarly has been involved by the Maoris and become a part of their legendary lore. Vide *Polynesian Mythology*, p. 97.

[5] The grandest of the sea-gorges of New Zealand is called Milford Sound. Combining precipices over 2,000 feet in height, the icy summits of the Southern Alps, and glaciers and waterfalls descending into valleys plumed with superb tree-ferns, it is not surpassed by any of the fiords of Norway in scenic magnificence and variety. It is supposed to have been cut wholly or in great part by a stupendous glacier.

[6] The glaciers of the Southern Alps are noted for their size and number, and especially for their comparative nearness to the level of the sea, as an illustration of the fact that the Southern Hemisphere to-day is passing through a glacial epoch: in one place, it is said, the ice descends to a point less than 800 feet above the sea.

[7] The geysers of the volcanic belt of New Zealand are in number legion, while in size they are less than those of the Yellowstone Park and Iceland. For the fullest account of them, and the infinity of phenomena involved, see the several

philosophic papers on the subject by Mr. Martin, referred to above, and others published since.

[8] Albeit the Terraces of Rotomáhana have been destroyed, New Zealand is not without noteworthy wonders still in the way of terrace formations, as they are one of the resultants of geyser action.

[9] Pounamu: The greenstone, or nephrite; resembling jade, but, I believe, a different mineral. It is found especially, if not wholly, on the Middle Island, which, accordingly, was called by the Maoris, the country of the greenstone.

[10] Awhato: Several species of fungus, *Cordiceps robertsii*, et al., which enter and occupy the bodies of certain larvæ which go into the earth in order to pass into the pupa state of their existence; and, curiously, while destroying the grubs, retaining intact to a remarkable degree their forms, as animal tubers to rush-like plants. The fungus attains a length of twelve or sixteen inches; and the larva, with which it has become incorporate and evolved from generally in a single stem from a point near the tail of the grub, so wonderfully preserved, that cross-sections under the microscope have revealed the delicate tissues of the alimentary canal and other organs involved in the vegetable growth without displacement.

[11] Ponga: A general name for the tree-ferns of New Zealand, belonging to the genera *Cyathea* and *Dicksonia*; the tallest attaining an altitude of forty feet.

[12] Nikau: A species of palm, *Arica sapida*: and one of the most remarkable of the living plants of New Zealand, representing the flora of the coal measures of Europe and America.

[13] Rata: An extraordinary plant, *Metrosideros robusta*, that begins life as a seed lodged in a crevice of a tree, which, before sending upward a shoot, sends downward to the earth, at whatsoever distance it may be, a clinging root. It then becomes a vinous parasite of rapid growth, clasping with numerous and strong arms the tree to which it clings for support, and in time killing it, and supplanting it as a magnificent crimson-flowering forest tree — in many instances, not only enveloping the trunk of its original support, but involving it in its very being and body.

[14] Kauri: A superb broad-leafed, cone-bearing pine, *Dammara australis*, attaining a height of 200 feet with a girth of 60; the grandest of the forest trees of New Zealand, and one of the monarchs of the vegetable kingdom; a glimpse into the glories of the Carboniferous Age of Europe and America; for it is one of the many plants of the evergreen flora of New Zealand

which approximate or are identical with the types of the coal measures. The kauri gum of commerce is the fossil turpentine of forest growths of this noble tree which have developed, decayed, and disappeared in the past.

¹⁵ Toke: Enormous earth-worms from one to three feet in length; formerly eaten and considered a great delicacy by the natives.

¹⁶ Tuatara: An anomalous reptile, peculiar to New Zealand, of a dirty brown color, and attaining a length of about eighteen inches; called, at one time, *Hatteria punctata*, and now *Sphenodon punctatum*.

¹⁷ Kakapo: One of the most extraordinary of the birds of New Zealand, a parrot, *Stringops habroptilus*.

¹⁸ Kea: One of the most remarkable birds of New Zealand, a species of parrot, *Nestor notabilis*.

¹⁹ Kiwi: A genus of anomalous birds, peculiar to New Zealand, and comprising four well-defined species, namely, the North Island kiwi, *Apteryx Mantelli*; the South Island, *A. australis*; the Little Grey, *A. Oweni*; and the Big Grey, *A. Haasti*; and a possible fifth, *A. maxima*, equaling in size a full grown turkey, while the others correspond in bulk to little and big varieties of the domestic chicken.

²⁰ Moa: A family of colossal birds which has become extinct during the past century; peculiar, as far as is known, to New Zealand, with the exception of one species, *Dinornis australis*, found in New South Wales, Australia; in height, ranging from four to eleven or twelve feet; wingless, or approximately so; and, in their relations with living birds, akin most closely to the kiwis, or the genus *Apteryx*, of New Zealand, and then, in the order mentioned, to the emus of Australia, the cassowaries of New Guinea, New Britain, and the neighboring islands, the rheas of South America, and the ostriches of south-western Asia and Africa — according to Hutton, however, "appearing to be intermediate between the rheas and the emus and cassowaries."

²¹ Kuri: A bushy-tailed yellowish variety of the common dog, *Canis familiaris*, found in New Zealand by its European discoverers, and supposed to have been introduced, along with a species of rat, by the Maoris, as they themselves assert in their traditions.

²² Maori: (Pronounced conventionally as if spelled Mowrie) The name given to the people found upon the islands of

New Zealand by their European discoverers, and to their descendants, now numbering about 40,000; a people belonging to the great Polynesian family which includes notably the Hawaiians, Samoans, Tongans, and Tahitians; warriors, cannibals, and communists in the fullest sense of the words. They came to New Zealand from a place called in their traditions Hawaiki, which, nominally, is the same as Hawaii, i. e., Hawa-iki, Little Java, and which is supposed, accordingly, to indicate Java as the fatherland of the several allied peoples of the Pacific. The first boat-loads of the immigrants, from the genealogies of several families preserved independently in as many parts of the islands, are inferred to have arrived not earlier than eight hundred years ago and not later than four hundred.

[23] Moko: The tattooing of the Maori. Not a generation ago preserved tattooed heads were an article of commerce in New Zealand; and to supply the demand, not only were murders committed and tribal wars carried on, but slaves also were tattooed in a superior style and then deliberately slaughtered — their preserved heads being more valuable than their living bodies: an evolution in the art of tattooing possibly the highest as well as the most horrible ever attained. Indeed, to such an extent was this trade carried on with its attendant evils of such a character as to require a special evolution of belief for their acceptance, that, upon taking possession of the country by the English, the most stringent laws were enacted immediately for its suppression and abolition, making the possessor or exhibitor of a tattooed head subject to a heavy penalty.

[24] Mere: A peculiar short double-edged sword, insignium of rank, sceptre of power, and the ocular and objective symbol of ownership in and right of occupation to certain districts or regions; made of wood, whale-bone, and several kinds of stone.

[25] Tiki: A symbolic image, worn on the breast by the Maoris, men and women, appended to a fillet around the neck; an image, in whale-bone, greenstone, or other material, of an ideal bisexual ancestral personage, typifying Man in the abstract and called Tiki.

[26] Tapu: The taboo; the highest evolution of law among the Maoris, and, I may say, too, the Polynesians in general; working at one time for the greatest good, and at another for the greatest evil. Its growth seems to have been the result of a necessity arising among a communistic people, for governmental, sacerdotal, and other special purposes, of isolating certain persons and setting apart certain places and things for them —

the backward swing of the communistic pendulum. The word ta-pu means literally priest-marked; from *ta*, to mark, or marked, as with a brush; and *pu*, a priest, or a representative of the gods in council, called also *pa*.

²⁷ Rotomáhana: Literally, *ro-to*, lake, and *ma-ha-na* (accented on the first syllable,) warm, the Warm Lake.

²⁸ Tárata: From *ta-ra*, a ridge, by contraction of a reduplication, *taratara*; the accent remaining on the original first syllable of each.

²⁹ Otukapuarangi: Literally, *o*, a place; *tu*, possibly for *te*, the; *ka-pu-a*, cloud; *rang-i*, heaven: the place of the cloud of heaven.

³⁰ Maui: One of the most popular and wide-spread of the mythic monsters, gods, ideal heroes, or what you will of the Polynesians, who plays, in general among his mythic associates, the rôle of a trickster, wonder-worker, dark horse, harlequin, Puck, serpent, and the like, and in particular at one time a curious combination of the parts of Loki and Thor in the mythology of the Scandinavians; at another a Jason, Ulysses, or Columbus; and at a third, Prometheus. The name signifies the Asker, the Enquirer; and taking the whole range of his actions, achievements, and adventures, he may be regarded as a personification of all the good and evil that attend the asking, seeking, investigating, and accomplishing of all things. In a mischievous prank through disobedience, which resulted in his own destruction, he is said to have brought death into the world; while one of his most glorious achievements during life was the hooking and bringing to the surface of the sea an enormous fish, which is none other than the North Island of New Zealand. Hence, according to the legend, or, figuratively speaking, the North Island particularly, or New Zealand generally, was termed *Te Ika a Maui*, the Fish of Maui; and curiously, Captain Cook and many of his successors, mistaking this metaphorical for a truly geographical name, have designated so the Northern Island. Among the Hawaiians, Maui, whose name is given to the island in which is found the monstrous crater of Haleakala, half a mile in depth and thirty-nine miles in circumference — Maui, similarly, is said to have hooked up the island of Hawaii, the largest of the group: did so, in fact: for I have been shown by the Hawaiians the very hook with which he did it, now in the form of a lava-islet between the island of Maui and Hawaii.

³¹ A rude hut built of slabs of sinter, near the White Terrace was a favorite lying-in room for the Maori women of the

neighborhood: the equable heat and humidity of the place producing relaxation and expediting delivery with minimum pain.

[32] Vide *Polynesian Mythology*, p. 30. Ohinemutu is a Maori village on Lake Rotorua; the name signifying *o*, a place, *hi-ne*, maiden, and *mu-tu*, last: the place of the last maiden. This village and Whakarewarewa, about two and a half miles distant, are the most extraordinary of all the odd and curious towns I have seen in my travels in the four quarters of the globe, not excepting the villages of the Arabs in the ruins of the subterranean grain-vaults of Carthage, like colonies of prairie-dogs. Situated in the midst of a myriad of steam-jets, boiling-pools, sulphur-lakes, geysers, and the like — the inhabitants making use of them in cooking, baking, washing, bathing, and in keeping themselves warm in winter — they can be compared to nothing within the range of my eye or imagination more appropriate than the nursery baked pie that revealed the four-and-twenty singing blackbirds, when, presumably steaming at every crack and crevice of the crust, it was set before the king and opened.

[33] A myrtle, *Leptospermum scoparium*, or *L. ericoides*.

[34] Grey's *Polynesian Mythology*, p. 72.

[35] Raupo: An aquatic plant, *Typha angustifolia*, recalling the calamites of the coal-measures.

[36] "Up to this time the vast Heaven [Rangi] has remained separated from his spouse the Earth [Papa]. Yet their mutual love continues — the soft warm sighs of her loving bosom ever rise to him, ascending from the woody mountains and valleys, and men call these mists; and the vast Heaven, as he mourns through the long nights of his separation from his beloved, drops frequent tears upon her bosom, and men, seeing these, term them dew-drops."— Grey's *Polynesian Mythology*, p. 9.

[37] So called by the writer in remembrance of his daughter.

[38] By reason of the earthy substances contained.

[39] The wad used by the savages of the Amazon in their blow-gun, is made of this exceedingly fine and light silk. It surrounds the poison-tipped arrow and is carried with it in its death-dealing flight.

[40] *Polynesian Mytholgy*, p. 3.   [41] *Ibid.*, p. 35.   [42] *Ibid.*, p. 41.

[43] The "CARLISLE P. PATTERSON," a small steamer belonging to the United States Coast and Geodetic Survey Department, Lieut. RICHARDSON CLOVER, Commanding, in making her first trip through the Straits of Magellan from the Atlantic to the Pacific coasts of the United States, in 1884-5.

AUSTRALIA: A CHARCOAL-SKETCH.[1]

PROEM — ACROSS THE BOWS.

Across the bows of the "ZEALANDIA,"
Betwixt the sea and sky, involved in haze,
I see a faint gray line — Australia!
An ancient, outcast island-continent;
An Ark adrift within the flood of Time,
Preserving through unnumbered days and years,
The fruitful pairs of a primæval life
Long vanished elsewhere and forgotten quite;
As well, as it hath happed, through Providence
Or Chance, a goodly portion of the Earth
Disjunct and set aside long ages since
For welling England's overflow to-day.

JUNE, 1885.

INTRODUCTORY.

"What is the dominant note of Australian scenery? That which is the dominant note of Edgar Allan Poe's poetry — Weird Melancholy. A poem like L'Allegro could never be written by an Australian. It is too airy, sweet, too freshly happy. The Australian mountain forests are funereal, secret, stern. Their solitude is desolation. They seem to stifle, in their black gorges, a story of sullen despair. No tender sentiment is nourished in their shade. In other lands the dying year is mourned, the falling leaves fall lightly on his bier. In the Australian forests no leaves fall. The savage winds shout among the rock clefts. From the melancholy gums strips of white bark hang and rustle. The very animal life of these frowning hills is either grotesque or ghostly. Great gray kang-

aroos hop noislessly over the coarse grass. Flights of white
cocatoos stream out, shrieking like evil souls. The sun sudden-
ly sinks, and the mopokes burst out into horrible peals of semi-
human laughter. The natives aver that, when night comes,
from out the bottomless depth of some lagoon the Bunyip rises,
and, in form like monstrous sea-calf, drags his loathsome length
from out the ooze. From a corner of the silent forest rises a
dismal chant, and around a fire dance natives painted like skel-
etons. All is fear-inspiring and gloomy. No bright fancies are
linked with the memories of the mountains. Hopeless ex-
plorers have named them out of their sufferings — Mount Mis-
ery, Mount Dreadful, Mount Despair. As when among sylvan
scenes in places
> 'Made green with the running of rivers,
> And gracious with temperate air,'

the soul is soothed and satisfied, so, placed before the frightful
grandeur of these barren hills, it drinks in their sentiment of
defiant ferocity, and is steeped in bitterness.

"Australia has rightly been named the Land of the Dawn-
ing. Wrapped in the mist of early morning, her history looms
vague and gigantic. The lonely horseman riding between the
moonlight and the day sees vast shadows creeping across the
shelterless and silent plains, hears strange noises in the primæ-
val forest where flourishes a vegetation long dead in other
lands, and feels, despite his fortune, that the trim utilitarian
civilization which bred him shrinks into insignificance beside
the contemptuous grandeur of forest and ranges coeval with an
age in which European scientists have cradled his own race.

"There is a poem in every form of tree or flower, but the
poetry which lives in the trees and flowers of Australia differs
from that of other countries. Europe is the home of knightly
song, of bright deeds and clear morning thought. Asia sinks
beneath the weighty recollections of her past magnificence, as
the Suttee sinks, jewel-burdened, upon the corpse of dead
grandeur, destructive even in its death. America swiftly hur-
ries on her way, rapid, glittering, insatiable, even as one of her
own giant waterfalls. From the jungles of Africa, and the
creeper-tangled groves of the Islands of the South, arise, from
the glowing hearts of a thousand flowers, heavy and intoxicat-
ing odors — the Upas-poison which dwells in barbaric sensu-
ality. In Australia alone is to be found the Grotesque, the
Weird, the strange scribblings of Nature learning how to write.
Some see no beauty in our trees without shade, our flowers
without perfume, our birds who cannot fly, and our beasts who
have not yet learned to walk on all fours. But the dweller in

the wilderness acknowledges the subtle charm of this fantastic land of monstrosities. He becomes familiar with the beauty of loneliness. Whispered to by the myriad of tongues of the wilderness, he learns the language of the barren and the uncouth, and can read the hieroglyphs of haggard gum-trees, blown into odd shapes, distorted with fierce hot winds, or cramped with cold nights, when the Southern Cross freezes in a cloudless sky of icy blue. The phantasmagoria of that wild dreamland termed the Bush interprets itself, and the poet of our desolation begins to comprehend why free Esau loved his heritage of desert sand better than all the bountiful richness of Egypt."— MARCUS CLARKE: *Preface to the Poems of Adam Lindsay Gordon.*

AUSTRALIA: A CHARCOAL-SKETCH.

Here rhyme was first framed without fashion,
Song shaped without form.— ADAM LINDSAY GORDON.

A Saunterer: poetic, philosophic, fanciful, facetious, or grotesque, as time and chance and circumstance determine: on the wallaby² a second time around the world:
Assuming for the nonce to be
A Seer and a Singer: all his senses to the sense of sight subordinate, involving his environment; and all his energies concentred and expended in his speech, evolving his environment in song:
I see and sing
AUSTRALIA!

The Austral World;
The World beneath the Cross, the Coalsack, and the Magellanic Clouds of Southern Skies;
The Nether World ;
The World below the Belt ;
The World Antipodal ;

The World of Shakespeare's Anthropophagi whose
    Heads do grow beneath their Shoulders for a
    verity;
The World Upset;
The World Turned Upside Down;
The World of Topsiturvia!

A Somewhere South to the Chinese for untold ages:
    whence trepang or beche-de-mer;
A Somewhere South and East associated with the Gol-
    den Chersonesus to the Greeks of Alexander's time
    and centuries succeeding: whence the vessels of
    the seas beyond the shores of India: deep-laden
    with the silks and spices of the Orient expanding
    North and South: fact-founded, fancy-formed: a
    stolen kiss evolved into a marriage-dream;
The Lochac of the mediæval Marco Polo: first of
    European wanderers to face the rising sun and
    point with left hand to a wondrous habitable
    North, Cipango, or Japan, and with the right hand
    to a wondrous habitable South, the world of Aus-
    tralasia!
Kai Dowdai: Little Country: to the natives of the
    Northeast Coast: from Muggi Dowdai: Big: New
    Guinea: Pápua: the flats of York Peninsula ap-
    pearing small beside the heights of Pápua: and
    that not in the eye of savages not in their speech;
The South Land of the Holy Ghost to the Pacific's
    pioneers, the pious Portuguese;
New Holland to the Dutch;
The Austral Great Unknown unto the English till the
    time of Cook;
AUSTRALIA from the days of Captain Flinders for all
    time!

I see and sing
The Seas Surrounding: sweeping, swashing, gnawing,
    gnashing: coming to and going from: a mighty

ravenous amœboid monster having in its maw a
continental animalculum: alternately devouring
and rejecting it; eternally digesting and ejecting
it: Amœba panpelagica!
The Arafura Sea: Molucca-ward;
The Coral: Micronesia-ward;
The South Pacific: Maori-ward;
The Indian: Wilkes' Land- and Madagascar-ward;
And all their inland reachings: friths and forths,
 creeks, inlets, sounds, bays, bights, and gulfs:
The Great Australian Bight;
The Gulf of Carpentaria;
Ports Jackson, Phillip, Denison — all, in a word the
 sound of which has been a falling clod upon a
 living sepulchre to millions of mankind,
The Bay of Botany!

I see and sing
The Great South Land,
In its totality and ultimate divisibility!

The largest of the fragments of the broken and dissev-
 ered continent of Australasia;
An area approximately kidney-shaped,
About the size of Uncle Sam's domain from sea to sea;
Astride the Line of Capricorn,
Half in the Torrid Zone and half in the South Tem-
 perate;
An almost rainless desert bowl irregularly rimmed and
 ridged with mediocral mountains: rain-condens-
 ing, forest-clad;
An Austral Great Sahara Desert, ringed and ridged,
 and flecked and fringed, with Atlas Mountains,
 Aspen Oasis, Nile Valley, and Algerian Tell!

I see and sing
Lake Amadéus: Dead Sea centre of the Austral
 World: Symbolic here of the ten thousand inland

fluctuating saline lakes and marshes, ponds, and swamps, and the lagoons along the sea-coast of Victoria: the correspondents of the Shotts of Algiers and the Bitter Lakes of Utah and Nevada: pools of ocean water left within the pits and hollows of the Continental Kraken when it came up from the bottom of the sea;

The Murray: Goolwa: Hume: the largest of the rivers of the Austral World: the correspondent in its course and current of the Orange of South Africa: in periods of drought decaying by absorption and evaporation as it nears the sea into a chain of stagnant pools: A symbol here of all the rivers of Australia evanishing in earth and air: and those, as well, the sea-board streams that hasten from the heights along the coast into the inlets of the ocean meeting them halfway;

Mount Kosciusko: highest of the summits of Australia: flecked with snow throughout the summer: cañoned grandly: showing scars of ancient glaciers: Symbol here of all the earth-ascendings and descendings of the Continental Isle;

The barren beach of the surrounding sea: the Utgard of Australia;

The dreary dunes along the coast;

The seaward grass-green mountain flanks;

The weathering walls and frowning precipices overhead;

The summit beauties and sublimities of the Australian Alps: the Asgard of Australia;

The dark depths of the gorges and defiles;

The withering widening wastes;

The parched plateaux;

The stretches strewn with fire-flaked flint;

The cracked and baked black bottoms of evaporated pools;

The blistering belts of rocks;

The burning sweeps of sand;

The simmering salt and soda sinks;
The dim delirious outlining of Lake Amadéus: a descent unto a depth below the circle of the all-surrounding ocean : down, down, down, through all the stages of a burning fever to delirium and Death! the centre of the Midgard of Australia!

I see and sing
The Riverina: 'twixt the Darling and the Murrumbidgee: richest of the austral regions: typic here of all the fertile oases that band and belt and dot the continental sink;
The Caverns of Jenólan: wondrous water-wormings through an ancient coral strand upheaved into a mountain: filled with stalactitic jets and pendants, stalagmitic pillars, beads, and buttresses, depending robes with crystal-diamonds spangled, and a myriad of fantasies of form besides: the concrete correspondent of the dreaming of the youth who fashioned at maturity the Taj Mahál: Symbolic here of all the antres of the Austral World;
The Cañons of Katoomba: Cowan's Cañon,[3] Govett's Leap, the Witch's Leap, and the ten thousand gaps and gorges, Fairy Dells and Devil Glens besides: romantic, picturesque, grim, ghastly, hellish: which compose in quarto the Grand Colorado Cañon Region of America in folio;
The Barrier Reef surnamed the Great: incomparable coral strand: the largest of the world: A symbol here of the infinity of reefs and bars, projecting points, peninsulas, capes, rocks, and islets which compound the shore-line of Australia.

I see and sing
The NEVER-NEVER COUNTRY: Word within itself an Epic of the Austral Continental Isle!

And therein of the Something-Nothing which the Eye
   must bring with it the Something-half to see at
   all:
The sea-like solitude of the primæval wastes;
The Inca-corse-like desiccation and decay;
The cavern-like vacuity;
The OM-like mystery;
The ever-present eldritchness;
The fixed and glassy eye-stare of ineffable despair;
The spectral shadows of the starving Burke and Wills:
   with staggering steps zigzagging on the burning
   banks of Cooper's Creek in search of Nardoo seeds:
   with feeble fingers clutching them spasmodically
   as their last resource: with gasping greed devour-
   ing them: with eating only famishing the faster
   and more horribly: a Barmecidal feast of most
   appalling ghastliness! the Austral tale of Tan-
   talus!
The melancholy memories of Leichhardt's fate: to
   fashion every stain of gray upon the yellow sand
   into the very spot where down the wanderer sank
   to rise no more: the sand discolored by his dis-
   solution and decay: his dust indissoluble with
   the desert: his eternal monument![4]
The ghost of Gordon galloping upon a phantom Favo-
   rite: the bright white moonlight entering the hole
   made by a self-directed bullet through his skull
   and streaming out a flame of spirit-burning blue:
   the while an echo of the beating of his heart is
   heard within his haunting rhymes!
And Spectral Shades of Sin and Crime: hulk-smelling,
   fetter-galled, demanhoodized: enough to demonize
   another Dante-Hell!
And scintillating over and amid the phantom forms,
   the hammerflush of Henry Kendall: master saga-
   smith of Australdom: his stithy in the bush be-
   neath a fire-charred stringy-bark: his bellows'-blast
   the buster and brickfielder: and the ghastly glow-

ing iron taking beauteous shape beneath his measured blows, or this or that: a brother murdered "in a far-off sultry summer rimmed with thunder-cloud and red with forest fires:" a kinsman slaughtered on "the windless downs: blue-gleaming like a sea of molten steel!"

I see and sing
The Record of the Rocks!
The Cosmic Elements of which the Continental Island is composed: forever changing their relationships with one another: coming, going: building up and breaking down: Protean! Symbol here of one and all, the King and Queen of Metals, Gold and Silver: now, diffused through land and sea, atomic: now, concentrated in dust and grain and ingot: now, composing the blood-globules — red and white — of the world-roaming monster, Commerce: now, returning by attrition to the indivisible atomic to begin another round anew;
The Movements and the Moldings of the Planet as a whole involving as a part the Continental Island: incidental to Rotation, Revolution, Cooling and Collapsing, Differentiating into divers densities: Evolving from a Unit into an Infinity: The Kidney-contour of the Continental Island here a type of all;
The Alternation of the Land and Sea: the going up and down of the vast area in part or as a whole: and all the incidents to the seesawing of the continent: upheaval into mountain and subsidence into sink: climatic change, organic change: erosion, drift: the dead o'erlaid with loam and hardened into stone: connection made or disconnection with adjoining lands: admitting or excluding plants and animals, or here or there, or now or then: effecting a peculiar isolation in the end, with

distant or long dead affinities elsewhere, most marvelous: commingling fossils elsewhere separated and defining geologic ages: puzzling scientists: The Great Dividing Range symbolic here of all;

The Alternation of the Geologic Seasons: Dry and Wet: an Eon-Summer baking the vast isle into the correspondent of the Great Sahara Desert, as to-day: an Eon-Winter drenching it into the correspondent of the Valley of the Amazon, as yesterday;

The hot and humid Eocene evolving through the Miocene and Pliocene into the cool and wet Post-Pliocene: the era of the elephantine in Australia as in America and other continental regions of the globe;

The cool and wet Post-Pliocene evolving through succeeding centuries into the Recent: hot and dry: A continental emperor decaying in his robes of state: his flesh and bones dissolving into desert-dust: his gorgeous forest-raiment vanished — all, save here and there, within a cool and humid mountain-gorge, a shred or patch: revealing in a part the grandeur and the beauty of the whole!

I see and sing

The Dykes and Overflowings of Basaltic Trap: the squeezing upward of the molten lavas of the centre of the cooling and collapsing crust: the paper-pulp to be transformed into the pages of the Record of the Rocks: decaying, forming soil of marvelous fertility: Mount Tomah symbol here of all;

The various Volcanic Vomitings: occurring at the intersection of the Earth-crust cracks: and differing from the preceding only in a concentration and continuance of action and discharge: cone-forming: Mount Canobolas the last and typic here of all;

AUSTRALIA.

The Granites and the Porphyries;

The Diorites and Serpentines;

The Old Silurian: the mausoleum of the Adam and the Eve of the biologists;

The Coral Strands compacted and converted into Marble Beds;

The Shales and Sands of the Devonian: entombing Scale-tree, Rhynchonellæ, Spirifers;

The Lower Coals: entombing ocean shells;

The Upper Coals: entombing air-plants: notably Glossopteris: and yielding Iron, Coal and Kerosene;

The thick Hawkesbury Sands: entombing Cleithrolepis: forming the grand mural precipices of the Austral Alps;

The overlaid Wianamatta Shales; Palæoniscus sepulchre;

The Clarence Beds;

The vast Cretaceous Strata: water-charged: great inland reservoirs awaiting but the Diamond Drill to make of burning sand a Paradise;

The Tertiary Rocks and Drifts: entombing plants approximating those of the same geologic age in other continental areas: a Flora rich and varied: tropical or semi-tropical: and not subordinated to one genus as the Flora of the Present to the ghastly Gums or Eucalypts;

The Present Depositions: aggregating and compacting film on film: by overflowing or evaporating waters: here distributing disintegrated quartz and sandstone far and wide o'er fertile valleys: there concentrating suspended marl and limestone in vast desert clay-pans: filling them with dazzling snow-white gypsum crystals: selenite: or other salt;

The Whole: the Record of the Rocks: the scattered leaves of the Cumæan Sibyl of the Ages of the Earth turned into Stone: a word on one: a letter and a fragment of a sentence on a second and a third: a mystic symbol on a fourth: each unintelligible in itself: but joined aright with this or that, Oracular: an utterance of an Eternal Truth!

I see and sing
The Ether Circumambient!
And therein of the Sun: to the observer, going round the earth from right to left: and casting shadows ever pointing southerly: a World of Widdershins;
The Seasons upside down: midsummer in December, midwinter in July;
The Autumn's aromatic breeze;
The Winter's ozone-bringing wind;
The wattle-perfumed zephyr of the Spring;
The Summer's furnace-blast;
The thermometric readings running up to Nine and Thirty plus One Hundred, Fahrenheit!
The noon and midnight variations reaching Ninety-nine degrees: the Eye of Heaven, the fiery eye of a hot-blooded warrior by day: the icy eye of an assassin in the night: forbidding hope: repelling prayer: transfixing in a gasp or shudder of despair!
The Buster and Brickfielder: austral red-dust blizzard and red-hot Simoom;
The Drought: a blast like that which smote the Assyrian host;
The pools diminishing from day to day becoming poisonous to bird and beast: attracting with deceitful glare for many miles around and leaving on their fatal shores the gasping staggering forms of myriads: their decomposing carcasses: their bones: a problem to the future scientist;
The pools becoming poisonous: to the surviving Black a terrible experience: a ghastly spectacle: an exhibition of mysterious malignity and might: the fact before his eyeballs to evolve into the fantasy

behind of this or that dread monster dwelling in
the venom-vats: or Bun-yip, Wan-gul, Myn-die,
Mul-ge-wan-ke, or the like: assuming this or that
familiar shape, or emu, snake, or kangaroo: the
austral correspondent of the Many-headed Hydra
of the Greeks;

The pools becoming poisonous: to the surviving Black
as well the cause compelling him, in order to al-
lay his burning thirst and live, to take the desert
frog from out its hole and squeeze into his mouth
the precious water-drops its bladder holds: the
fact, as well, before his eyeballs to evolve into the
fantasy behind of this or that inexplicable fable
otherwise: the Tiddalick, a giant frog, that, laugh-
ing at a dancing eel — prosaically, croaking at the
Black's unearthing crooked stick,— disgorges water
to supply mankind, create a deluge, or the like;

The heated air uprising from the burning deserts:
swirling, sweeping, gathering the dust and sand
and withered herbage: forming lofty, swaying, fast-
revolving desert-spouts: inverted spiral cones:
now, scattered o'er the plains a score or more of
merry waltzing Brobdingnagian sylphs: anon,
evanishing: succeeded, haply, by an all-involving
overwhelming hurricane: a demon-god of in-
exsuperable rage, malignity, and might;

The Rain: the chief of all the wonder-workers of the
Austral World: where, haply, for a time beyond
the memory of man, naught but the glare of burn-
ing sands appeared, behold! before the 'cloud-
rack of an adventitious desert-drenching storm
has vanished from the sky, a myriad of pale-green
sprouts uprising from as many earth-secreted seeds:
and then a maze of dark-green foliage: a crazy-
quilt of floral bloom spread over countless leagues:
a wilderness of sweets: a broad-cast scattering of
seeds to sleep again mayhap for centuries! the fa-
ble of the falling show'r of gold into the lap of

Danaë a grand and glorious fact!
The Whole the Song of Solomon Unsung: in chaos; hottest of hot breaths commingled with the rarest perfumes: kisses: swelterings: exhaustions: Life and Death!
The while — O wonder of the World Turned upside Down! — the Southern Hemisphere of the revolving Earth is in a Glacial Age!

I see and sing
The Bush: the Flora of the Austral World!
The Stag-horn Fern: its fronds expanding like the flat palmated antlers of the moose of Maine;
The Bird's-nest Fern: its canna-leaf-like fronds encompassing the trunks of lofty trees: composing fitting capitals unto the columns of the forest Parthenon;
The Arborescent Ferns: Alsophila australis running up to forty, sixty, eighty feet before expanding into a gigantic parasol of vegetable plumes, or metamorphosing into a fount of sea-green water: passing into spray and air before descending to the earth;
The Pherosphœra: intermediate between a Lycopodium and Juniper;
The Kangaroo-grass: from the sea of salt surrounding to the sea of salt enclosed, enticing ever on and on the hungriest of the flock and herd: the shepherd and the stockman following: and then the town and city: wanting which, the continental island were four-fifths a blank to-day;
The Microzamias: half fern, half palm: the austral substitute of the symbolic palm of Rome;
The Cocoanut, the Fan, and Cabbage Palms;
The Grass-tree: Black-boy: Yellow-gum: a monstrous arborescent Rush: anear, resembling tussocks of coarse overarching grass upon a stunted, stumpy, blackened branching palm: afar, a native Black: its flowering spike, his spear: of divers uses and diverse: from dyeing silk to making an

illuminating gas;

The gorgeous Illawarra Lily: Doryanthes: bearing crimson floral clusters on a lofty spike: from ten to twenty feet in height;

The glorious Cyrtosia: the orchid marvel of the austral bush: its myriad of beautiful and fragrant flowers strung along a trailing stem for thirty feet!

The Cherry Tree: with fruit turned inside out;

The Bunya-bunya: noble representative of a most ancient gens of pine: broad-leafed, big-coned: its nut-like seed a store of fattening food: a grove the only heir-loom of the Black;

The She-oaks: Beefwood: Austral Larch, or Fir: in lieu of leaves, the termination of the branches subdivided into pendent tufts and tassels of attenuated and articulated twigs: like the antennæ of a beetle or a prawn! a spectral arborescent Equisetum! smoky-green, funereal: The curtained chamber of the dead, the tasseled pall, the hearse's drooping plumes, the melancholy of the cypress-shaded grave, the closing lashes wet with tears, the blank hereafter — all organic in a tree!

The Murn or Mallee-oak: in times of drought its hollow stems supplying life-sustaining water to the Black: competing as a fountain with the dew-conserving bladder of the desert-frog;

The Mulga-tree: its water-yielding roots another rival of the bladder of the desert-frog;

The Giant Nettle-tree: a hive of bees in every leaf;

The Banyan-tree: the grandest of the Figs: in its expansion and extension, self-supporting its long arms with outward-leaning, life-renewing, supplemental props: the fable of Antæus in the form of tree: or, happily, the British Empire symbolized in its expansion and extension round the world: adventurous dependent filaments here taking root and there, and, in the course of time, becoming independent props and nourishers, and passing the o'erspreading and o'ersheltering sway to farther points: until the branches, North and South and East and West, o'erlap and interlace: the grandest governmental growth the globe has ever seen!

The Big-leafed Fig: related closely to the last: its sprawling, widely buttressed base, compounding and confounding root and trunk and twisting limb, a wonder of the vegetable world;

The Boabab: the Gouty Stem, the Monkey-bread, Sour Gourd, or Cream-of-Tartar-tree: of all the vegetable monsters of the earth, the chief: a huge, aërial, arborescent yam! a bulb become a tree without a bole! a root, compounding sponge and mucilage, Barbadoes'-leg and the deformities of gout, rejected by the earth, and heaved and humped up in the air into a tree! defying ax, drought, fire, and time: endowed with a shark-heart vitality: deciduous: its gourd-like fruit filled with a mealy melting acid mass: a desert substitute for lemonade!

The Desert Pea: the floral beauty of the Midgard scrub;

The Wattles: many kinds of many qualities: of some, the footstalks simulating leaves and substituting them: in the evolvement of the Leaf, a stage beyond the She-oak, with its leafless terminals divided into jointed threadlike twigs;

The Lilac or White Cedar-tree: deciduous: its purple bloom, night-scented, beautiful;

The Flame-tree: all the beauty and the splendor of a conflagration in its bloom!

The Salt-bush of the inland flats;

The Christmas Tree: the holly of the Austral World;

And chief among the world of wondrous worts besides,

The Eucalypts: bark-shedding, camphor-scented, gum-exuding, fever-frighting evergreens: a probable suggestion of the Boomerang within their leathery leaves: vertical suspended: shadowless;

The Eucalypts: their bark depending from their naked
   limbs and trunks in swaying, fraying ribbons, tat-
   ters, shreds: Stripped to the waist, a forestful of
   grizzled, gaunt, and haggard gaberlunyie-men: A
   myriad of outcast Lears: The summer dream of
   Sydney Smith: stripped of his flesh and sitting in
   his bones: here realized in grim and grotesque
   forestry;
The Eucalypts: of the Black Spur, with slightly taper-
   ing trunk, high-reaching slender branch, long,
   light, and airy limb, and spectral finial twig, up-
   rising to a point o'ertopping the Big Trees of Cali-
   fornia: A formula objective of the operations of
   the human brain: evolving, ramifying, and at-
   tenuating Thought into an ultimate: a point in
   philosophic or poetic fantasy ne'er reached before!
The Whole: the Austral Bush in its totality: The
   spectral shadows of the dead and buried Miocene
   of Europe still within the wood: A musty medi-
   æval folio on Demonology perused alone at dusk:
   the savor and the subject of the volume giving to
   the wilderness of the blackletter text an all-pervad-
   ing eldritchness: a woodcut here and there impart-
   ing shape and visual reality unto the diabolic and
   the weird: and the illuminated letters serving rath-
   ed to intensify than to relieve with their bright hues
   the all-involving spectre-haunted gloom!

I see and sing
The Fauna of the Austral World—
The Fauna of the Water and the Land!
The Idia: a symbol here of all the lowest forms of
   ocean life;
The Giant Earthworm: six feet long: the Anaconda of
   the Annelids;
The rare Trigonia: a Mesozoic memory: a baby kiss
   in an objective unobjectionable form in its oppos-

ing pinkish pearl-lined shells: an idyll of the
young world's beauty, innocence, and purity;

The Case- or Lictor-moths: Metura: marvelous among
the marvels of the insect world;

The Wattle- and the Grass-tree-boring Moth-grubs:
fried or roasted, luscious morsels: titbits for the
gastronomic gods of old: the Blue Point oysters
of the Austral World;

The Honey-bee: about the bigness of the housefly:
stingless: black: before the bigger armed incomer
with the Colonist fast disappearing with the Black:
one savage weakling going with another everywhere upon the advent of the civilized and strong;

The Dromia conchifera: a stalk-eyed crab upholding
with a supernumerary pair of walking legs a mollusk half-shell as a shield: a grotesque little Ajax
Telamon;

The Cobble-toothed Port Jackson Shark: Cestracion:
crab-crushing, mollusk-munching: old-world ocean
ghoul: organic shadow of the Secondary Seas forecast into to-day;

The Burnett Salmon of the Queensland streams:
Ceratodus: nor fish, nor flesh, nor good red herring: Fish-branch of the Zoölogic Tree just at the
point of forking into Frog: and like the last and
the Trigonia, belonging rather to an early Mesozoic age of the Earth's history than this!

The Leafy Dragon-fish: Phyllopteryx: the most fantastic of all piscine forms: the ultimate of the
bizarre and Japanesque: the fancy of the heretofore incomparably whimsic artist Hokusai out-Hokusai'd in fact! The male pouched somewhat
like a female kangaroo: enveloping the eggs laid
by the female in a soft subcaudal sack, and thus
transporting them till hatched!

The Crested Serpent-fish: Regalecus: a length attaining — fifteen, twenty — who can say how many
feet? the dorsal fin extending its whole length and

rising from the head into a long back-streaming crest: a sea-chimæra or sea-serpent for a verity!

The Pygopods: with rudimentary fore-limbs: three-quarters lizard and one-quarter snake;

The Lialids: with no external trace of limbs: one-quarter lizard and three-quarters snake;

The dread Death Adder: typic here of all the austral snakes: an ultimate depending and perverted offshoot from the Reptile-branch of the great Zoölogic Tree: the fore-and hind-legs of the lizard gone, and its innocuous saliva turned into the venom of a tooth-formed sting;

The Long-necked Turtle of the inland creeks: reptilian crane;

The mighty Megalania: a monstrous, many-horned, gigantic saurian of old: in miniature within the living Moloch horridus;

The Lizard ruffed or frilled like pictured Queen Elizabeth: Chlamydosaurus: hopping on its hind-legs: Frog-branch of the Zoölogic Tree just at the point of forking into Bird;

The Emu and the Cassowary: and the huge extinct Dromornis: desert-formed into an avian giraffe: its energies expended in evolving legs and neck in lieu of wings: the needful for the not: the Bird-branch of the Zoölogic Tree just after forking from the Reptile: pelvis, sternum, cranium Reptilian;

The Mound-birds: Megapods: as yet which have not learned to build a nest and hatch their young themselves, but still, remembering their reptile origin, when they have scratched and scraped together a great mound of sand and herbage-mold, depositing their eggs therein, and leaving them to be brought forth by the engendered heat and moisture of the heap fermenting in the sun: the new-born chicks, like new-born crocodiles, requiring not a mother's care: like China's symbol sage, born hoary-headed, worldly wise;

The Bower-birds: with voices not yet specialized in song and art-ideas not yet fixed and fashioned in fair nests: unto the typic Bird, as prattling, play-house-building children unto Man and Woman: present fiction fingerings tow'rd future facts;

The Crested Cockatoo: the golden-crowned White Parrot Czar of all the Russias of the Austral Continent;

The Piping Crow: the magpie of the South;

The Lyre-bird: wondrous-tailed, mimetic, shy: afar in the seclusion of the bush involving its environment and then evolving it in vocal correspondents to the wondering world: the symbol of the austral Son of Song;

The Sable Swan: beneath the Southern Cross, the night incarnate, as the White, beneath the Northern Bear, the Day;

The Honey-suckers: feather-tongued: Australia's humming-birds;

The Curaduck: a kind of crane: in quaker garb a pantomimic clown: from grave to gay alternating in a surprising manner: now, as solemn as a self-subduing saint: anon, a flighty and fantastic Merry Andrew! dancing, kicking, pirouetting! turning, tumbling, twisting, twitching! halting, hopping, moping, stalking! Spider-monkey metamorphosed into Bird!

The Cereopsis: bird compounding goose and crane: and yet not of the water but the land!

The extinct Phillip Island Parrot: cousin-german to the honey-sucking, sheep-destroying and -devouring kea of Zealandia;

The Great Kingfisher: alias, the Gogobera: alias, the Laughing Jackass: alias, the Settler's Clock! robbed of its birthright as a fisher by the Buster-bandits of the Austral World — its occupation gone, turned scoffer, mocker, loon, in the expression of its unavailing rage and all-involving feelings of revenge: an avian demoniac Democritus: its laughter loud, chaotic, and maniacal: a voicing of the wild, the weird, the eldritch, and the ghastly of the Never-Never Country not to be encompassed by the mutterings of Man: a desert dirge inimitable, unapproachable, unique!

I see and sing
The Monotremes: egg-laying, suckling at the waist: the halves of the cerebrum not connected: the Reptilian-branch of the great Zoölogic Tree just at the point of forking into the Mammalian!
The Cogera: Echidna: hedgehog-shaped, fossorial, shade-loving, myrmecophagous: the Austral World's Ant-eater, Aard-Vark, Hedgehog, Porcupine, and Mole in one;
The Tambreet: Duck-mole: Platypus: Ornithorhynchus: fur-clad, duck-billed and web-footed, sun-abhorring, water-haunting, and earth-burrowing: half-bird, half-beast! Old Mother Nature mentally confused: compounding and confounding her new Bird and Mammal types!

I see and sing
The Myriad of Mammal-makeshifts of the austral Fauna: The Marsupials: (albeit, some with pouches, some without: some with pouch-bones, some without:) the Mammal-branch of the great Zoölogic Tree just after forking from the Reptile: inchoate, chaotic, monstrous: Nature-dreams incorporate;
The Kurboroo: Koala: Phascolarctos: bunty, bobtailed, big-paunched, browsing bugaboo: the mythic wise beast of the fictions of the Black: a makeshift Monkey, Bear, and Sloth: the most grotesque of all the gargoyles of the old cathedral of Australia;
The Wombat: thickset, chisel-toothed, fossorial: a

makeshift of the Groundhog of America, the weather-wise " Old Probabilities ; "

The huge, extinct Diprotodon and Nototherium: the makeshifts and contemporaries of the Megatherium and Mylodon;

The Phascogals: not pouched: the makeshifts of the Weasels, Minks, and Stoats;

The Phalangers: prehensile-tailed: the makeshifts of the Monkeys of America;

The Bandicoot: a makeshift of the Mole: " as miserable as a Bandicoot," a popular comparison of problematic truth and odious accordingly to man and beast;

The Belideus and the Petaurist: the makeshifts of the Flying Squirrels — rather, Squirrel-parachutes;

The Myrmecobius: not pouched: a puny makeshift of the Great Anteater of the Amazon: resorting, it is said, to strategy to supplement its lack of strength and claw: instead of tearing up an anthill and devouring its inhabitants within their subterranean cells, enticing them without, by running rapidly around the hill, and licking up a legion ere they can return!

The Dasyures: the makeshifts of the little cat-like carnivores;

The Thylacine: without pouch-bones: the makeshift of the wolf-like carnivores;

The jaw-determined, fierce, extinct Thylacoleo: makeshift and contemporary of the Sabre-tooth;

The Kangaroos, the Wallaroos, the Wallabies, and Pademelons: makeshifts of the Deer and Antilopes: their evolution back and downward into tail and hind-legs, the reverse of that which has effected Man: In this the correspondents of the Spider Monkeys of the Amazon: depending and distorted off-shoots from the Mammal-mainbranch of the Zoölogic Tree: corrupted lines of the grand Iliad of Life descending into doggerel, or muttered backward, like a witch's prayer, converted into senseless gibberish!

I see and sing
The Orders of the Mammals not included in the Monotremes and the Marsupials, indigenous:
The curious Hapalotis: a little rodent in the form of kangaroo: in Kangaroodom doing as the kangaroos;
The Land-rats and the Water-rats: for such there be in Netherdom as in the Upperdom of Avon's Bard;
The great, gregarious Bat: the Flying-fox;
The Eared and Earless Seals;
The Dugong: Halicore: the oriental Manatee: the father of the fiction of the half-man half-fish monsters of the sea;
The yellow-sided delphic Bottle-nose;
The Whales: Balænidæ: organic tanks of oil sea-piped around the world: a score or more: among the small, the Diplodon and the Mesoplodon: with long and tapering beak: and in the lower jaw two pairs of teeth: that meeting, as they sometimes do, above the upper jaw prevent the animal from opening its mouth and causing thus its death;
The Dingo: dusky, brush-tailed, fox- and wolfish: howling, screeching: barkless: tamable: allied to the Coyote of Nevada and the Dhole of Bengal: the Wolf-twig of the Mammal-branch just at the point of forking into Dog!
And last of all the Mammals to the manor born, I see and sing
The Black: the Austral Man: an offshoot from an ancient Asian Man-branch of the Zoölogic Tree, depending, withering, decaying, almost leafless now: a figure in the grand Dissolving Panorama of the Earth evanishing into a memory: a myth: a mystery for aye;

The Black: brown-mud-black skinned: thin-armed, thin legged, and bottle-pouched: small-handed and small-footed: finger-toed: dark, cavern-eyed, flat-nosed, maw-mouthed: with burnt-black waving hair and full crisp beard: well-shouldered and high-chested: savoring of phosphorus: keen-visioned, sharp-eared, agile, and alert: precocious babe: aborted man: a sweenied, swarthy, savage scrub: a weasened, wolfish wanderer forever on the wallaby: on: on: himself, and his belongings all and singular, into the Never-Never Country of Eternity!

His Gin: a woman, wife: Symbolic here of all pertaining to the woman-half of his humanity: his loves and hates, his jealousies and feuds, his virtues and his vices as a Man in his totality among his kind: especially, his partiality for adipose combined with femininity to supplement his want of fat combined with masculinity!

His Boo-hoop: babe: first cradled in a hole scooped in the warm dry sand: then folded in a bag of 'possum skin and slung upon the mother's back: then set astride a shoulder or her neck: and then, as soon as it can crawl, provided with a digging-stick and started out in search of roots and frogs: to feast or famish as it may henceforth! Symbolic here of all the stages of his growth from birth to premature maturity: his struggle for existence in his wretched world from first to last: escaping this destruction to encounter that: his cradle and his grave the self-same desert sand: his life a ling'ring living burial!

His Coo-ee: a peculiar call: Symbolic here of all his mimicries and mutterings: his speech, his songs. his war-cries, and his dying groans: Primæval Man Mort-Mumblings: incoherent: lapsing into whisperings: lip-quiverings: death-rattleings: and there an end;

His Chir-rin-chir-rie: knocking out the upper front teeth: Typic here of all his mutilations and disfigurements: his scoring, scarring, gashing, slashing, piercing, lopping, clipping — all;

His Yin-ka: string of human hair three hundred yards in length wound round the waist: A symbol here of all his dress and ornaments: of skins and feathers, bone and shell, bark, rush, and hair;

His Nar-doo-flour: the crushed seeds of the Cloverfern: the one extreme of his variety of food: a Stranded Whale the other! This, the latter, haply once within a life-time: an Australian Oil-strike! incommensurable, overwhelming, maddening! exalting and expanding for the moment the emaciated famine-haunted wretch into an open-handed and big-hearted benefactor of mankind! fire-signaling afar to share his feast the very enemy perhaps whom but the night before he sought to stun in sleep and rob of his prized kidney-fat ere he recover and awake to linger through succeeding days and nights in an unutterably agonizing death! The Fern and Whale symbolic here of all his food;

His Gun-yah: Wur-ley: Mi-am: lean-to, hut: but one remove from the Bornean ape's arboreal retreat: Symbolic here of all his artificial bields and shelterings against the winter's cold and rain;

His Won-guim: Boomerang of play: an Eucalyptus-leaf-like toy of wood: a form compounding bend and twist, convexity, and flattening, (suggesting a propeller-screw with parabolic blades,) and when impelled by skill, rotating and revolving in a most eccentric orbit: going through the air a hundred yards and half again as far and coming back: alighting as it has been willed behind the thrower's back or at his feet: gyrating, swirling, forward, backward, upward, downward, like a merry waltzing thing of life and play: a rondo of the mirth and joys of youth reëchoing among the tombs and sepulchres of the illimitably vast God's-acre of Australia! Symbolic here of all his toys and games and sports besides: among them, notably, his Weet-weet: Kangaroo-rat: second only to the Won-guim as a toy-projectile: antedating the Fish-bullet as a special form designed to meet the least resistance in the air;

His Barn-geet: Boomerang of work and war: Symbolic here of all his weapons, tools, and implements: of wood and bone and stone and shell: his spears and clubs: his Wammerah, or Throwing-stick, increasing wondrously the length and leverage of his right arm: his axes, chisels, knives, and hooks: his fire-drills, baskets, nets, and weirs;

His song-and-dance Cor-rob-bor-ee: by firelight in the forest: Naked women seated in a semicircle singing and hand-beating on a skin stretched tight between their spread knees: Leader in the centre with two signal-sticks, click-clacking, striking, waving: droning, humming, chanting: pacing to and from the women and the dancers: Dancers decked with bent-bough anklets, 'possum pinafore, and ringed and streaked and striped with pipeclay: simulating skeletons: with clacking sticks: arranged in line or lines in front of women: all together as a unit swaying, bending, jerking, twisting: leaping this way, leaping that way: chanting, clacking: kicking, jumping, stamping: fast and faster: loud and louder: high and higher: imitating dingo, emu, kangaroo, or curaduck: enacting fishing-, hunting-, warring-, wiving-scenes: fantastically, diabolically: culminating in the highest leap and loudest shout of all: then disappearing in the dark: ere long to reäppear in a new guise, with voice and vigor as before: Symbolic here of all his concertings and caperings in the expression of his social pleasures, savage rage, religious rite, and eldritch demonism: in the ex-expression of his wild and weird environment: in emulation of the Laughing Jackass, Bird, and Dingo, Beast: in rivalry of each and every living thing that has involved the Never-Never Country in its flesh and blood;

His Be-a-ma: exchanging wives: A symbol here of all his marriage customs and restrictions, and his complicated Tamil system of relationships;

His Kidney-fat Diablery: the chief of all the involutions of his horrible environment into his mind and body and its evolutions thence in horrible imaginings and practices: his desert life depriving him of all his adipose save that about his kidneys and their capping glands: his hunger forcing him betimes to feed upon his fellows and discovering to him the luscious morsels of the loins: his murderous propensities and anthropophagous proclivities becoming growth-inwrought, developing in this or that direction thence to the most diabolic of extremities! Symbolic here of all his sorceries and mystic demonism: his Mur-ro-kun: a magic bone; his Bulk or Mur-ra-mai: a talisman or magic stone: imparting a mysterious and awful pow'r to its possessor, a Co-rad-jee, doctor, priest, or sorcerer: a piece of quartz, chalcedony, a crystal, glass decanter-stopper, or the like: concealed especially from woman's eye: enclosed in yarn and net, hid under arm-pit, in the mouth, or otherwise: The austral correspondent of the Cannel Coal of Dr. Dee, the mythic Urim-Thummim of Joe Smith, the meteoric Blackstone of the Kaaba of Mecca, and the like;

His Ten-di: judgment council: Symbol here of all his rude and crude imaginings of law and government: his punishments with Waddy Blow upon the Head: Spear Thrust through Arm and Leg:

and chief of all his Ordeal of Spears: the culprit
with a narrow shield exposed to a succession of
swift-flying well-directed darts: or slain outright
or famous ever after for his bravery and skill;

His Koot-chee: mythic monster: many-visaged, many-
voiced: chaotic concept of the baleful in the form
of a tormenting and destroying devil: growling in
the thunder: moving in the whirlwind: building
fires in the Aurora Austral: causing sickness:
carrying contagion: material and immaterial: to
be opposed as well as with won-guims as with
witchery: Symbolic here of all his gods and
devils fashioned by his wants and wishes, hopes
and fears, in the mirage of his imagination: mir-
roring eternally the desert wilds and wastes: The
mental correspondents of the malagrugous Mex-
ique images conceived but not yet cut in black
basalt: as well, the air-drawn monsters of the
drunkard and the maniac;

His Moo-ra-moo-ra: smallpox: Typic here of all the
ills to which his flesh is heir and thief;

His Grin-ka-ri: flayed corpse: A symbol here of all
his rites and customs appertaining to the dead;

His Mirrn-yonk: shell and refuse heap, or kjökkenmöd-
ding: last of all his monuments and memories to
disappear: incorporate indissolubly with his island
sepulchre!

The Whole: the Fauna of the Austral World in its to-
tality: the Shadows of the Fauna of the world be-
sides commingling and compounding in peculiar
forms: fantastic, weird, grotesque: familiar,
strange, chimerical: a hashish-dream menagerie!

I see and sing
The Slayer and Successor of the Black:
The Master of the Austral World to-day:
The Problem of the Centuries to Come:
The CORNSTALK: Man compounding millions of

mankind: from all the airts the wind can blow:
of all conditions, colors, creeds, shapes, sizes, aims,
and ends: invading, over-running, and appropriat-
ing: dwelling, killing, tilling: digging, delving:
muliplying, ramifying, modifying all;

The CORNSTALK: Man involving and evolving an
enlarging universe: inverting, and everting: in-
teracting: many, one: colonial, intercolonial: de-
pendent, independent: national, and international:
corporeal and incorporeal: Composite Cosmopoli-
tan;

The CORNSTALK: Man of the To-Day expanding
and extending into the To-Morrow's Homo-Ulti-
mate: inheriting the World within his Blood and
Brawn and Brain and parting with his Birthright
only with the Mooning of the Earth;

The CORNSTALK: People-Pyramid of Austral Egypt:
course on course contracting from a base of savage-
ry deep-buried in the desert-sand unto an apex of
enlightenment bright-gleaming in the æther of the
tiptops of the Black Spur Eucalypts;

The CORNSTALK: People-Poem in a Word: the
Kalevala of the Suomema of the South: the Fin-
land, not of Frost, but Fire!

I see and sing
His Grasses, Flowers, Fruits, and Grains, now fringing
the vast sepulchre of Dingodom with mind and
body sweets and surfeitings: now fringing Hell
with Paradise!

I see and sing
His baneful weeds: Sweet-briar, Thistle, Vervaine,
Milkweed, Sida, Furze: the Devil that aye lurks
behind the Cross;

I see and sing
His Singing, Game, and Table-birds: now frighting to

the Never-Never Country fast the Laughing Jackass with its eldritchness and demonism!

I see and sing
His Beasts of infinite subservience and use:
The Dog: the first slave of the Master of the World: the first extension of the tooth of Man into a substitute to catch and kill for him: the point at which the Man-branch of the Zoölogic Tree forks from the wholly Beast into the Barbarous: the first stage in the evolution of the Cosmopolitan: the first scene of the drama of the Hundred-handed son of Ouranós and Gê, Briáreos;
The Cat: the second servant of the Master of the World: the first extension of the noonday sense of sight of Man into a substitute to guard at night his precious stores while he is fast asleep;
The Pig: the waste and kitchen refuse of the Master of the World compacted, purified, and put again upon his pantry-shelf;
The Rabbit and the Hare: fast-breeding, inland-pressing, irrepressible: slaves that would fain be masters: typic elsewhere of the timid, here the terrible! out-leaping in the race for life the Kangaroo and Wallaby;
The Sheep: the first and foremost of the beasts to equalize the everchanging hot and cold winds of the earth: to keep the Master of the World within an artificial favored clime at the equator and the poles: now multiplying marvelously in the austral wastes in spite of their Sahara heat, aridity, and barrenness: converting fast the Never-Never Country into Colchis — Country of the Golden Fleece;
The Ox: the Back and Belly of the Master of the World in an infinity of outside supplemental forms;
The Ass: the first-draft of the Drama of the Centaur: myth compounding Man and Horse;
The Camel: desert-dune incarnate: desert-junk;

The Horse: the thews and muscles of ten men or more
subordinated to the will of one: the prototype in
an organic form of the infinity of Steel and Steam
combined in the World-master's engines and ma-
chinery to-day: all which I see and sing here in a
word,
The Iron-Horse!

I see and sing
The Mob of Millions who compose
The CORNSTALK: mythic Man: supposititious per-
sonality: ideal individuality: the counterfeit pre-
sentment of a multitude in one;
The Mob of Millions: each a Leaf upon the Man-
branch of the Zoölogic Tree: the universal Ygg-
drasill;
The Mob of Millions: each an Iliad: an actual epit-
ome of all: a sum organic of the world!

I see and sing
Them in their Finite Individuality
And Infinite!

One, picking cotton on the Brisbane plains: a turkey-
foot of tribal or totemic scars upon each cheek,
and down his forehead and his nose a line of art-
ificial ornamental warts as big and round as peas:
a Negro, from the western coast of Africa: sym-
bolic of the African in his totality;
Another, hoeing sugar-cane hard by: his skull com-
pressed and conified with bandages in infancy, old
Inca-like in shape: a Black from Mallicollo, one
of the New Hebrides: a type of all the Melanesi-
ans;
One, bending sail, aboard a Labor Trading Schooner:
Yankee Stars and Stripes tattooed with other fig-
ures on his brawny fore-arms: a Kanaka from
Hawaii: typic of the Polynesian;

Another, taking beche-de-mer in Roebuck Bay: a kris scar on his neck: his left eye out: a lithe Malayan from Malacca: typic of the great Malayan multitude;

One, in the suds at Collingwood: new-saddle hued: his head in shape, like the great cooling and collapsing Earth, according to the figurings of Green, a compromise between a sphere and tetrahedron: round it coiled the pigtail badge of his political minority: a Chinaman: symbolic of the Mongol third or fourth of all mankind;

Another, with a Trio of Gilt Balls above his door in Perth: an angler-fish in human guise: his head upheld and half turned round by a carotid aneurism: a Jew from anywhere, except Jerusalem: a type of all the Wandering Tribes of Israel;

One, mining kerosene at Hartley Vale: a leather thong about his wrist to fend against rheumatic joints: a Stonehenge Briton handed down unto to-day, from Basingstoke: a typic Celtic Aryan;

Another, mining silver in the Sunny Corner Mines: club-footed, ambidextral, deaf: a Cymric Welshman from the Clwyd: another typic Celtic Aryan;

One, personating Peace and Order in the City of the Plains: auroral-haired, pockmarked, pugnosed, long upper-lipped, and monkey-mugged: a bobby with a Bishop Barker in his hand, hobnobbing with a cattle-duffing lag: an Irishman from Inch-a-Goill: a third type of the Celtic Aryan;

Another, paper-making and fellmongering at Liverpool: as neckless as a fish, bow-legged, and pigeon-toed: a Gaelic Scot from Aughnasheen: a fourth type of the Celtic Aryan;

One, selling snuff, tobacco, and cigars in Armidale: a musty, mouldy shadow of the-man-that-lost-his found: consumptive: dieting on dugong oil: a Spaniard from Valencia: a typic Latin Aryan: a

Diego: commonly prefixed with Damned, by
Gringo tars;

Another, making wine at Germantown: forever swallowing the Adam's apple in his neck alternately with twirling his moustache: a Frenchman from Boulogne: another typic Latin Aryan;

One, bullock-punching on the Cambridge downs of Kimberly: a stammerer, and stutterer: afflicted with St. Vitus' dance: a sore affliction at a pinch: a Portuguese from Santerem: a third type of the Latin Aryan;

Another, fiddling in the streets of Ballarat: a green silk blind before his sightless eyes, and golden buttons in his ears, in lieu of rings: an old Italian of Mantua: a fourth type of the Latin Aryan;

One, shipping copper-ore at Wallaroo: strabismic to accommodate a wryneck twisting to the right and a peculiar nasal turning to the left: a Swede from Gottenburg: a typic Teuton Aryan: a Gringo, in the Diego lingo of the sea;

Another, in the office of the telegraphic company at Palmerston: his left arm off at upper third of humerus: homesick: a Dane from Elsinore: another typic Teuton Aryan;

One, mining gold in Bendigo: a flaxen-haired Apollo Belvidere: tormented with a tapeworm for ten years: a Dutchman from the Hague: a third type of the Teuton Aryan;

Another, rolling iron at the Eskbank works in Lithgow Vale: Thor-bearded, shaggy-browed, loquacious, bibulous, and quarrelsome when drunk: an old Norwegian from Hammerfest: a fourth type of the Teuton Aryan;

One, building a great iron railway bridge across the broad Hawkesbury: long, lank, leathery, and lantern-jawed: a mule-kick scar between his eye-

brows: Sankey-hymn-book singing, and profane:
a Yankee from Sang Hollow, Pennsylvania: a fifth
type of the Teuton Aryan;

Another, pen-depicting a new Gonodactyl from Port
Jackson: laying his forefinger to the left side of
his nose, in emphasizing "Yes; I know," or as a
sign in lieu thereof: a Holstein cowlick over his
right eye cascading his unkempt, long, silvery
locks into a fishtailed fountain playing silently and
ceaselessly upon his thinking-heated brow: a German from Aschaffenburg: a sixth type of the Teuton Aryan;

One, in the parliament of New South Wales: round-headed and round-bodied: pinkish-skinned: well-clad: the parting of his hair, moustache and beard, midway between his ears symbollically indicating him in his essential legislative individuality: divided into hemispheres, a Northern and a Southern, or, a Home and a Colonial: a positive and negative: "My word!" one minute, and "No fear!" the next: an Englishman from Liverpool: a seventh typic Teuton Aryan;

And all the millions of the people of Australia besides in the infinity of the expression of their individuality: the all-involving one idea of existence: each to be

What he has never been;

What he is not;

And what none other than himself can be —

A further evolution of the Finite in Himself into the Infinite!

The Lifer: for the term of his existence in the flesh a banished branded man: a gnarled and crook'd and twisted scrub, transported from the densely crowded forest of the British Islands to the open empty wastes of Topsiturvia, to straighten out, untwist, and grow erect: to be reversed from bad to good if not by homilies and hulks, by the machinery that turns and twists the Earth itself and the infinity of circumvolving spheres — or killed in the attempt;

The Lifer: haunted by a hopeless hope: a happy dream by night, a harrowing thought by day: to go back Home: to breathe the air of England and of Liberty: to be a Man: the sky above his head, the earth beneath his feet, and North or South, or East or West, an open way for him to walk in manly strength and pride;

The dread Bushranger: austral outlaw: Robin Hood: Frank James: succeeding the extinct Thylacoleo as the greatest of the austral beasts of prey;

The Larrikin: the Hoodlum of the Austral World: (The word from *Lark*, the same as *Hark!* the outcry of our language-forming sires on *hearing* the melodious and joyous bird high overhead, a tiny twinkling song-star in the sun-lit heavens; thence, through metaphoric *Lark*, a noun, extreme hilarity, and *Lark*, a verb, to riot — or, from *On a Lark*, *Out Larking*, and the like, to the last phase of its development and lowest stage of degradation, *Larrikin!* a word that may be likened to the Kangaroo, developed down and backward into a monstrosity!)

The old Beachcomber: gaunt, grim-visaged, eager-eyed, tar-smelling, and tattooed: a ship-deserter, runaway: the jetsam and the flotsam of the waters of the world in human guise;

The Whaler: of the Murrumbidgee and the Darling: when it suits his pleasure and convenience, a dolce-far-niente outcast in the fertile valleys of the rivers named, beyond the running of a warrant or a writ: a fisher, hunter, cut-throat, thief, or what he will, time, place, and circumstance suggesting and determining: by day affrighting phantoms of remorse with Thatcher's songs: by night, with rum;

The Swagman: bed and board upon his back — or, having humped his drum and set out on the wallaby, the austral tramp: in search of work, or, haply, aimless, trudging on and on into the Never-Never Country: lifting listlessly his hat in silent awe and clammy-skinned, heart-sinking introspection while he halts before a gaunt, gigantic, ghost-white gum, graved with the mystic, fateful letters, L'-D-T: the ghostly hand of Leichhardt beckoning to him from out the yawning all-involving sepulchre beyond!

The sly Sundowner: swagman timing his arrival at a station that the time, the place, and circumstance, appealing to the hospitality of worthy pioneers, may never fail to get for him a supper, bed, and breakfast ere he trudge again;

The Bushman: eking out a weird existence in the spectral forest: dwelling in an endless eldritch dream: half in the world of Something, half in that of Nothing: *Gunyah,* his bark hovel; *Skillian,* his bark lean-to kitchen; *Damper,* his unleavened bread baked in the ashes; *Billy,* his tea-kettle, universal pot and pan and bucket; *Sugar-bag,* his source of saccharine, a bee-tree; *Pheasant,* his facetious metaphoric euphuism for Liar, quasi Lyrebird; *Fit for Woogooroo,* for Daft or Idiotic; *Brumby,* his peculiar term for wild horse; *Scrubber,* wild ox; *Nuggeting,* calf-stealing; *Jumbuck,* sheep, in general; an *Old-man,* grizzled wallaroo or kangaroo; *Long-sleever, Bishop Barker,* and *Deep-sinker,* synonyms of Yankee Schooner; *Station, Run,* a sheep- or cattle-ranch: and *Kabonboodgery* — an echo of the sound diablery forever in his ears, from dawn to dusk of Laughing Jackass and from dusk to dawn of Dingo — his half-bird-and-beast-like vocal substitute for Very Good;

The Squatter: camping for a week, a fortnight, or forever, where he finds none to dispute his right: ignoring title-deeds: in blissful ignorance of judgments, liens, and mortgages: a retroversion to the Bedouin-nomadic stage of his forefathers on the desert wastes and steppes of Asia;

The Stockman: austral Cowboy: by the magic of a whip-crack herding cattle half a league away;

The manor-born Moonlighter: austral Guacho: fearless, skillful, breakneck, rider: in the bush and in the open: over stones and thorough marshes: lassoing the Scrubber and the Brumby, when, at night, to slake their thirst, they leave the scrub or bush to find a pool, a water-hole, or billybong;

The Dummy: man of straw in buying land;

The Jackaroo: the austral Tender-foot;

The Cockatoo: the austral small freeholding tiller of the soil; his house, belike, with roof of thatch, and walls compounding stones and sun-baked mud, whitewashed within and -out, and decked within with lyre-bird tails and emu eggs; upon a shelf above an open hearth, a Bible, Yankee clock, and Clarke's blood-curdling novel: dog-eared, thumb-worn, brown; his paddocks fenced with overlapping tree-trunks, interlacing limbs, and upturned roots — a ghastly spectacle!

All, one and all the Mob of Millions who compound and aggregate
The CORNSTALK: Mythic Man:
The Laborer:
The Miner, Metallurgist, Manufacturer;
The Carrier by land and sea;
The Builder, Engine-driver, Agriculturist;
The Druggist, Surgeon, Counselor;
The Actor, Author, Editor;
The Soldier, Statesman, Scientist;
The People scattered o'er the Land, like Seeds Broadcast;
The People gathered in the Cities and the Towns, like

Garnered Stores —
All, one and all,
The Man-half and the Woman-half in One: all comprehending, all-idealizing, and all-uttering,
The BARD!

I see and sing
The Evolution of the Austral World,
Effected by
The CORNSTALK: the Norwegian Thor turned topsy-turvy with the world around him: crushing not the skulls of the Frost-giants of the North, but, strange mutation! hurling his fell hammer at the Fire-gods of the South: the Warmth, the Light, and Life of Muspellheim: his olden good gods metamorphosed into monstrous fiends!

I see and sing
The Evolution of the Austral World
In general and in detail:
From Desert to Domain;
From Mallee-scrub to Orange-grove;
From Cockatoo to Cock and Hen;
From Kangaroo to Cotswold Sheep;
From Black to White: from Lowest Type to Highest Type of Man;
From Solitude to Cityful;
From Want to Wealth;
From Bunya-bunya seed to Bread;
From Billybong to Beer;
From 'Possum Pinafore to Silken Gown;
From Boomerang to Armstrong Gun;
From Shanksmare to the Iron-horse;
From Message-stick to Universal Mail;
From Red-hand-daubing to Photography;
From Coo-ee-ing to Telegraphing round the World;
From Song-and-Dance Corrobboree to Parliament;
From Noon-day Nightmares to Grand Galleries of Art;

From Agony to Anæsthesia;
From Memory to Monument;
From Laxity to Law;
From Demonism to Darwinism;
From Chaos-Speech to Kosmos-Song;
From all the Negatives of the sepulchral No-Man's-
   Land, the Never-Never Country, to the Positives of
   Queensland, New South Wales, Victoria, Australia
   South, Australia West — collectively,
The Hand Five-fingered of the Mistress of the Seas that
   grasps the Grand Prize of the Southern World;
The Paw Five-taloned of the Lion of the North that
   takes the Lion's Share of the Huge Carcass of the
   South ;
The YANKEELAND beneath the Southern Cross;
Among the Nations of the Earth, a Nation of Enlight-
   enment, the blazon of whose glorious banner has
   not been an empty boast, ADVANCE!

---

[1] The first edition of this poem was published in 1886, at Greenesburgh, Pennsylvania, in the form of an octavo pamphlet containing 40 pages. It was dedicated "to the venerable DR. GEORGE BENNETT, F.L.S., F.Z.S., ETC., of Sydney, New South Wales: to whom the world is indebted for much that is known of Australia; and to whom the world bows in grateful recognition." The notes included a number of quotations from the poetical works of THOMAS BRACKEN, HENRY KENDALL, CHARLES THATCHER, ADAM LINDSAY GORDON, and others.

[2] ON THE WALLABY: An Australianism signifying traveling, wandering, tramping, on the go: wallaby being a generic term of native origin for a number of kangaroo-like animals specifically distinguished as the rock-wallaby, black-gloved-wallaby, nail-tailed-wallaby, and the like.

[3] COWAN'S CANON: The weird and picturesque gorge in which the new bridle-path has been made from Katoomba to the Caves of Jenólan. Dingo-haunted: laughing-jackass-echoing: tree-fern-shaded: orchid-scented: glow above and gloom below: here an overhanging iron-stained cliff: there a multiple waterfall: presenting a novel interest and fascination at every

turn of the tortuous path descending nine hundred feet in a becline distance of half a mile. So named, in July, 1885, by Mr. George E. Cook, of Lithgow, N. S. W., Superintendent of Roads, while on the wallaby with the writer: exploring, geologizing, botanizing: hungering, thirsting: every muscle aching: burning the bush of Australia to make the charcoal for the preceding sketch.

'The stain produced by the decomposition of the carcase of a man, a sheep, or other animal of equal bulk, on the sandy plains of Australia, is discernible for many years — practically indelible.

AT BEIRUT.

    Hard by the spot St. George be-swinged the Dragon.

THE GERMAN WAR-GOD.

The triune war-god of the German creed,
Old Kaiser Wilhelm, Bismarck, and Von Moltke.

NEW JERSEY.

Pervaded with the perfume of the peach.

THE COLUMN AND THE ARCH.

The grandest monument of Greece, the Column;
The grandest monument of Rome, the Arch.

IN NAGASAKI.

A Petrarch in Japan? Impossible!
And wheresoe'er the end of passion is
Attained before the evolution of
The feelings into fancies hath begun.

THE BRAVE, OLD BURG OF GREENE.[1]

It was the turning of the year. Before a glowing grate,
In my good, old mother's cushioned chair, alone, at
ease, I sate;
At my elbow, a stand, and a crystal cup, whence aris-
ing, a rare perfume
Commingled its might with the golden light, in the
glamour of the room.

The merry bells of the passing sleigh had ceased their
tinkling sound;
The purr of the cat on the rug had passed into silence,
in sleep profound;
The click! click! alone was heard, of a clock in the
corner encased,—
Like a grotesque and grim personation of Time,— to
mimic the heart in my breast!

When hark! as the clock struck twelve, a knock!
Come in, come in, I cried;
And the king of good fellows came bounding in, and
sat down by my side.
A light in each eye like a living star, shedding gleams
from heaven on earth,
And a smile on his lips circling round and round, like
a planisphere of mirth!

Now, away with the cares of the work-a-day world, and
the carks of his work-a-day wife!
Let us live while we may, like a sunburst of light,
through the lowering clouds of life—

Let us fill to the brim and drain to the dregs, and the
 de'il take the golden mean,—
Come, give us a toast! My royal guest said — To the
 Brave, Old Burg of Greene!

To the brave, old burg of Greene! Aye, aye; to the
 brave, old burg of Greene!
The dearest spot in the wide, wide world, the loveliest
 ever seen!
Where the air, with the breath of the living, is sweet,
 as if violets did abound,
And the very earth, with the dust of the dead, is holy,
 holy ground!

Aye, aye, let us drink to the brave, old burg, our all in
 all on earth,
That bears a name, and embodies a fame, was won by
 well-tried worth;[2]
And let us swear, as our glasses clink, the day will nev-
 er be seen,
When the spirit will die among her sons, of "the con-
 quering genius, Greene!"[3]

Good hap befall the man of mark, who leads an honest
 life,
And, in good time, takes a woman of worth to be his
 wedded wife;
That in their home, the brave, old burg may ever re-
 new her youth,
And wax, as the seasons come and go, in virtue, love,
 and truth!

And evil hap befall —— Nay, nay! this is nor time
 nor place,
To wish a woe, or wreak a wrong, on the vilest of the
 race;

For why, God wot, it is the tide, the turning of the
    year,
Of peace and good will unto all, and universal cheer!

Then let the toast go round and round, To the brave,
    old burg of Greene!
Among the fair towns of the land, a crowned and scep-
    tred queen,
Enthroned upon a mighty hill, in token of her force,
Like England's virgin queen of old, astride a warrior's
    horse!

Ha! a blessing hath he in his birthright, who points to
    this town as the place of his birth!
Ha! a blessing hath he in his fireside, who sees, in this
    cluster of earth-stars, his hearth!
Ha! a blessing hath he in his winding-sheet, that is
    wrapped in the good, old town!
And a blessing hath he in his epitaph that gives and
    takes renown!

St. Clair, the Brave but Unfortunate![4] And many a
    sacred score,
Whose names are echoed from out the earth, of the
    glorious days of yore,—
Whose names are muttered by marble mouths, or
    mumbled by mutes in the sod,
Where the sink is seen, and the grass is green, in the
    tear-bedewed Acre of God!

These are the names that are heard in the heart, when
    the name of the brave burg is spoken!
These are the ties that are bound in the blood, that are
    only with life itself broken!
These are the subtleties sunk in the soul, that are felt
    though they may not be seen,
Till the king of good fellowship takes up the glass —
    To the brave, old burg of Greene!

Aye, these are the words of the Wizard of Dreams,
    when the eye-lids are closing in rest,
That raise from the depths of the sea of the mind the
    uncharted Isles of the Blest! —
A vision of beauty and bliss upon earth, to the eyes of
    the flesh only given,
When Himál'ya's height comes out of the night, above
    the storm-cloud, in heaven!

I've wandered north and I've wandered south, in the
    world of wonders untold;
I've wandered east and I've wandered west, in the
    world of the New and the Old;
But in farthest Ind and remotest Cathay, with the girth
    of the globe between,
The nearest spot to my heart of hearts was the brave,
    old burg of Greene!

There was a fabled fount of old, that drink of it who
    would,
And wander thence for many a day by forest, field or
    flood;
Still must he turn, in weal or woe, to quench a burning
    thirst,
With an enchanting second draught whence he had
    ta'en the first.

But what is the fable but fact in disguise — a thought
    for the thing, in mask —
Like the genie of Araby's marvelous tale, in the fisher-
    man's new-found flask? —
I had drunk long and deep of the magical spring,
    whence all the enchantment has been,
When my lips were pressed to my mother's breast, in
    the brave, old burg of Greene!

Ye Winds that wander round the world, oh, bring your
	sweetest breath,
From hawthorn hill and violet vale, and scent-com-
	mingling heath,
That when, with her lint-white locks ye play, and
	fevered furrows, fan,
She may close her eyes and kiss again her babe in the
	bearded man!

And thou, O Sun, thou warmth of the world, here
	gleam with a summer's ray,
In her winter of winters that knows no spring, and set
	far hence the day,
When the snow that is piled on the trembling height,
	in an avalanche will start,
And deep in the Valley of Shadows below, encase in
	ice her heart!

Oh, who will not drink to the brave, old burg that em-
	bodies his being in others?—
The love that links, from the life-lighted dawn, the
	hearts of sons and mothers!
The love that links, from the white-veiled vow, the
	hearts of man and woman!
The love that links, from a first-born's cry, the hearts
	of all that are human!

Oh, who will not drink to the brave, old burg, in which
	his being is bounded—
Not a sentient sphinx in uncertain suspense, between
	two seas unsounded,—
Nor a riddle relation 'twixt matter and force, in mysti-
	cal, mind-mixing mud,—
But a man among children and women and men, in
	flesh and bone and blood!

Oh, who will not drink to the brave, old burg, the rare
 old burg, and the dear,
When the Spirit of Peace and Good Will unto All, at
 the turning of the year,
In the guise of the King of Good Fellows will come,
 and sit in the open heart's room,
And recall with a toast, in the mind of its host, What
 a heaven on earth it is, Home!

Home! the brave, old burg of Greene! Among the
 hoary hills,
Where the Appalachian mountains appear in a form
 my fancy fills —
An outcast King Lear of the Mountains of Earth, in
 the storm wand'ring, wasted and worn,
While the Alps and Himál'yas, in pitiless pride, share
 the crown from his temples torn![5]

Home! the brave, old burg of Greene! Among the
 humid hills,
Where the Mississippi's roar is heard, in the ripple of
 the rills —
The Father of Waters who warrants the word, of the
 Stars and Stripes unfurled,
Come, ye hungry and homeless, wherever ye be, here's
 a welcome to the world!

Home! the brave, old burg of Greene! Where, afar,
 in the untold past,
The mammoth strode in the wild, wild wood, like a
 whirlwind in muscle amassed;
Until hark! to the roar of the last of his race, as the
 Era of Mind began,
With the burning brand and the flint-flaked barb, in
 the earth-freed hand of Man![6]

Home! the brave, old burg of Greene! Where, anear, in a later age,
The Redskin followed the leaf-turned track, a wolf-head war to wage;
Till Guyasootha sank in gore, the bravest of the brave,
And the tomahawk and the scalping-knife were laid in the warrior's grave![7]

Home! the brave, old burg of Greene! In the circle of vision set,
Where the armies of England and France of old, in bloody battle met;
Oh, fell the day, when the Lion at eve, all red, with gore and spent,
Uprooted the Lily transplanted here, and won the Continent![8]

Home! the brave, old burg of Greene! Without or lines or laws,
Till George the Third declared the word, and lo! Westmóreland[9] was!—
The farthest stretch of the King's long arm, from the Isle of Isles in the sea,
Till lopped off with a sword, in a new-coined word, the Land of Liberty![10]

Home! the brave, old burg of Greene! In the very venue, where came
The wondrous youth to found the worth that won the Father's fame!—
In the lowliest cot, oh, how blest is the lot of the sire who can say to his son,
Here, on this spot, the deeds were wrought, that gave to the world, Washington![11]

God prosper long, in all that gives to life the charms of
    health,—
God prosper long, in all that gives to love its untold
    wealth,
The man that prays, God bless our Home! and the
    woman that says, Amen!
When the glasses clink, and the guest and host drink,
    To the Brave, Old Burg of Greene!

L'ENVOY.

There is a tomb, where the wealth of the world and
    the art of man are combined,
In a rival gem to the Koh-in-oor, in the crown of im-
    perial Ind;
In whose guarded glory, the senses sink, in a surfeit of
    sweets, to sleep,
And the soul in a dream sees another Taj that makes
    the wanderer weep!

Oh, when his wandering shall have ceased, and an end
    have come to time,
May the humble bard, whose heart is heard reëchoed
    in his rhyme,
Be laid in the tomb of his hallowed home — in the Taj
    in fantasy seen,
For aye to rest, among the blest, in the Brave, Old
    Burg of Greene!

---

[1] This poem first appeared as the New Year's Address of the Greenesburgh Press, 1st January, 1883.

² NATHANAEL GREENE, of Rhode Island, a Major General of distinction during the Revolution.

³ From a poem by PHILIP FRENEAU, the Poet of the Revolution.

⁴ ARTHUR ST. CLAIR, a Major General of the Revolution, the BELISARIUS of America. He is buried in the cemetery which bears his name in Greenesburgh.

⁵ Geologically speaking, the Alleghany or Appalachian Mountains are infinitely older than the Alps and the Himalayas, and are estimated to have been, at one time, over six miles in height. Nothing now remains but a wasted and disjointed skeleton of their former greatness.

⁶ An imaginary account of the destruction of the last of the mammoths is given in the initial poem of the writer's *Song and Story in Southwestern Pennsylvania*, 12mo., Greenesburgh, Pa., 1876.

⁷ For a brief account of the distinguished Redskin warrior, GUYASOOTHA, and a number of the most thrilling episodes of the "wolf-head war" waged in the Forks of the Ohio, the River of Blood, see *ibid, sparsim*.

⁸ An account also of the incidents of this fateful war is given in the volume referred to.

⁹ The accent of this word in Pennsylvania is invariably on the second syllable: in England, on the first. *More*, being a form of *mare, meer, mere*, or *mael*, (as in maelstrom,) meaning the sea, a lake, or other similar body of water, the American pronunciation is preferable to the English, laying as it does the stress on the more important of the descriptive syllables.

¹⁰ The county of Westmoreland was erected just before the breaking out of the war of the Revolution, and is remarkable for being the first county formed west of the Alleghany Mountains and the last by the fiat of a British king. The lines of the poem, accordingly, are literally correct. For further on the subject, see the volume referred to above.

¹¹ The theatre of many of the remarkable actions of the early manhood of WASHINGTON was in Southwestern Pennsylvania: notably while on his mission to the French on the Allegheny, and while serving under BRADDOCK and BOUQUET. See volume referred to, for particulars.

AT GETTYSBURG.[1]

"The Battle of Gettysburg, as an agency in determining the result of the contest between the Government and its assailants was the most important of the war [of 1861-5.] It was the beginning of the end. The little crown of saplings which Pickett made the mark towards which his troops were to aim, and which a part of them did actually reach, has been styled 'the high-water mark of the rebellion.' The star which, at that moment, had appeared in the ascendant, began to pale and move to its setting."—SAMUEL P. BATES: *Martial Deeds of Pennsylvania*, p. 325.

With low-bent head and wonder-lighted eyes,
The soldier listened to the story of
My wayward wand'ring twice around the world;
And therein of the strange, the wonderful,
And the sublime of every sea and land,
It was my good or evil hap to make
A part of my existence evermore:
A myriad of match-like memories,
Betimes to kindle feelings of delight,
Inflame the passions of my bosom, and
Illume the mystic midnight of my mind,—
Now, with weird shimmering auroral dreams;
Anon, with flashing incandescent thoughts—
The lightning-scissored silhouettes of God
Within the storm-rack of the intellect!

My tale of travel told, the veteran,
Tumultuously moved, a moment stood
With heaving bosom and with trembling lip;
Then, grasping my right hand, and glancing from

My eyes to Heaven as his gathered thoughts
Found utterance in gesture, look and speech,
Pronounced these words with solemn emphasis:
"My friend! But to have been where you have
    been,
And to have seen what you have seen, by God!
I would have been a louse upon your head!"

This happened hence a year or more. Since then,
The soldier and his speech have haunted me;
And ever and anon I find myself
Confronting him in fancy with a change
Of parts upon the world-wide stage of life —
I having heard his story, as he mine —
Assuming his emotion as my own —
Appropriating gesture, look, and speech —
"My friend! But to have been where you have
    been,
And to have seen what you have seen, by God!
I would have been a louse upon your head!"

And why? The soldier wore a coat of blue,
And fought among the brave at Gettysburg!
While I — O cruel fate! — was far away!
While I, a son of Pennsylvania!
Was not among the first to stand or fall
Before the foe, beneath my mother's roof
And on her holy hearth, at Gettysburg!
Unworthy I — the soldier's peer in age!
Ignoble I — the soldier's peer in strength!
Benothinged I — a vagabond beyond
The pale of immortality for aye!

O soldier of the country of my birth!
All would I give that I have gained within
The worlds of wonder of the New and Old,

Had I thy history within my heart!
That I might thrill as I have never yet,
While I read what is written there in blood:
I faced my country's foe at Gettysburg!
I fired a shot — I drove a bayonet —
I clubbed an empty gun at Gettysburg!
Or, glory of all glories of the earth !
I bore the shot and shell betattered flag —
I bore the blood and brain bespattered flag —
I bore the Stars and Stripes at Gettysburg!

Aye! veteran of the United States!
All would I give that haply I have gained —
Alone in eldritch Australasian wilds,
Or mingling with the millions of Cathay;
Aghast among the Ganges' floating dead,
Or gloating o'er the Kremlin's gems and gold;
Crazed 'mid the wrecks of a Biscayan storm,
Or musing on the moonlit Amazon;
Racked with surróche on Andéan height,
Or swooning in New Zealand's baths of bliss;
Wasted with want and sickness in Brazil,
Or surfeited with sweets in Malay-land;
Death-doomed before a half-drawn Niphon sword,
Or senseless dragged from an Egyptian mob;
Fate-fixed across an alpine glacier-chasm,
Or wave-washed mangled 'mid Hawáiia's crags;
Scaling Corea's wall against the world,
Or stayed by storms in Patagonian wastes;
On the Atlantic mountained 'round with ice,
Or Lucy's Isle within a boiling sea;
Before a coming South Sea waterspout,
Or on an earthquake-shattered South Sea isle;
Returning the stone-staring of the Sphinx,
Or bowed before Japan's begodded Buddh;
Dreaming the dream of marble of the Taj,
Or thinking the eternal thoughts of Rome;

AT GETTYSBURG.

Ear-turned to bulbul's song, or jaguar's scream,
Or Wisdom's word from agèd Owen's lips;
Within the glare of Afric's glowing sand,
Or gloom of India's mount-enchiseled fanes;
Where Muni twirled the wheel that turns for aye,
Or Plato taught the ages yet unborn;
Where Grecian keel conveyed the Golden Fleece,
Or Spanish prow cut from the waves a world;
Where mighty Genghis conquered in the East,
Or Cortes and Pizarro in the West;
Where ancient Greek and Trojan met at Troy,
Or modern Goth and Gaul at Waterloo;
Amid Himál'ya's heaven-kissing heights,
Or Hálemáumau's hell-ignited fires;
Agape in London's inwalled wonder-worlds, —
Elate before a list'ning Emperor, —
Or awed at the Anointed's Holy Tomb! —
All! all! had I as thou swelled with my voice
The shout of victory at Gettysburg!
All! all! could I as thou now say in truth,
I share the glory of IMMORTAL MEADE!

---

[1] Read at the Camp-fire of the Grand Army of the Republic, in Fifth Avenue Music Hall, Pittsburgh, Pennsylvania, October 4th, 1887.

END OF THE RIME OF A RAMBLER TWICE AROUND THE WORLD.

LIKE FERN-LEAVES FOUND IN SHALE:

OUTLINING LIFE

AGAINST A WORLD TURNED INTO SUNLESS STONE.

LIKE FERN-LEAVES FOUND IN SHALE:

OUTLINING LIFE

AGAINST A WORLD TURNED INTO SUNLESS STONE.

THE ATLANTOSAURUS.

"Near the base of our Cretaceous formation, in beds which I regard as the equivalent of the European Wealden, the most gigantic forms of this order (Dinosauria) yet discovered have recently been brought to light. One of these monsters (*Atlantosaurus montanus,*) from Colorado, is by far the largest land animal yet discovered; its dimensions being greater than was supposed possible in an animal that lived and moved upon the land. It was some fifty or sixty feet in length, and, when erect, at least thirty feet in height. It doubtless fed upon the foliage of the mountain forests, portions of which are preserved with its remains." — PROF. O. C. MARSH: *Popular Science Monthly,* vol. xii, p. 524.

Indubitable dinosaur, Atlantosaurus, hail!
Thou, gecko aggrandized into a quadrupèdal whale;
I marvel at thy magnitude, I wonder at thy weight,
I bow me down before thee, thou organic ultimate!

Big, bulky, Brobdingnaggian beast! exceeding in thy size
All living things upon the land e'er seen by human eyes! —
Illimitable lizard, incommensurable newt,
Interminable tadpole, inexsuperable brute!

Poetic symbol of the grand in heaven, earth, and hell;
Rhetoric type of the immense and unapproachable;
And all the better, too, perhaps, for being vague as vast,
An image of stupendous size that cannot be surpassed!

There's Samuel Johnson — to what beast, besides thyself on earth,
Can he the better be compared for comprehensive girth?
Among the English bards and scribes, in his productive time,
As thou among the birds and beasts of every age and clime!

So Koong-Foo-Tse, the Chinese sage — to what organic thing,
Wise men wage wordy wars about, and gentle poets sing,
Can he be likened better, in his philosophic bulk,
Than to thy huge, enormous, indeterminable hulk?

So Genghis Khan, the ruler of one-third of all mankind,
Incomparable till the day Chance, Marsh and Cope combined
To hale thy mighty carcase from the mesozoic mud,
And put thee on thy monstrous legs as whilom thou hast stood.

So Cuvier in science, and Napoleon in war;
So Shakespeare as a dramatist, and Garrick as a star;
And Washington, a patriot — each peerless and alone,
Until thy mountain mass emerged from out the world
    of stone!

Yea, hail! Atlantosaurus, hail! superlatively great,
The measure of the mightiest in thee incorporate —
The measure of the mightiest in worth and wicked-
    ness! —
May thy colossal shadow never grow a shade the less!

THE GLACIAL EPOCH.

The winters waxed as the summers waned,
    And colder blew the blast,
Until land and sea appeared to be
    A common world-wide waste,
And bird and beast to struggle ceased
    In the gathering ice encased.

Until beneath the floor of the cave,
    To the eyes that stared within,
The southern sun at noon sank down,
    And the northern night set in —
The longest night without the sun's light
    The earth had ever seen.

And over the hill-tops from the pole,
    The ice-flood came in its might,
Till, over the mouth of the cave op'ning south,
    It rose to a towering height —
A jutting cliff of ice, as if
    To signal the coming of light.

And one by one of hunger and cold
    The cavern-dwellers died;
The baby first, and the mother that nursed,
    And the stranger that made her his bride —
Till all were gone save a father of bone,
    And a daughter of skin by his side.

Till all were gone save the two alone
    To gnaw at the frozen dead —
At hand and foot, at breast and throat,
    And then at a ghastly head;
Until no more food for flesh and blood
    Remained in scrap or shred.

When, sinking to the cavern floor,
    The famished father slept —
In delight to dream that the sun's bright beam
    Had into the cavern crept;
While the daughter, as gaunt as the spectre of
        Want,
    In her horrible hopelessness, wept.

When — was it the sun in the cave that shone,
    To open the dreamer's eyes?
Or the inturning light from the towering height
    Of the overhanging ice?
Until, at length, it gave him strength
    Upon his haunches to rise.

"Up! up! my daughter! the sun's returned!
    Behold the light and believe!
The night has flown and winter gone,
    And one of us can give
In flesh and blood the needful food
    That the other still may live!

"Up! up! my daughter! and drink my blood
    As it bubbles from my heart!
Quick! quick! with your lip to catch the drip
    That will follow this eager dart!
Quick! quick! that I may feel while I die
    That from thee I do not part!"

The father raised a flake of flint —
    It flashed above his head,
In the shimmering light from the towering height
    Into the cavern shed;
It tapped the flood of his bounding blood,
    And quivered in him — dead!

But the daughter's lip never caught the drip
    Of the blood that followed fast. —
While the father slept, her tears, as she wept,
    Into ice on her lids had amassed;
And an indrawn breath between parting teeth
    Had cooled in a corpse aghast!

O doubly deluded dreamer of old, —
    Sacrificing thyself to save
A life that had flown before thine own, —
    Sleep, in thy hillside cave,
Till the melting height of the ice in the light
    Has fallen and closed thy grave!

Sleep, with the flint between thy ribs,
    Beside thy daughter's bones,
Until the last of the ice has swept past
    And scored above thee the stones —
Recording the date of thy self-wrought fate,
    With gruesome, grinding groans!

Sleep, in the dust that gathers where'er
    Time gnaws with tireless tooth,
Until the sage, in a future age,
    In imparting his wisdom to youth,
Shall leave logic and lore, and point to the score
    In the stone, in tracing the truth.

Sleep, in the distant poet's dream
    Of the evolution of art,
Till he shall have passed like an echoing blast,
    In life performed his part —
Indelibly wrought in the score his thought,
    And hid in the stone his heart!

Sleep! sleep! with the sanctified sires of old,
    And never, never wake,
To learn how vain are the dreams of man
    That dies for another's sake,
Lest that noblest end to be attained
    Mortal man nevermore may make!

THE SAVAGE MOTHER AND THE CAVE BEAR.[1]

A PRE-HISTORIC INCIDENT.

With antlers interlocked and fast, two elks embattling
    stood,
Their flanks agape with every gasp, their dewlaps dripping blood;

While, leaderless, their scattered herds ranged 'round
    in doubt and fear,
Pursued by gaunt and gurly wolves that gathered far
    and near;
While crows flit through the limbs o'erhead, with an
    impatient caw,
And hovered o'er the trembling prongs with out-
    stretched beak and claw.
When hark! the shout of savages, repeated west and
    east,
Announced the coming of a horde to share the forest
    feast!

Anon, the weaker of the elks sank lifeless to the
    ground,
And brought the stronger to his knees, their heads to-
    gether bound;
When, quick as hunger thinks and acts, in crow, and
    wolf, and man,
The gathered throng upon the twain to feast and fight
    began.
The crows, upon the antlers perched, picked at the clos-
    ing eyes;
The wolves, upon their haunches set, pulled at the life-
    less thighs;
While, armed, one with a jasper knife, another with a
    dart,
The savage horde the hamstrings cut and pierced the
    living heart.
Then, with a shout that stilled the crow and hushed
    the wolf in dread,
The wild men leaped upon the elks — the living and
    the dead —
And smote the crow and speared the wolf, till, driven
    from the prey,
A circling fire of crackling wood kept them in fear
    away.

Anon the horde upon the ground, with greedy, greasy jaws,
Sate thoughtless of all else besides the filling of their maws,
When o'er the embers of the fire neglected in the feast,
There strode an unexpected guest, a huge and monstrous beast —
A bear, from out the mountain-side's cavérnous bat-hung pit!
A mockery to manhood's might, a wonder to his wit!

The roar from out the monster's throat such sudden terror gave,
As if the thunder of a storm had bellowed from a cave!
The savages, in wild affright, fled far into the wood,
Nor turned to see, save each to learn if he might be pursued —
Save one, a naked suckling that had from its mother crept,
And, while she feasted on the flesh, upon the warm hide slept.

But hark! what fearful shriek is that, that pricks the monster's ear,
Just as the baby wakes against the cold nose of the bear?
It is the mother backward bound, heart-wrung with grief and wild,
To snatch from out the jaws of death the future in her child!

The embers crossed, the mother stooped, and seized a glowing brand,
Then leaped before the monster's face, and made a threatening stand.

The monster on its hind feet rose, and, with uplifted
    paws,
Stood like a huge hide-bearded man, and oped its aw-
    ful jaws.
Between the ragged rows of teeth, the mother thrust
    the brand,
And snatched the baby from the ground, with an uner-
    ring hand;
And while the monster crunched the fire, a pain-dis-
    tracted beast,
The mother passed beyond pursuit, her baby on her
    breast!

A mother's love! Oh, it is this, in the eternal
    strife,
That links the Future with the Past in everlasting
    life!

---

[1] According to Vogt, every gradation between the Cave Bear and the common species, *Ursus arctos*, may be traced; while Busk asserts that the remains of the bear, found in the British caves and gravels, is identical with the Grizzly Bear of America. In this country, there are two fossil species, *U. americanus* and *U. amplidens*, found in the southern part of the United States.

"The Grizzly is the most ferocious and terrible of all American animals. He exercises absolute terrorism over every living creature that comes in his way. It is said that even the hungry wolf will flee at the sight of his track, and no animal will venture to touch a deer that has been killed and left by him. His strength is such that, even the powerful bison falls an easy prey, and a single blow from one of his paws has been known to remove the entire scalp from a man's head. He is the only member of his family that will venture to attack man unchallenged, but it is said that he will retreat at the scent of a man, if he can do so unobserved." — W. E. SIMMONS, JR.

ATLANTIS.

"Among the great deeds of Athens, of which recollection is preserved in our books, there is one that should be placed above all others. Our books tell us that the Athenians destroyed an army that came across the Atlantic ocean, and insolently invaded Europe and Asia, for this sea was then navigable; and beyond the straits where you place the Pillars of Hercules was an immense island, larger than Asia and Libya combined. From this island one could pass easily to the other islands, and from these to the continent beyond. The sea on this side of the straits resembled a harbor with a narrow entrance, but there is a veritable sea, and the land which surrounds it is a veritable continent. On this island of Atlantis there reigned three kings with great and marvelous power. They had under their domain the whole of Atlantis, several of the other islands, and part of the continent. At one time their power extended into Europe as far as Tyrrhenia, and uniting their whole force they sought to destroy our whole country at a blow, but their defeat stopped the invasion and gave entire freedom to the countries this side of the Pillars of Hercules. Afterward, in one day and fatal night, there came mighty earthquakes and inundations, that engulfed that warlike people. Atlantis disappeared, and then that sea became inaccessible, on account of the vast quantities of mud that the engulfed island left in its place. — PLATO.

The sovereigns, sitting side by side, upon a central
    mound,
Looked down upon a level plain for many miles
    around,
Where gathering the people came in joy to cele-
    brate
The union of the rival realms in one harmonious
    state —

The realms that for an age had been at war without
　　surcease,
Until this happy, happy day of universal peace.

At the right elbow of the king that ruled within the
　　north,
His son, the heir apparent, sate, a prince of proven
　　worth;
And at the left hand of the king that ruled within the
　　south,
An only child, a princess in the budding bloom of
　　youth:
A man and woman round and full in their organic
　　growth
To join the human halves of life in a new birth of
　　both;
A man and woman far apart, as man and woman are,
Until their love had wrought the change to peace from
　　world-wide war.
Albeit they had never met, save in entrancing dreams,
In which the fancy fondles with the fiction of it
　　seems;
And never will until the sun, now rising, shall have
　　set,
And they in marriage shall have been conjoined to
　　crown the fête.

Till then, to the impassioned pair, and time-tormenting
　　twain,
How weary move the moments with the people on the
　　plain —
How dreary drag the hours along with the succeeding
　　parts
Of the procession heedless to their aching, yearning
　　hearts!
With scarce a glance in secresy into each other's eye,

And only once above the din a sympathetic sigh !
But every end to be achieved its time it must abide,
And so the consummation must the bridegroom and
    the bride.

First came afoot a horde of slaves, in the procession's
    van,
With all the substances of earth that minister to man;
Next came a legion burdened with the products of the
    plants
That in a myriad of shapes subserve to human
    wants;
And then a countless multitude with every bird and
    beast;
Of use to man and woman, from the largest to the
    least;
Then came the races of mankind, the white, and black,
    and red,
From every quarter of the earth where man and
    woman wed;
Next, all the craft and tradesmen, in a dense and dusky
    cloud,
And all the servants of the kings commingled in a
    crowd;
Then, borne above their children's heads, a host of
    hoary sires
Rejoicing in the union that determined their desires;
Next, bearing each a babe or twain upon her bosom
    bared,
A myriad of mothers in the great procession fared;
Then, hand in hand, as many men and women happ'ly
    wed,
Their several lives eternal in the issue of their bed;
Then, last of all, ten thousand youths, clasping as
    many maids,
Came whirling in a mazy waltz — and then away as
    shades:

Since, from the mountain's highest peak, the crimson afterglow
Had faded into deep'ning shades of brown and black below.

When lo! the kings uprising, in a transport of delight,
The hands of prince and princess joined with the approach of night.
A whisper, from the youths and maids attendant on the twain,
Speeds to the guard surrounding and the crowd upon the plain;
And, hark! the whisper bursts into a loud and lengthened cheer
That rises to a mountain-top to an attentive ear;
And lo! as quick as sound and sense and action can unite,
There flashes from the highest point a ruddy beacon light;
And as the heart beats quick with joy, from peak to peak afar,
The tidings leap the valleys as the star succeeds to star!
Till, speeding thus from north to south, and from the east to west,
The island of Atlantis is the Island of the Blest!

At length the universal shout, reëchoing, decreased,
Till in the middle of the night it altogether ceased;
When, in a chamber still and dark, their worth in life to prove,
The lips of prince and princess met and lingered long in love;
Their interlacing eyelids closed; and, in the lengthened kiss,

The world without departed from the world within of
   bliss!
When suddenly the palace walls were leveled to the
   earth,
That shook as if it struggled in the painful throes of
   birth;
Till, splitting here and splitting there, with each suc-
   ceeding spasm,
A ragged rock was left apeak, encircled with a
   chasm,
Where, separated from the world, the prince and prin-
   cess lay —
The future severed from the past — the all in all for
   aye!

And upward rose the island of the future firm and
   fast,
As down a thousand fathoms sank the island of the
   past,
Rent with the earthquake's force and crossed with
   many a ragged crack
In which a flood of fire appeared like lightning in the
   rack —
A flood of fire that dashed and splashed, till, rising in
   its might,
The island of Atlantis was illumined with the light —
The island of Atlantis was aflood with lava streams
That followed fast and furious from out the ragged
   seams.
Then, from the sea surrounding, came a wave of
   mountain height,
A wall of sparkling splendor in the lava's vivid
   light;
Until it met the molten mass in an engulfing flood,
And lo! where stood Atlantis was a seething sea of
   mud!

From which a mighty steam arose that melted in the
    sky,
And lo! Atlantis was an isle alone of fantasy:

The ragged rock, within the sea of universal death,
On which the prince and princess lay with a com-
    mingled breath;
Till, rising with the morrow's sun, within themselves
    they found
The source of their salvation from the sea of death
    around;
And recognizing each in each a supplemental good,
They symbolized themselves within the worship of
    their God.

Erect, with his right hand upheld, the prince looked
    to the sky:
And God extended from himself into infinity;
The princess, kneeling, with clasped hands, looked
    downward to the earth:
And God extended from herself into a finite birth —
A naked, new-born babe, a Christ, the Saviour of man-
    kind,
Descended from a sire above, within the prince's mind.

And as it has been, so it is, and shall be evermore,
The island of Atlantis is at war from shore to shore,
Until the halves opposing cease in the eternal strife,
The North becoming husband and the South becoming
    wife;
And from their union issues, as the isle sinks in the
    sea,
The Future severed from the Past: the all in all for
    aye!

PLOT AND COUNTERPLOT IN THE PALACE OF PALENQUE.

Palenque![1] To the archæologist, what a volume is involved in this single word Palenque, an aggregation of ancient art that has won the admiration of the world! I cannot assume, accordingly, that the reader is not familiar with its wealth of wonders, to such an extent at least as to obviate the necessity of an extended introduction to the following romance in rhyme, written to make quick with life, sentient with understanding, and sympathetic with the great heart of humanity, the City of the Dead of untold centuries: to people once more the wonderful Palace, and, deep in its mysterious recesses, to catch the whispered secrets that separate in the struggle for existence the sovereign and the subject, the father and the daughter — all, save the twain whom Love hath made bold enough to risk the mortality of the present for the immortality of the future — the life eternal in the issue of their union.

"Thou liest!" the king to the courtier said;
  "For, liefer[1] than love this slave
Of a sculptor, though fair as his genius is rare,
  My daughter would go to her grave!"

"My life the forfeit for falsehood be;
  But come with me, my lord,
And thou shalt behold, as I have told,
  In witness of my word."

Behind the screen, pierced with the point
  Of a stealthy, quivering blade,
The royal spy strained an eager eye
  To see as the courtier had said.

Before him stood the sculptor at work,
　　With his chay-stone chisel[3] in hand,
Upon a face of grandeur and grace —
　　The face of the lord of the land.

When lo! the princess appeared in the hall,
　　Upon her arm a bird,
To which she talked and sang, as she walked,
　　As if nobody saw or heard.

Until, hark! the sound of the sculptor at work! —
　　The parrot frightened flew
Into the gloom of an inner room,
　　And the princess abashed withdrew.

And before the sun sank in the west,
　　That stood then in midsky,
The king commands, and the courtier stands
　　Condemned for his falsehood to die.

Four slaves outstretch his arms and legs,
　　While a fifth, about his neck,
Hangs a collar-like[4] stone to stifle the moan
　　The victim of justice may make.

And a sixth unsheathes a glittering blade,
　　In the exercise of his art —
And behold! in the gleam of the setting sun's
　　　　beam,
　　A beating, bleeding heart!

And while the heart throbs in the air,
　　Adown the altar's height,
The corpse is cast, agape and aghast,
　　A feast for the dogs in the night!

"So be it ever with him that speaks
    A falsehood to the king!
Resound the trumpet and the drum,
    And let the welkin ring!"

———

The seasons came, and the seasons went
    As speechless as they came,
Till the royal ear again must hear
    Another tale of shame.

"Thou liest!" the king to the courtier said;
    "For, liefer than lie with this slave
Of a sculptor, though fair as his genius is rare,
    My daughter would lie in her grave!"

"My life the forfeit for falsehood be;
    But ere thou decreest my doom,
Let the king's own eye this night espy
    All that may hap in her room."

Again the king, with the courtier, sate
    Behind the piercèd screen,
Where all that might befall in the light
    Of the full moon might be seen.

And lo! as the light and shade grew apart,
    The sculptor, with a torch [5]
Of beetles aglow with a living lowe,
    Appeared upon the porch.

And, with a slow and stately step,
    Passed through the curtained door, [6]
And thence, till he stood in a thoughtful mood,
    His unfinished work before.

Then, fixing his torch to illumine his work,
    He took up his chisel of chay,
And began to scratch about a sketch
    Upon the stone in clay.

And thus he worked with careful skill,
    Until the middle night,
When, crossing the floor, he passed the door,
    And disappeared with his light.

The king and courtier, then, in stealth,
    Crept to the princess's bed,
To find her deep in a dreamless sleep,
    As if among the dead.

And at her side, a fretful child,
    In the innocence of youth,
To awake in affright at the stir in the night,
    And cry with the tongue of truth!

And ere the morrow's rising sun
    Shone in the height of heaven,
The courtier's warm but heartless form
    To the dogs of death was given!

"So be it ever with him that speaks
    A falsehood to the king!
Resound the trumpet and the drum,
    And let the welkin ring!"

The time sped; till a good old man,
    Attendant on the throne,
Made bold to proclaim the princess's shame,
    The country's grief and his own.

"Thou liest!" the king to the old man said;
  "For, liefer than bear to this slave
Of a sculptor, a son, and slay it as soon,
  My daughter would rot in her grave!"

"I am an old, old man, O king,
  And dearly love I life;
But if I lie, so let me die
  Beneath the bloody knife.

"But come with me to the garden wall,
  Where the grass is sere and red,
And thou shalt behold as I have told —
  The babe in secrecy laid."

With long and hurried strides, the king
  Into the garden sped;
The sod was raised; and the old man gazed
  In vain to find the dead!

Upon his knees the old man fell,
  "Three days, O king, I crave
To find the corse taken hence perforce
  And laid in another grave."

"Thy boon I grant," the king replied,
  And, in a troubled mood,
From the garden wall to the palace hall,
  With stifling anger, strode.

"Make haste, my sons!" the old man said;
  "Into the wild wood hie,
And fetch a gaunt she-wolf with want,
  That your father may not die!"

Within the wood the seven sons
    In stealth and silence sought,
Until a gaunt she-wolf with want
    Was to their father brought.

Within the garden walls, the beast,
    With hunger fierce and keen,
Was cast, perchance, with its sharpened sense,
    To scent what couldn't be seen!

"Come, now, O king," the old man said;
    "And where the famished beast
Digs in the ground, there will be found
    The baby laid at rest."

Now here, now there, about the yard,
    The eager she-wolf ran,
Until she found a scent in the ground,
    And to dig at once began.

"Quick! kill the beast!" the old man cried;
    "Before she eats the corse!"
But ere the dart could pierce her heart,
    The wolf had torn perforce —

From out the ground a feathered bird,
    Of green and yellow and red,
A ribbon about its resplendent throat,
    The princess's parrot, dead!

The old man fell upon his knees;
    "My life, O king, is thine;
It was for her bird, the weeping I heard;
    I did the princess malign."

And before the sun sank in the sea,
    The old man's heartless breast,
Filled the gaping jaw and the hungering maw
    Of the gaunt and gurly beast.

"So be it ever with him that speaks
    A falsehood to the king!
Resound the trumpet and the drum,
    And let the welkin ring!"

Ah, me! the weary hours the king
    Sate in his palace of stone;
A million among, the thought of the throng,
    And yet in his heart alone![8]

The only wight that approached at will,
    Without a regal command,
An old, old slave on the brink of the grave,
    With a broom in his trembling hand.

"Come hither, slave!" the monarch said,
    "And tell me truly why
Thou comest alone unto the throne
    And fearest not to die?"

"It is because," the old slave said,
    "My duty never goes
Any nearer thy thought than the sole of thy foot,
    Or nearer thy heart than thy toes."

"Is is said and well," the king replied;
    "But happily now, it appears,
That head and feet together must meet —
    The king and his slave as peers.

" Come, sit thee down upon this couch,"
    And talk as a brother with me;
And what I may that thou canst say,
    That will I do for thee."

The old slave sate beside the king,
    And spake with freedom and ease,
Of shadows that crept on the floor as he swept,
    And of dust that made persons sneeze.

" And nothing more," the old slave said;
    " Than only this, will I say,
That, if thou would'st prove thy daughter's love
    I might suggest the way.

" Condemn the sculptor to be slain
    Within the princess's sight;
And as her heart will play its part,
    So let thy mercy or might.

" And what thou mayest that I can say —
    I trust, I do not presume;
I pray thee, my lord, be as good as thy word,
    And buy me a new broom! "

The guards and executioners
    Were summoned to the king;
And as his word was spoken and heard,
    Arranged was everything.

The day arrived; on the palace porch,
    The king and princess sate,
The bloody mound in sight and sound
    Of the eye and tongue of state.

Oh, pale, pale was the princess's face,
    And ashen were her lips;
While her eyes were bright with a muffled might
    That moved at her finger-tips.

But never a sigh escaped her breast,
    Her beating heart to check,
Till the collar of stone was taken down
    And hung on the victim's neck.

When hark! as the flash of the uplifted blade
    Gleamed in the staring eye,
What a rousing cheer divides the ear
    With a baby's piercing cry?

And lo! three thousand men of might,
    With swords and arrows drawn,
Appeared before the palace door,
    A menace to the throne!

And in their midst, in a woman's arms,
    A baby richly dressed,
A brilliant red plume on its head,
    And gold upon its breast!

Before the king the princess fell;
    "My father, lord of lords,
Withhold thine hand and thy command,
    And listen to my words.

"I am thy child, borne by thy queen,
    A princess by birth-right;
But, as a slave, O king, would'st thou have
    Me ever in thy sight!

"Within thy palace walls confined,
    A trembling, troubled thrall,
Beneath the hand of thy command,
    In blood, on every wall!"[10]

"Till, of all the evil things of earth,
    I shunned thee, growth-inwrought,
A thing apart from thee, my heart,
    And a dream undreamed, my thought!

"And when thou would'st repress my love,
    As truly told to thee,
Thou taught'st me how to thee to do,
    As thou did'st unto me.

"When, with the spy behind the screen,
    Thou taughtest me deceit,
It was I, apt I, that made the bird fly
    By pinching hard its feet!

"And not its fear of the scratching chay,
    Familiar to its ear,
As the warning word in the sound I heard,
    When I drew listlessly near!

"And when, O king, beside my bed,
    Thou stolest in the night,
It was I that shook the child till it woke,
    And cried out in affright —

"A child that never before nor since,
    Within thy daughter's bed,
Has mocked the charms of another's arms,
    Asleep in another's stead.

"And when, O king, the gaunt she-wolf
    Tore the parrot from the earth,
It was I that made the mock parade
    To conceal my baby's birth.

"For why, my lord, the jealous bird
    Flew at the baby's eyes,
And repeated the word of endearment heard,
    And mimicked the baby's cries."

"And when a servant killed the bird,
    For its tell-tale tongue and spite,
I wept indeed, as the old man said,
    And buried the bird in the night—

"Cutting here the sod, to deceive the slaves
    That skulked in my path as spies,
And laying it where the wolf might tear
    It out before thine eyes.

"And now, O king, lest thou might'st slay
    The sculptor in my sight,
It did behoove me in my love
    To summon all my might.

"Hear then, O king, and mark each word;
    These three things have I done,
To guide thy hand and give command
    And secure the crown for my son.

"First, I have bound thy body-guard,
    With their trust in a mother's love,
More firmly to me than their fear of thee,
    At their mercy, can remove.

"And in their midst, I have placed my child,
    That, whatsoever hap
To him beneath the dagger of death,
    Their future king may escape.

" Next, I have found a culprit slave,
    For the ransom of his head,
To risk his life beneath the knife,
    In my baby's father's stead —

" Who, in the guise of thine old slave,
    That sweeps with a new broom,
At thine elbow stands with a sword in his hands
    To determine, if need be, thy doom!

" While, third, my lord, I have closed the door
    Behind thy unguarded back,
That thou mayest give what I will receive,
    Or, otherwise, will take —

" Thy crown, in trust for the sculptor's son,
    The issue of my womb,
In exchange for what revealed thy plot,
    The reward of thy slave, this broom! "

The king uprose in a murderous mood,
    And hurled to the ground his crown;
Then, stamping his plume, he seized the broom,
    And sank into a swown.

The princess tore from the sculptor his mask,
    While the welkin loud did ring,
And placed upon his head the crown,
    And pronounced him her husband and King!

And hark! what word is that that cuts
    Like a knife through the startled air?
A word of command to stay a hand,
    And the culprit's life to spare!

And that faint cry afar in the throng
    That rises above the din?
The fleetest run and fetch the son
    That has made his mother the Queen!

With the prince upon her bosom laid,
    Before the surging crowd,
The queen, endeared to all, appeared,
    And spake to them aloud.

"So be it ever with woman and man,
    When they all risks will run,
Their faithful love in each other to prove,
    And save or daughter or son!

"So be it ever that plot will meet
    Its counterplot in turn,
That the strong from the weak and the harsh from
    the meek,
    The rule of right may learn!

"So be it ever as it has been
    Unto the slave and king!
Resound the trumpet and the drum,
    And let the welkin ring!"

---

[1] Palenque! Yes; it is a word of Spanish origin and signifies a stockade, an enclosure of palisades, or, if you will, a corral. But what of that? Does not our word *Court*, the palace of a king and all its appurtenances, persons, plate, politeness, pusillanimity, and power — does not our own word Court signify, etymologically, a stockyard, or cattle-pen?

[2] "In *lief* . . . . we have a positive which has lost, almost beyond recovery, its once very popular comparative degrees, and is itself fast growing obsolete. It has been so completely set aside that few are aware of its close relationship with the Anglo-Saxon verb *leofan*, our *love*, and its connection with the Old English *leman*, once *liefman* and *lefman*, the dear one, and as such continually used of both sexes." — SCHELE DE VERE.

[3] "Don Miguel had a collection of chay or flint stones, cut in the shape of arrow-heads, which he thought, and Don Miguel was no fool, were the instruments employed (by the

sculptors of Copan.) They were sufficiently hard to scratch into the stone. Perhaps by men accustomed to the use of them, the whole of these deep relief ornaments might have been scratched, but the chay stones themselves looked as if they had been cut by metal." — STEPHENS: *Central America, ect.*, i. 154.

⁴ "The High Priest had in his Hand a large, broad, and sharp Knife made of Flint. Another Priest carried a wooden collar wrought like a snake. The persons to be sacrificed were conducted one by one up the steps, stark naked, and as soon as laid on the Stone, had the Collar put upon their Necks, and the four priests took hold of the hands and feet. Then the High Priest with wonderful Dexterity ripped up the Breast, tore out the Heart, reeking, with his Hands, and showed it to the Sun, offering him the Heart and Stream that came from it. Then he turned to the Idol, and threw it in his face, which done, he kicked the body down the steps, and it never stopped till it came to the bottom, because they were very upright." — COGOLLUDO, cited by STEPHENS: *Travels in Yucatan*, i. 317.

As far as the knowledge of the writer goes, this is the only instance of the use of wooden collars; whereas a number of stone collars have been brought from Ceneral America, the use of which — a puzzle to archæologists — is presumed to have been that ascribed to them in the poem.

⁵ That it was possible to engrave by the light of the fire-fly (*Elater noctilucus*) of Central America, several of the beetles being fastened to a stick to make a torch, or confined in a cage to constitute a lantern, see COWAN's *Curious History of Insects*, pp. 51-4. Curiously, too, by the light of a single beetle, in the Palace of Palenque, were the scene of the poem is laid, STEPHENS reports that he was able to "read distinctly the finely-printed pages of an American newspaper." — *Central America, ect.*, ii. p. 302.

⁶ " The principal doorway (of the Palace of Palenque,) is not distinguished by its size or by any superior ornament, but is indicated only by a range of broad stone steps leading up to it on the terrace. The doorways have no doors, nor are there the remains of any. Within, on each side, are three niches in the wall, about eight or ten inches square, with a cylindrical stone about two inches in diameter, fixed upright, by which perhaps a door was secured. Along the cornice outside, projecting about a foot beyond the front, holes were drilled at intervals through the stone; and our impression was, that an immense cotton cloth, running the whole length of the building, perhaps painted in a style corresponding with the

ornaments, was attached to this cornice, and raised and lowered like a curtain, according to the exigencies of sun and rain. Such a curtain is used now in front of the piazzas of some haciendas in Yucatan." — *Ibid.* ii. 312. On the doors at Uxmal that opened and shut, see STEPHENS: *Travels in Yucatan*, i. 324.

⁷ *She-wolf:* a clumsy combination to express sex, of ancient and honorable usage, but now no longer employed by careful writers. FULLER has *she*-saint and *she*-devil; SHAKESPEARE, *she*-Mercury; ADDISON, *she*-knight-errant and *she*-Machiavel; and BYRON, *she*-parade and *she*-condition.

⁸ In writing these lines the presence of ANDREW JOHNSON, the President of the United States, was ever before me, as I have described him in an article entitled *Reminiscences of his Private Life and Character*, published in the Pittsburgh *Leader*, Sunday, 22 August, 1875, the concluding paragraph of which I reproduce here:

"In conclusion, I may say that during the last years of his presidential term of office, MR. JOHNSON, on account of his physical suffering, his domestic cares and anxieties, and his hard, inflexible, and persistent manner of thinking, reasoning, and talking, of working, of doing everything, was lonely in the centre of forty millions of people, and unhappy even to miserable, on that pinnacle of power, of one of the mightiest nations of the globe, to which the eyes of myriads are turned as to the greatest happiness on earth! He was too great to be companionable, and his own philosophy teaches that he paid the penalty of his greatness in loneliness and misery."

⁹ For lack of a better word, let "couch" pass for the seat which is represented among the sculptures at Palenque and elsewhere. The principal figure, supposed to be a queen or princess, represented in the elliptical tablet at Palenque, sits cross-legged on a couch the arms or sides of which are ornamented each with a panther's head. The leg and foot of another couch, with panther's head and feet, in stucco at Palenque, are said by Stephens to be "elegant specimens of art and models of study."

¹⁰ Concerning the Red Hand, depicted, on the walls of the palaces and temples of Central America, as if an open hand smeared with paint had been pressed against the plaster or stone, see STEPHENS: *Travels in Yucatan*, ii. 46. The Indians say it represents the hand of the master of the building, which, I presume, signifies, a mark of individual ownership or authority, analogous to the indenture of the olden time in England, and the signature to-day.

"The writer has known a Mexican parrot to exhibit its jealousy in the manner detailed in the poem, biting children caressed in its presence, and then imitating their cries of pain and fear.

FREYDISA.

After Biarne had coasted along the shores of America, (in 986,) and Leif had effected a settlement in Vinland, (in 1000,) and Thorwald had sailed to more southern regions of the new found land, (in 1002,) and Thorstein had made his unsuccessful attempt to bring back the body of his brother from its resting-place at Crossness, (in 1005,) and Thorfinn Karlsefne, commanding one ship, and Biarne Grimolfson and Thorhall Gamlason commanding a second, and Thorvard, intermarried with FREYDISA, the natural daughter of Eric the Red, commanding the third, had returned from their memorable expedition, (in 1007-11,)—after these events had taken place, in the year 1012, FREYDISA, the aforesaid, the half-sister of the brothers Leif, Thorwald, and Thorstein, prevailed on two Norwegian brothers, Helge and Finboge, to make another expedition to Vinland, in partnership or as a joint venture: (the gray mare being the better horse, evidently,) she and her husband, Thorvard, fitting out one ship, and the brothers another; the number of men being limited to thirty each, and the number of women left indefinite. FREYDISA, however, contrived to secrete in her vessel five more men than her complement. And so they set sail from Greenland. And no sooner had they landed than they began to quarrel, FREYDISA compelling the brothers to build new boothes for themselves, and leave to her those which Leif had built twelve years before; and so they continued in strife, until, before the winter was over, FREYDISA incited her husband and men to murder the rival crew. This was done in the most atrocious manner. While asleep, the victims were surprised and bound as prisoners; and while they were led one by one from the booth, FREYDISA found a willing hand to slaughter the men, but neither her husband nor one of her crew would kill the women, five in number, who belonged to the Norwegian vessel: for reasons which served only to exasperate FREYDISA the more. Whereupon, she seized an axe and butchered them herself.

This is the first tragedy of America of which there is an authentic account. It is related in the Codex Flateyensis, a memorable MS. of the fourteenth century — a history which Rafn has reproduced in part, with Danish and Latin translations, in his quarto, published in 1837, to which the curious reader is referred for sufficient evidence to warrant the following idealization and elaboration of the character of our horrible heroine of the North.

There is one characteristic of the FREYDISA of the poem, however, of which there is no hint in history beyond the fact that her father, old Eric the Red, whom she seemed to repeat in the guise of a woman, was very reluctant to exchange his old religion and familiar, namely, the worship of the gods which had been evolved from the terrible objective conflicts of Frost and Fire in the north of Europe, for the new and strange, namely, the worship of the Christ Crucified which had been developed from the equally terrible but subjective conflicts of passion and penitence in central Asia: a fact which fancy has seized to make FREYDISA, accordingly, the last of her race to represent the religion of the North in opposition to the religion of the South which was introduced into Greenland but a few years before her departure for Vinland: the circumstance of her sex, moreover, being of significant avail in the antithesis.

While, for the doom of FREYDISA, this only is recorded: that after the confession of three of her crew, who had been put on the rack, by Leif, he said, " I cannot be induced to turn against my sister; but this I will divine, that her issue will never have the prosperity of their peers." "And so it came to pass," the saga-smith has added, "that from that time they were held in detestation."

Oh, for a sip of Kvasir's [1] blood,
 With a draught from Mimer's [2] well,
Or the tuneful tongue with which Bragi [3] sung,
 My terrible tale to tell!

But the blood is spilt and the well is dry,
 And wishing no help affords;
From the Ragnarok [4] of the past to invoke,
 Now nothing remains but words.

But words, vague sounds with a vaguer sense,
    Instinct with thought no more
Than the shapes of bones in shattered stones
    Are the beasts and birds of yore.

———

Freydisa stands on the sandy shore
    Of Vinland's new-found coast,
And with many a curse in nautical Norse
    Begins her blasphemous boast.

"It is time that Christ has come upon earth,
    Proclaiming Peace and Love,
Life's strength to the weak, death's delights to the
        meek,
    The eagle's prize to the dove!

"For of all the men and women of old
    To rejoice when the deed is done,
And to ride on the blast that has wrecked the past,
    There now remains but one!

"But one upon earth to murder for mirth,
    As well as for lust and gain;
To bathe in the flood of the hot gushing blood,
    And rejoice in the ruddy stain!

"But one to slaughter from dawn to dusk,
    And from dusk to dawn carouse;
With blood to fill full a foeman's skull,
    And drink Valhalla's[5] joys!

"But one, the daughter of Eric the Red,
    On this strange island cast,
With a Christian groom to determine her doom,
    Of the viking race, the last!

"Unless in a storm the red-bearded Thor[6]
    As a worthy wooer will come,
And, while thunders crash, with a lightning flash
    Illumine with life her womb!"

The while, in the gleam of the midday sun,
    Freydisa gloats in glee
O'er a sight — since unseen in Vinland, I ween,
    For which, Christ glorified be!

Full five and thirty shallow graves
    Upon a bloody strand,
With, uncovered there, a mass of hair,
    And here a foot or hand.

And here, upon a woman's face,
    An eyeball staring wild,
And there agape a mangled shape —
    A belly big with child!

While beast and bird and slimy slug,
    Left by the ebbing tide,
Together feed with ravenous greed
    On the corpses side by side.

"Come, come, ye little wolves and weak,
    Come, gorge your gullets in haste,
Lest ye may see there remains with me
    A wolf-whelp of the past —

"A Garm[7] to gulp ye down in a trice,
    While his howl is still in your ears;
Or a Fenrir[8] to feed with insatiate greed
    Till this island itself disappears!

"Come, come, ye puny crows and vile,
　　Come, gorge your gullets in haste,
Lest ye may see there remains with me
　　A raven of the past—

"One of the twain that over the world
　　Take their diurnal flight,
That Odin's[9] ear all things may hear,
　　When they rest on his shoulders at night—

"A Hugin to swoop, in his hurried flight,
　　And clutch ye in his claw;
Or a Mugin[10] to break ye in his beak
　　And mince ye in his maw!

"Come, come, ye shriveled shrimps and prawns,
　　Come, gorge your gullets in haste,
Lest ye may see there remains with me
　　A Kraken of the past—

"Lest ye may see this island sink,
　　And above it the Maelstrom come,
With its widening whorl and seething swirl,
　　To wash ye into foam!

"Come, come, ye degenerate things of earth,
　　Ye fit companions of Man,
Who kneels and prays, in these latter days,
　　Afeared to do what he can!

"While of all the men and women of old,
　　To bury the dead with more dead,
There remains but one, a woman alone,
　　The daughter of Eric the Red!"

The while bold Thorvard and his crew
    Sit in Leif's boothes near by,
At their noonday board with food well stored
    From the murdered Norwegians' supply.

When behold! Freydisa, the Bloody, appears!
    Advancing from the strand,
An axe upon her shoulders of brawn,
    A woman's head in her hand!

Upon the board she lays the head —
    " Here is the face so fair,
The promised meed to ye all for the deed —
    Now, let each take his share!

"What! will ye flee from Beauty's self
    In horror and affright?
Ye, caitiffs base, of a pitiful race,
    Go, get ye from my sight!"

Freydisa stands, in the light of the moon,
    On a rock of Vinland's coast,
And with many a curse in nautical Norse,
    Resumes her blasphemous boast.

The rising tide in billows rolls,
    Till, sweeping o'er the strand
The surging waves lay open the graves
    And lift the dead from the sand —

And lift the mangled dead from the sand,
    And toss them about in their might,
The lightest of toys and the brightest of joys
    Within Freydisa's sight.

The wind howls with increasing din;
    The clouds close fast and thick;
The lightnings crack the black lid of rack;
    The thunder follows quick.

A jutting crag, of ragged rock,
    High-hanging overhead,
With a deaffening crash and o'erwhelming splash,
    Falls among the floating dead!

The very earth sways to and fro,
    The sea goes up and down;
Still, unmoved by the shock, on the quivering rock,
    Freydisa stands alone!

"Hurrah! hurrah! for the giants of old,
    In whose majestic mirth,
There is one to rejoice with a human voice,
    The last of her race upon earth!

"But higher still, rise higher, ye waves —
    Into the sight of Thor,
These dead uphold their tale to unfold
    Of Freydisa's valor in war!

"Yea, higher still, as if enraged
    The Midgard Serpent shook —
As if again he felt the pain
    Of the Redbeard's barbèd hook!"[11]

"And louder still, roar louder, ye winds—
  Lift up Freydisa's voice
Above the cloud to resound aloud
  And make the Æsir [12] rejoice!

"Yea, louder still, ye roaring winds—
  As if Hræsvelgur [13] spread
His wings to sweep across the deep
  And strengthened ye as ye sped!

"And nearer still, ye lightnings strike,
  That ye may be caressed,
Till I feel the fire of a worthy sire
  In the blood that burns in my breast!

"Yea, nearer still, ye lightnings of Thor!
  Come, make my bosom your bed,
That I live not the last of a race of the past,
  The daughter of Eric the Red!"

The while bold Thorvard and his crew
  Cower in the boothes in fear;
As if Ragnarök were in every stroke
  Of the lightning so threatening and near.

Until lo! Freydisa, returning, appears,
  Revealed, in the dazzling light,
A giant in stature, in form, and feature,
  In their bewildered sight!

When, with a common terror seized,
  They flee into the storm,
Perchance behind a rock to find
  A screen to the fearful form!

"What! will ye flee from a woman's charms —
    A bosom bared at midnight?
Ye, caitiffs base, of a pitiful race,
    Go, get ye from my sight!"

For Greenland, ho! the sail is set,
    And what though the sea be rough,
Freydisa stands with the helm in her hands
    And bids the boat be off!

Away the ship Skidbladnir[14] speeds
    Before the bellying blast,
Till, in the foam of her northern home,
    At anchor she lies fast.

When, amid the greetings and merry meetings,
    A score of voices cry,
"But where are they of Noroway?"
    We cannot their sail descry?"

Then up and speaks Freydisa forthwith,
    And answers one and all,
"Wrecked off the coast of Vinland and lost,
    And now in Hela's[15] hall."

"But where got ye these well-known arms,
    And the jewels your neck bedeck?"
"We stripped the dead, in the white sand laid,
    Recovered from the wreck."

"But why this bloody, bloody axe,
    And this mat of a woman's hair?"
"I severed a vein to ease my pain,
    And cast my combings there."

But many shake their heads in doubt,
    And gather in groups afar,
Where the muttered word cannot be heard
    By the terrible woman of war.

And when Freydisa sleeps, behold,
    Ten daring men and true,
Creep along the sands, and, with smothering hands,
    Bear away three of her crew.

And afar hence in a secret place,
    They break them on the wheel,
Till, with gasping breath in the fear of death,
    Freydisa's deeds they reveal.

"Ye lie! ye lie! ye cowards accursed!"
    A voice cries in the night;
And with the word Freydisa's sword
    Gleams in the flickering light!

Surprised and aghast, the torturing ten
    Into the darkness flee;
The light is quenched — and Freydisa's sword drenched
    In the blood of the tortured three!

"And ye, Freydisa and her crew
    To her enemies would betray?
Ye cowards accursed, of my foemen the worst,
    Get ye to Hela, away!"

The days and weeks and months and years
    Speed in their ceaseless flight,
Till Freydisa stands with a staff in her hands,
    And in rags and tatters bedight.

When a little old hag, not as high as her hip,
    Before Freydisa appears,
And mocks the alarms in her trembling arms
    And the tortures in her tears.

Freydisa grapples with the hag
    To hurl her in the hall,
But falls herself before the elf,
    And breaks her staff in her fall.

And behold! as she rises in her wrath
    And gasps for breath and fast,
She bends on the half of her broken staff
    At herself in horror at last!

Her face scored with the hag's long nails;
    The hairs of her head torn out;
Her every brawn and thew and bone
    An ache from head to foot.

Albeit, she grapples the hag again,
    To fall, as she fell before;
But on all fours to rise, with sightless eyes,
    And her teeth scattered on the floor.

When, lifting a feeble, faltering hand,
    To grope for the hag in her rage,
She falls, nevermore to rise from the floor
    To wrestle in vain with Old Age!

To wrestle in vain with Elli,[15] like Thor,
    In the olden, olden time,
When the gods, begot in the saga-smith's thought,
    Wrought wonders in runic rime.

Freydisa writhes in her wretched plight,
　　Deaf in the thunder's din,
And blind in the gleam of the summer sun's
　　　beam,
　　But not in the dream of Sin!

She sees, in Náströnd's [17] venom vat
　　Afloat a horrible head,
With the face of the last of her race of the past,
　　The daughter of Eric the Red!

While, from a wicker-woven roof
　　Of serpents of monstrous size,
The venom drips from lurid lips
　　Into the upturned eyes!

And three long fingers point at the face,
　　As if, from out the gloom,
The Sisters [18] of old in silence foretold
　　Freydisa's eternal doom!

But still she mutters the curse of her youth,
　　Till her lips and tongue are dumb —
Till, with latest breath, she mumbles to Death,
　　"It is time that Christ has come!"

The while, nor man, nor woman, nor child
　　To succor or soothe comes near;
But keeps aloof from the outcast's roof,
　　In shuddering horror and fear.

Until, upon a heap of bones,
　　The rotting rafters fall,
And the mould of years in turn appears,
　　A cover to one and all —

To one and all of the women and men
   Of the olden, olden time,
When the gods, begot in the saga-smith's thought,
   Wrought wonders in runic rime.

Leaving nothing behind in fancy to find
   But an echo that never is dumb,
Repeating the last of the words of the past,
   " It is time that Christ has come!"

---

[1] Why poetry is called in Scandinavian lore, Kvásir's blood, Suttung's mead, the dwarf's ransom, Odin's booty, Odin's gift, the beverage of the gods, ect., is told in the second part of the *Prose Edda*, commonly called the *Conversations of Bragi*.

[2] " But under the root [of the ash Yggdrasill] that stretches out towards the Frost-giants there is Mimir's well, in which wisdom and wit lie hidden. The owner of this well is called Mimir, [Memory, Mind.] He is full of wisdom, because he drinks the waters of the well from the horn Gjöll every morning. One day All-father came and begged a draught of this water, which he obtained, but was obliged to leave one of his eyes as a pledge for it." — *The Prose Edda*.

[3] "'There is another god,' continued Har, 'named Bragi, who is celebrated for his wisdom, and more especially for his eloquence and correct forms of speech. He is not only eminently skilled in poetry, but the art itself is called from his name *Bragr*, which epithet is also applied to denote a distinguished poet or poetess.'" — *The Prose Edda*. See poem on Valhalla, *ante* p. 87.

[4] Ragnarök: literally, the gods beracked, or beclouded : hence, the end of the world, the destruction of the universe.

[5] See poem on Valhalla, or the Hall of the Chosen, *ante* p. 85.

[6] See poem on Norway, *ante* p. 39.

[7] In the Grímnis-mal, st. 43, Garm is styled the first of hounds, as Bragi is of bards, the Yggrasill of trees, Odin of

the Æsir, etc.; and in the Eddaic account of Ragnarök, he is described as a fearful monster. "That day the dog Garm, who had been chained in the Gnipa cave, breaks loose. He is the most fearful monster of all, and attacks Tyr, and they kill each other."

⁸ See poem on Norway, *ante* p. 38.

⁹ Etymologically considered, Odin, Wodin, or God, is the Sense of Sight idealized, personified, and deified. It is synonymous with the Seeing One or the Wise. See poem on Valhalla, *ante* p. 85.

¹⁰ Hugin and Munin are Spirit and Mind mythologized — the former being confounded with or compounding Thought, Reason, and the like; and the latter, Memory. And wherefore symbollized in the form of ravens, see poem on Valhalla, *ante* p. 86.

¹¹ How Thor went to fish for the Midgard Serpent is told in *The Prose Edda*. This mythological reptile is not only a reminder of the Asiatic origin of the Scandinavians, but an involution of the great cuttle-fish of the Norwegian seas: its long serpent-like tentacles converting the real serpent of the land into an ideal monster of the ocean — the horizon symbollized. See poem on Norway, *ante* p. 36.

¹² Etymologically, Æsir means the beings; mythologically, the Gods of the Scandinavian Creed. Cf. our word *is*.

¹³ See poem on Norway, *ante* p. 37.

> "Hræsvelgur's the giant,
> Who on heaven's edge sits
> In the guise of an eagle;
> And the winds, it is said,
> Rush down on the earth
> From his outspreading pinions."—
> *Vafthrudnis-mál*, st. 37.

¹⁴ So called after the mythological ship of the Scandinavians.

"'What hast thou to say,' demanded Gangler, 'of Skidbladnir, which thou toldst me was the best of ships? Is there no other ship as good or as large?'

"'Skidbladnir,' replied Har, 'is without doubt the best and most artfully constructed of any, but the ship Naglfar is of larger size. They were dwarfs, the sons of Ivaldi, who built Skidbladnir, and made a present of her to Frey. She is so large that all the Æsir with their weapons and war stores find room on board her. As soon as the sails are set a favorable breeze arises and carries her to her place of destination; and she is made of so many pieces, and with so much skill, that when she is not wanted for a voyage Frey may fold her together like a piece of cloth, and put her in his pocket." — *Prose Edda*.

[15] Hela, etymologically the same as English *Chill*, Latin *Gelu*; mythologically, a personification of the chill and rigidness of death, the Goddess of the Frigid Regions of Death; and strangely now — the whirligig of time ever making the globe and all which it inherit a world of widdershins — our Hell, where, according to popular notions, the souls of the wicked are punished by *fire*.

[16] How Thor wrestled with Elli, (a personification of Old Age,) is told in the narrative of his adventures while on his journey to the Land of the Giants, in *The Prose Edda*.

[17] "In Náströnd there is a vast and direful structure with doors that face the north. It is formed entirely of the backs of serpents, wattled together like wicker-work. But the serpents' heads are turned towards the inside of the hall, and continually vomit forth floods of venom, in which wade all those who commit murder, or who forswear themselves, [or commit adultery.] As it is said in the Völuspá, st. 34, 35 —

'She saw a hall
Far from the sun
In Náströnd standing.
Northward the doors look,
And venom-drops
Fall in through loopholes.
Formed is that hall
Of wreathèd serpents.

'There saw she wade,
Though heavy streams,
Men forsworn
And murderers,
And those who others' wives
Essayed to blandish.'" — *The Prose Edda*.

[18] The Weird Sisters. "Near the fountain which is under the ash, [Yggdrasill,] stands a very beauteous dwelling, out of which go three maidens, named Urd, Verdandi, and Skuld, [*i. e.*, the Present, Past, and Future.] These maidens fix the lifetime of all men, and are called Norns. But there are, indeed, many other Norns; for, when a man is born, there is a Norn to determine his fate." — *The Prose Edda*.

THE WITCH TRAGEDY OF SALEM.

To the physiologist, the popular delusion with respect to witches which culminated at Salem, Massachusetts, on the 22nd day of September, in the year 1692, presents the most striking and instructive example in the annals of America of the subversion of human nature that results whenever the subjective idea — the "thought" of the following poem — becomes more potent than the objective reality — the "thing" — in moving mankind to attain their ends. At the place and time mentioned, eight persons, who had been condemned as witches, (albeit, of both sexes, and "persons of knowledge, holiness, and devotion," as admitted by the Reverend Mr. PARRIS, the most distinguished of the deluded divines who played a part in the tragedy,) were executed on the gallows; after perhaps a score or more had been hung, or pressed to death beneath weights, during the development of the delusion in the Puritan settlements of New England: for the details of which the reader is referred to the *Records of Salem Witchcraft*, copied from original documents, and printed for W. ELLIOT WOODWARD, at Roxbury, Mass., in 1864, and the two volumes of CHARLES W. UPHAM, a monograph on the subject, published in Boston, in 1867; before the publication of which works, it seems the subject was regarded generally rather as a jest than a matter of serious contemplation for the historian and philosopher, and the most improbable event in the memory of man to inspire the pen of a poet.

Whirling in and out, the world without
    Becomes the world within;
The thousand things a poet sings
    Another course begin
In the brain of man, as whims and dreams
    Of sanctity and sin.

Thus, all the things that lengthen Life,
　　In every form of food,
Of earth and air, of water and fire,
　　Become so many thoughts of good,
That gather upon a good king's throne
　　And evolve into a God.

While all the things that shorten Life,
　　From the whirlwind and the weevil,
To the tortures accursed of hunger and thirst,
　　Become so many thoughts of evil,
That jump to ape the worst man's shape
　　And develope into a Devil.

Until, side by side, within the brain,
　　At constant jog and jar,
These shadows engage in youth and age
　　In everlasting war;
For so without the human thought
　　In conflict all things are.

Until, turning inside out the man —
　　The slave of the shadows within —
Divides the world around him whirled
　　Into halves that never have been:
A heaven above of goodness and love,
　　And a hell below of sin.

And all mankind this slave as well
　　Divides into bad and good;
His self-esteem ever ranging him,
　　With a most complacent nod,
Albeit imbrued with a victim's blood,
　　The first in the service of God.

And all that doubt and differ with him,
    He damns as the Devil's own,
Albeit flesh of his fruitful flesh
    And bone of his bodily bone;
His might making right to kill at will
    His sister, sire, or son.

Until, behold! the City of Peace [1]
    The City of War become!
The virtue and worth, the music and mirth
    Of the goodman's happy home
Converted to ill-will and woe,
    The dungeon and the tomb!

Until Murder, in mask, in the pulpit stands,
    The vicar of God, to tell
Of the secret marks that stand for the sparks
    Of the burning brands of hell,[2]
And of the reward in heaven prepared
    For him that to quench will quell!

Until Guilt, in disguise, sits on the bench,[3]
    And Innocence pleads in vain,
While Malice and Spite, Revenge and Hate,
    Ill-will and Greed of Gain
The jury compose in human clothes
    To do the deed of Cain!

Until, behold! upon the hill,
    Against the midnight sky,
Eight gibbets swing in the storm, and sing,
    And dance as the blast sweeps by —
Was ever God so debased to the sod,
    And the Devil exalted so high!

Eight gibbets swing and eight gibbets dance!
    Albeit burdened each
With a victim of Vice, condemned in a trice,
    And hung without halt or hitch —
Incorporate evil in league with the Devil,
    A shadow of shadows, a Witch!

Not a thing that exists in the world without
    The human skull and brain;
But a monster begot in the womb of thought
    And born again and again,
Until the fact confronts an act
    And proves it abortive and vain.

Until, behold! in the pulpit, now,
    In sackcloth and ashes cast,
Repentant Remorse bending over a corse,
    From the gibbet agape and aghast,
And with many a moan and gruesome groan,
    In vain recalling the Past![4]

While, in ermined state and with wisdom's wig,
    Sits Reversal in Judgment, distraught,
In vain with wereguild to compound for the killed,
    And untie the gallows'-knot
By annulling the law unable to draw
    The line between Thing and Thought![5]

Until, behold! the City of War
    The City of Peace, forsooth;
The Thing and the Thought together brought
    Into the relation of Truth;

2P

And the Witches of Old, a tale to be told
By Age in teaching Youth.⁶

---

¹ The signification of the word *Salem*.

² When, on the fearful 22nd of September, the Reverend MR. NOYES, the worthy coadjutor of MR. PARRIS and COTTON MATHER, stood looking at the execution, he exclaimed that it was a sad sight to see eight firebrands of hell hanging there!

³ When the delusion had abated and the prisoners were discharged by proclamation by SIR WILLIAM PHIPPS, Chief Justice STOUGHTON retired from the courts in obstinate rage at his conflicts with Satan having been cut short.

⁴ The Reverend MR. PARRIS said, "I do humbly own this day, before the Lord and his people, that God has been righteously spitting in my face; and I desire to lie low under all this reproach," etc.

⁵ Judge SEWALL, in full assembly, made a penitential acknowledgment of his error. The excommunications of REBECCA NURSE and GILES COREY were canceled. While in 1711, the authorities of the Province, with the sanction of the Council of QUEEN ANNE, made a grant to the representatives of REBECCA NURSE of £25; to those of MRS. EASTY, £20, etc.

⁶ "This Salem story is indeed shocking in every view — to our pride as rational beings, to our faith as Christians, to our complacency as children of the Reformation. It is so shocking that some of us may regret that the details have been revived with such an abundance of evidence. But this is no matter of regret, but rather of congratulation, if we have not outgrown the need of admonition from the past. How does that consideration stand?

"At the end of nearly three centuries we find ourselves relieved of a heavy burden of fear and care about the perpetual and unbounded malice of Satan and his agents. Witchcraft has ceased to be one of the gravest curses of the human lot. We have parted with one after another of the fetish or conjectural persuasions about our relations with the world of spirit or mind, regarded as in direct opposition to the world of matter. By a succession of discoveries we have been led to an essentially different view of life and thought from any dreamed of before the new birth of science; and at this day, and in our own metropolis [London,] we have Sir Henry Holland telling us how certain treatment of this or that department of the nervous system will generate this or that state of belief and experience, as well as sensation. We have Dr. Carpenter disclosing facts of incalculable significance about brain-action without consciousness, and other vital mysteries. We have Dr. Maudsley showing, in the cells of the lunatic asylum, not only the very realm of Satan, as our fathers would have thought, but the discovery that it is not Satan after all, that makes the havoc, but our own ignorance which has seduced us into a blasphemous superstition, instead of inciting us to the study of ourselves." — *Edinburgh Review*, July, 1868, p. 24.

Curiously, too, in the able review of Mr. Upham's work, here cited, the writer makes no allusion to the fact that, during the seventeenth century, for every person executed as a witch in America, a thousand were executed in England alone for this imaginary crime: Mr. Mackey, in his *Memoirs of Extraordinary Popular Delusions*, estimating the number of those sacrificed in the course of the century specified in England at forty thousand!

END OF THE POEMS LIKE FERN-LEAVES FOUND IN SHALE.

SAGE, RUE, AND THYME.

The old saw's Sage and Rue,
That, in my garden grew,
With "pun-provoking" Thyme,
On the rocky Ridge of Rhyme.

SAGE, RUE, AND THYME.

—1864—

THE LEGEND OF THE WEEPING WILLOW

The maple leaves were weaving shrouds
    Of colors bright and gay,
From Autumn's gold and purple clouds
    That deck the dying day.

When down the way a lady fair
    Rode merrily with me;
While loosely hung her auburn hair
    From ribband fetters free.

Near Fanny's Wood, then, as we rode,
    The lady, pointing, said,
"See yonder willow[1] by the wood
    That, weeping, bows its head!"

"Yes," answer'd I. Continued she,
  "A legend touching, true,
Has made the same tree dear to me —
  Would like it told to you?"

"Yes; thanks. A tale but told by you
  Was ever dear to me."
She, sighing, told this Legend true
  Of the Weeping Willow-tree.

———

When, two and fifty years ago, (1812)
  The fearful tocsin rung,
War! war! against an English foe,
  To right our country's wrong!

A soldier, young and gallant, rode
  To bid a last adieu
To one who dwelt within this wood,
  A maid, his sweetheart true.

Down yonder hill, with slackened rein,
  His way he sadly led;
The horse partook his master's pain
  And lowly hung his head.

A lithe and slender willow wand —
  The rider's only goad —
Hung loosely in the soldier's hand
  As on he slowly rode.

And as he passed this flowing spring,
  He startled at a sound, —
He heard his loved one sweetly sing, —
  The switch fell to the ground.

THE LEGEND OF THE WEEPING-WILLOW.

To yonder oak the horse was tied;
  The rod, unthought-of, lay
Till found by the intended bride,
  And waves this tree to-day.²

" Farewell. Within the coming year,
  If then the Briton's fled,
I'll come again to thee, my dear,
  If not, believe me dead.

" A soldier idly speaks of death,
  Then start not at the name;
With him 'tis but an empty breath,
  Another word for fame.

" But if I live — a happy life,
  Return I then to lead,
To live, to love, with thee, my wife — "
  Her thought of death was fled.

For th' hope of love dreams not of death,
  Of happiness alone;
It twines not in its flowery wreath
  The weed of deadly tone.

Her eyes, though tearful, quickly shone
  With inward love-warmth true:
Like blue-bells turning to the sun
  When wet with morning's dew.

" Then fare thee well. A woman's love
  Hopes, prays the same come true,
Yes, nightly prays to Him above
  To keep from danger you.

"A year, though long the time it seems,
    And much of sorrow brings,
Yet, happy thoughts and happy dreams
    Will lend it swiftest wings.

"And if, forsooth, you come not then?
    See yonder ivy spread
Its leaves so fresh and green, e'en when
    The oak it clings to's dead."

"A noble vow," the soldier said,
    "Of faithful love out-spoken;
To keep my heart from fear and dread
    I need no other token.

"'Twill cheer me when the winter's blast
    Blows chilly through the camp,
And warm the sod on which I'm cast
    Though deadly cold and damp.

"The stormy wind its force has sped,
    The winter frost's no harm,
The frozen ground's a downy bed,
    When all within is warm.

"A farewell kiss of love? — one more? —
    Oh, had some Indian drug
Prolonged that bliss forever more,
    No other Heaven I'd beg."

Many years their flight had ta'en:
    The Briton long had fled:
Yet, came the soldier not again,
    For he was with the dead.

The faithful maid yet knew this not,
    And still her dreams were bright:
The day of hopeful woman's thought
    Has neither cloud nor night.

And upward looked the maid to God,
    As the dead her heart still kept;
And upward grew the willow rod
    And drooped its head and wept.

And now this willow weeps above
    The maiden's lonely grave,
An emblem of her faithful love, —
    And long such may it wave.

An honest tear for the faithful maid
    Came trickling down my cheek,
When 'neath the weeping-willow's shade
    The lady ceased to speak.

---

[1] The weeping-willow, to which the legend refers, since the publication of the poem in 1864, has falled before the axe. It stood at the spring on the Salem road half a mile north of Greenesburgh.

[2] A branch of the weeping-willow, *Salix Babylonica*, when stuck into moist soil will take root and grow into a tree: each branch of a tree being in fact a tree in itself at a certain stage of development.

—1866—

THE LOVE-LORN LADY'S LAMENT.

I saunter on the sandy shore,
    Where the waves seemed merry girls,
Bedecking themsel's with seaweed and shells,
    And flowers of foam in their curls;
Where now I see in the foam a shroud,
    As if tossed on eternity's bed,
And here a moan from the depths unknown —
    Alas! he is dead! he is dead!

I wander through the wooded glen,
    Where Nature seemed a child,
That prattled among the birds in song,
    And in the flow'rets smiled;
Where now the deadly nightshade grows,
    And the owl echoes, over head,
The clods' mournful sound as they fell in the ground —
    Alas! o'er the dead! o'er the dead!

Ah! there is no beauty again to the eye
    That bedews a lover's mould,
And no more music again to the ear
    That has heard a lover knolled;
When the heartstrings are struck by the Harper of Death,
    And the soul to the discord is wed,
    The head and the heart are forever apart,—
Alas! he is dead! he is dead!

— 1869 —
THE REBUKE OF THE SAGE.

"Within this book the universe is planned,
Read it, if ye the whole would'st understand!"
Cried out the boastful Spirit of the Age
Unto the hoary-headed Hindu Sage.

SAGE.
"From this bold crag, what seest thou in the ocean?"
SPIRIT.
"I see naught but the waves in wild commotion,
Their upreared ragged crests snow-white and bright
With a strange, lustrous, phosphorescent light."

SAGE.
"Look up, now into the great vault of heaven?"
SPIRIT.
"I see the stars — the Crown, the Polar Seven,
The Pleiades, and that broad band of light,
The Milky Way, across the brow of night.

SAGE.
"Presumptuous man, and would'st thou bid me look
Within the narrow compass of thy book,
To know the universe, its moving cause,
Its ultimate design and governing laws;

"When, 'twixt a mite and world, thy piercing eye
The smallest difference cannot descry;
When to thy keen discriminating sight,
In myriads they both appear as light!

"Go, take a drop of ocean's sparkling brine,
And make its hidden secrets wholly thine,
And thou hast, of the universal plan,
Learned more than ever yet has vain, vain man.

"Write down the Individual alone,
Before the sum of the Unknown and Known;
The Known Finite will tell whenever writ
All knowledge of the Unknown Infinite."

— 1871 —

THE TWO TOWERS.

I.

THE TOWER OF FIRE.

Stern Winter lifts his heavy hand!
His brow a scowl
In the lowering cloud;
His voice a howl,
Wild, high and loud,
In the storm that sweeps over the land —
Over the hilltop, and over the heath,
Giving to every cranny a breath
To mimic the wail of woe unto Death.

The timid leaves, at the first faint sound,
Fly, fluttering, helpless, to the ground,
And, for shelter, look
Into every nook,
Even into the watery wards of the brook.

The lordly oak and the lowly bramble
Together tremble;
And the lapped up lake and the burly river
Quake and quiver,
Shudder and shiver.

Flown are the warblers of holm and hedge;
And, a living wedge
To the warm South driven,
Flock after flock of geese[1] has riven
The troubled heaven.

Withered and wind-strewn are weed and flower;
E'en the thistle,[2] bold
In his stronghold —
His thorny castle and prickly tower, —
Has lost the ruddy glow of his face,
Shrank to a ghost,
And wanders about like a spirit lost,
Wind and storm tossed,
Anywhere —
A flitting flake of the pallor of fear
Blindly seeking a resting place.

And Man, who alone wields the weapon of wit —
Who saddles and bridles the ocean horse,
And with stream for a spur, a compass a bit,
Rides where he lists on the wide-world course;
Who yokes the oxen of water and wind,
His corn to grind;
Who changes the dart, by the lightning hurled,
To a carrier-dove;
Who soars, on the pinions of gas, above
The woe and the wail of a wicked world,
To that good and happy land of love,
Where holy spirits are feigned to move, —

Even Man, the bold,
Grows chill and cold,
When Winter uplifts his heavy hand, —
When his scowl
And his howl
Darken and deafen the 'frighted land, —
Even Man, the bold,
Grows chill and cold,
In dread of stern Winter's icy ire,
And bolts and bars his main stronghold,
His TOWER OF FIRE!

———

Stern Winter has struck with a heavy hand!
Frozen and numb,
Palsied and dumb,
Stark and stiff a corpse lies the land!
The pallor of snow is over all,
And icicles tassel the funeral pall.

Congealed is the blood of river and lake.
Yet hark! from the depths profound,
Where Winter can neither strike nor 'wound,
You can hear the billows' surge —
A coronach wild, a dismal dirge,
At the dead land's wake.

Now, where is Man,
Who dares the demons and devils of nature
As no other creature
Can?
Unscathed, unscarred,
By Winter's blow,
Dealt heavy and hard
With shot and shell of ice and snow,
Aloft he stands in his Tower of Fire;

And the terrible ire
Of Winter dire,
The little hero now dares to defy,
You can read these words in his flaming eye,
" I'll conquer thee yet before I die;
This Tower shall be thy funeral pyre!"

The worldly reel turns round and round,
The yarn of time is wound and wound,
Till a six-months' hank is run;
When lo! the Sun,
In a blue and balmy midday sky,
Stands high!

And Winter has gone and Summer come!
No icy daggers on cottage eaves,
But nourishing rain in gentle showers;
No midnight hoar-frost skeleton-leaves;
But bright and blooming noonday flowers;
And the tempest drum
And the wild wind fife,
That led stern Winter to war and strife,
Are drowned in the brown bee's peaceful hum;
And Death, perforce,
Himself is a corse,
For all is aglow with the lustre of life!

And the death of the land,
By a blow of stern Winter's heavy hand,
A fiction — a dream —
A poet's theme!

Nought but a fiction — a dream —
A poet's theme!

Yet such things may fall in the scales of the mind,
And kick the beam
To good or evil:
Less, by far,
Can make or mar
A golden harvest to rustic hind —
Rain-drop or weevil![3]

For though the Mind
Is a wizard king,
To draw in the skull his magic ring,
And raise the spirits of water and wind —
Kelpie, goblin and ghost, —
Aye, and the genii of earth's dark caves,
And the fiends of fire —
A host
Of willing, abject, able slaves,
To make a deed of their master's desire;
Yet it seldom can rule that little elf,
Itself;
But, with nimble motion,
At the prick of a whim, or the spur of a notion,
It turns it about, with supple joint,
To one or the other cardinal point
Of the moralist's compass, good or evil,
God or Devil.

II.

THE TOWER OF PRAYER.

Age, like a dancing fay,
Tiptoed lightly from day to day —
The stepping stones laid in the stream of time —
And the sound of his footsteps fell

THE TWO TOWERS.

Like the faintest notes of a distant bell
Ringing an evening's chime.
Yet, step by step he grew
In size and strength, till every thew
Was hard and stiff as the archer's yew;
And from a child,
With manners mild,
He waxèd wrathful, warlike, and wild.
And still, unheeded he stalked by the side
Of Man in the height of a victor's pride.
Till lo! looming up like a tower on high,
Or Brocken spectre⁴ against the sky,
Before his victim he takes a stand,
And raises a stern and heavy hand!

The Eye that shone like the sun of Spring,
High overhead,
As a waning moon now glimmers through
A lurid brugh —⁵
A halo crimson, a circle red,
The shadow of Age's signet ring.

The Ear that rang with the laughter of youth,
And garnered the lessons of wisdom and truth;
That treasured the accents of friendship and love,
And grew spell-bound
At the magical sound
Of the song-sorceress of the grove;
That gladdened
At the wedding of music of lute and guitar,
And maddened
At the fearful alarm-bell, the tocsin of war;
Now strives in vain its door to unlock,
When words — old friends and old neighbors —
    knock;
Strives in vain, though a helping hand
Be hollowed, and at its elbow stand.
For age has gnawed, with the brown tooth of rust,

The latch,
The spring, the bolt, the ward, and the catch,
And cast
The key
Into the dark sea
Of the past!

The Voice, that defied the tempest's wrath
With a scoff,
Now gasps for breath,
And in whispering slippers shuffles after
A harsh, dry cough —
Age's demoniac laughter.

The Back, Man's proud totemic [6] sign,
That towered erect as a mountain pine,
Now droops
And bends and stoops,
Till, in the brook's
Still mirror, it looks
Like the curvèd scythe
With which Old Time, like a mower blithe,
Cuts ever and ever his world-wide swath.

The brawny Arm and the sinewy Leg
Assistance beg
Of each other,
And give it like brother to brother.
The leg on its knee rests the feeble hand;
And when the legs in turn aid crave
To walk or stand,
The hand, of the burden takes the half,
With a staff —
The finger of Age that points to the grave!

The Heart, deep-rooted in Christian soil,
That grew like Norway's sturdy pine,
With arms reaching far and wide

On every side
In the happiness, welfare, and life,
Of cherished children and worshiped wife;
Till mankind, weary of sorrow and toil,
To rest in its shade would calmly recline,
And point to the top towering high above,
To index the way to the land of love;
Now, lopped of its limbs, since daughter and son,
And wife are gone
To the grave,
It sways to and fro in the cold world's blast,
Like a man-of-war's mast
Battle-scarred,
Blackened, charred,
Unrigged and unsparred,
Forsaken and shunned and dreaded by all;
For in its fall
To the parting deck,
Is wreck,
And death beneath the wave!

Squandered long since are Youth's treasures
On tops and toys
Of sports and joys,
And rattling baubles of pleasures;
And squandered long since the wealth
Of Manhood's health,
On crowns of ambition and laurels of fame,
On ribbons of praise and the scroll of a name,
On trinkets of vanity, feathers of pride,
And on hobbies of whim and opinion to ride.
But what! can the spendthrift Jew
Spend all his silver and gold,
That Age, the inquisitor old,
Cannot get
A guinea or two from the heretic yet?
No.
Then go,

And draw one by one the teeth by decay,
And in each foul socket a hot coal lay;
On the thumb put the torturing screw;
On the ankle and foot
Wedge the tight Spanish boot;
And break
The arms and the legs on the wheel of ache;
And straighten yon ugly, crooked back
On the rack;
And on each great toe
Give a blow
With agony's cruelest weapon, the knout
Of gout;
Then, then must the miser his hoarded pelf
Of strength and endurance discover,
And eke out the mangled mass of himself
Till the very last coin is paid over!
If he die, if he do not, all's well —
A territion' 'twill be of the torments of hell!

But surely the Mind of Man
Still looms like El Capitan,
A mountain rock in its firmness grand,
Though Age before it will stand,
And point with his heavy hand,
To the great Yosemite cañon of death
Yawning a thousand fathoms beneath!
Ah, no! Its mountain base
By the earthquake of fear's rent asunder;
And his face
Is black with the dark clouds of doubt —
The lightning of hope darting in and out,
And despair rolling after in thunder!
And in the deep cañon of death,
That yawns beneath,
The magic mirage unrolls the weird
Panorama of all that on earth is feared,
Now magnified and distorted by fancy,

The mind's self-deceiving necromancy.
Here hells are depicted in every hue,
And unrolled to the view,
Where fire and water, earth and air,
In all their awful forms appear;
And even a round
Of life, for a sinful soul is found,
Through the hideous forms
Of toads, and lizards, and worms. —
The boldest must view it, with bated breath,
The fearful mirage of the cañon of death!

Ah, where shall he go now, Man, the mortal?
What power
Appeal to, and crave
Himself to save?
Or cast e'en a firefly's glimmer of light
At this midnight hour
Of the dark and fearful and terrible night,
That breaks beyond the grave?

Before him there stands a feudal tower
With open portal,
Low and narrow and small,
But yet may enter all,
Who will bend the knee,
In humility;
The head of its helmet uncover;
And lower
The neck for the stroke of a sword;
And clasp the hands, without gauntlet or glaive,
For the chains of a slave;
And with heart laid bare,
Fealty and homage swear
To the LORD:
It is the holy TOWER OF PRAYER![8]

Here tapestries hang from hall to hall,
Where all
The good and lovely on earth that has proven,
By the loom of the happiest vision is woven.
And what heavens of bliss, in this web, for the dead,
Inwrought in pearls and golden thread!
Here, angels and bright cherubim;
Here, saint singing psalm and hymn;
Here, the sea-rover's wild Valhalla joys,
A midday battle, a midnight carouse;
Here, the classic elysium of Jove;
Even God's holy presence,
A life eternal of light and love;
And absorption into the Holy Essence,
Nirvâna;
And many
A fiction — a dream —
A poet's theme.

The old Man enters the Tower of Prayer;
His fear now banished,
His care now vanished
Into air;
And to and fro through the tapestried halls
He creeps,
Till, weary with visions of heaven, he falls,
And sleeps —
Sleeps in death in the Tower of Prayer!
For Age has followed him even there,
And before his victim taken a stand,
And struck the death-blow with a heavy hand!

Food for worms! —
Back to the elemental forms

Of Matter, Man goes, as science affirms;
But the life — the soul —
The Force that pervaded the whole,
Where is it? or here or there?
On earth? in air?
Or bound with matter to shift and change
In its infinite range
Of forms that the chemist can measure and weigh,
As a farmer can reckon his wheat and his hay?
Or apart from matter, a force unique,
This world or a better again to seek,
And live as a spirit eternally,
From sin, and sorrow, and death made free?

But what say the sextons, old and grey,
As they dig the grave through the frozen clay?
Says one —
"Aye, Winter and Age are born of one mother,
Are brother and brother,
And as Spring follows one, so youth must the other.
In faith,
After death,
Again we will both be boys,
And, perhaps, in the height of our youthful joys,
And fun,
Leap over the graves, with nimble foot,
Where our old bodies moulder and rot."
The other, nodding his hoary head —
"'Tis said,
The seed
In Spring will sprout and grow
Best, where the old stock, withered and dead,
Falls over —
A leafy cover
To melt away with Winter's snow,

And cherish,
And nourish
Its new-born self, a flower or weed."

Nought but a fiction — a dream —
A poet's theme.
Yet such things fall in the scales of the mind
And kick the beam
To good or evil;
Less, by far,
Can make or mar
A golden harvest to rustic hind —
Rain-drop or weevil!

---

[1] Plutarch, in his comparison between land creatures and water creatures, says, "Cranes, at their first setting out, cast themselves into a triangle with the point forward, thereby to cut and pierce the wind that bloweth before and about them, to the end that their rank, thus arranged and set in order, might not possibly be broken." — *Morals*, Holland's translation, folio, London, 1657, p. 787.

The truth, however, lies in this: The eyes of the crane are situated on the sides of the head, so that the bird cannot see an object directly in its front: hence, to follow its leader, it is obliged to keep a little to one side in order to see it. The same is true of the wild-goose of the poem, *Branta Canadensis*.

[2] *Cirsium lanceolatum.*

[3] See *Cowan's Curious History of Insects*, pp. 71-2, where an account is given of a lawsuit between the Commune of St. Julien and a species of weevil which continued for more than forty-two years, during the Fifteenth century.

[4] The gigantic spectre of the Hartz mountains in Hanover, and seen at sunrise from the Brocken, the loftiest peak of the range, is the shadow of the observer cast upon the thin vapors then floating in the sky.

[5] This old word *brugh*, applied to the hazy circle sometimes seen around the disc of the sun and moon, and generally considered a presage of change of weather, has been overlooked by our standard lexicographers. It has been derived from the Greek *Brochos*, a chain about the neck, possibly our *brooch*. Other forms of it are *brogh* and *brough* — the latter occurring in the old poem *The Farmer's Ha'*, st. 28:

> "Meg cries she'll wad baith her shoon,
> That we shall hae wet very soon,
> And weather rough;
> For she saw about the moon
> A mickle *brough*."

Another word applied to the lunar halo and not found in the dictionaries is *burr*. — Vide Brande, Jamieson, et al. The "*lurid brugh*" of the poem refers to the *arcus senilis*, or red circle about the ball of the eye of aged persons, the result of fatty degeneration of the cornea.

[6] *Totemic* — characteristic, specific, an adjective from *totem*, an Indian word for a picture of a bird, turtle, or other animal, used by the North American Indians as a family, or tribal symbol or designation — a rude kind of heraldic coat-of arms, and so termed by early writers.

> "Each his own ancestral *totem*,
> Each the symbol of his household." — *Longfellow*.

The signification of the upright back of Man is elaborated in the initial poem of the writer's *Southwestern Pennsylvania in Song and Story*, entitled "The Last of the Mammoths."

[7] *Territion*, another useful word not found in our standard dictionaries. Its meaning is apparent from the following quotation from Lieber's *Encyclopædia Americana*, *sub voce* Torture: "The mere threat of torture is termed *territion*, and is distinguished into *verbal territion*, in which the accused is given up to the executioner, who conducts him to the engines of torture, and describes, in the most appalling manner possible, the sufferings which he may endure, and the *real territion* in which he is actually placed upon the machine, but is not subjected to torture."

[8] At the time this poem was written, the writer had not made an especial study of the science of symbolism. In the poems "Atlantis" and "Chautauqua," the signification of the attitudes of prayer is given correctly.

— 1874 —

THE JEWELS I PRIZE.

Let the miserly hoard up their symbols of self,
    Their copper and silver and gold,
Their jewels and gems — base, mineral pelf,
    Inanimate, senseless, and cold!
But to me give the treasures of life's tidal flood,
    Impassioned and sentient, and warm,
That burst into being and beauty with blood,
    In woman, life's loveliest form!

To me give the jewels of mirth and delight,
    With which nothing earthy can vie —
The diamonds that flash with a welcoming light,
    And gleam in a fond woman's eye;
To me give the jewels of gladness and bliss,
    The heart's fondly found treasure-trove —
The rubies that flush with a passionate kiss,
    Instinctive, responsive to love!

And the golden metal called precious is dross,
    When compared to the golden net,
Which Nature has woven of light-flowing floss,
    And out in the stream of life set;
And oh, to be caught in that golden mesh,
    And tangled with love's deftest art,
To feel as it tightens the quivering flesh,
    And the beat of a fast throbbing heart!

— 1875 —
MAID OF MAHONING.

Maid of Mahoning,¹ asleep in thy bower!
    Beauty as cold as if chiseled in stone —
Or as the colorless wax-petaled flower³
    Drooping in dread of the pine-forest's moan;
And as impassionate! Maid of Mahoning,
    Stilled would the aspen leaf be in thy breath!
Hast thou no moments of sighing and moaning?
    Art in the Vale of the Shadow of Death?

Hark! 'tis a voice from the lips, that, close-pressing,
    Oft to thine own, behind secresy's veil,
Glowing with rapture's protracted caressing,
    Measured the moments of bliss, like a snail!
Know'st thou that voice in the wild night imploring?
    Yea, though the tempest and torrent combine —
Drowning all sounds in the flood of their roaring —
    Sleeping or waking, that voice thou'dst define

Maid of Mahoning, a faint flush is creeping
    Over thy white neck and over thy brow;
Crimson thy face is — oh, canst thou be sleeping?
    Canst in thy dreaming again hear his vow?
Maid of Mahoning, ah, why dost thou tremble,
    And thy breath quicken — at what fond alarms?
Cannot the heart in thy bosom dissemble?
    Sleeping or waking, wouldst be in his arms?

Maid of Mahoning, oh, dream on forever;
    Web after web weave in fantasy's loom;
Wake not to wail that realities sever —
    Wake not to weep at mortality's tomb!
Maid of Mahoning, in dreams with thy lover,
    Limpet thy lips in a soul-scaling kiss;
Then let the tide of time rise and roll over,
    Thou wilt be ever the Spirit of Bliss!

---

[1] "The next spring, we moved to a town about fifteen miles off, called *Mo-ho-ning*, which signifies a lick." — *McCullough*.

[2] The wax-pipe, *Monotropa uniflora*.

THE DEMON LOVER.

From ten, when she kissed her fond mother good-night,
    Until twelve, Isabel, at the window, has sat,
In the shaded light's gloom of a still, curtained room.
    When lo! through the casement there flutters a bat!

A bat, in a suit of the unseen at night,
    On a wing of the silence that will not alarm,
When behold! in the gloom of the still, curtained room,
    The wing of the bat has become a man's arm!

The wing of the bat has become a man's arm,
    That encircles the form of the fond, watching maid,

In a silent embrace that is throbbing and warm,
    Till a hot breath has left and lost all in a shade!

But behold! the bright sun of midsummer has risen,
    And gone with the bat are the shades of the night;
E'en the mocking-bird swings in its bright gilded prison,
    And merrily sings in unfeignèd delight!

But thrice has the breakfast-bell rung in the hall,
    Ere Isabel tremblingly trips down the stair,
With her hand on the baluster, lest she may fall,
    And the flower of yesterday still in her hair!

"My daughter! my daughter! what aileth thee, tell?
    As the dead thou art cold, as the dead thou art white!"
"O mother! O mother! I'm happy and well —
    I have seen but a bat in my room the past night."

"But a bat?" "Yes, a bat." "Only that?" "Only that."
    "Then a bat let it be and thou happy and well;
But, my daughter, beware, lest the flower in thy hair,
    That has faded o'er night be not burnt — where bats dwell!"

Aye, call him a bat, and a bat he becomes,
    As many old fables of fantasy tell:
He that sucks the warm blood of inflamed womanhood,
    Is well understood in the Vampire of Hell!

LOVE'S HOLY GRACE.

Yes, bright be the dew that bespangles
    The spider's gauze web in the grass,
Reflecting the dawn as it dangles,
    In its fairy-formed, globular glass;
But brighter my darling's eye beaming
    With the fire of a lip-quiv'ring kiss,
Its sparkles a galaxy gleaming,
    Illuming a heaven of bliss.

And red be the maple buds [1] breaking
    When Spring awakes frost-nipped at dawn,
When ice-beaded branches are shaking,
    And showering pearls on the lawn;
But redder my darling's cheek-blossom
    That bursts into loveliest charms,
When Winter has fled from her bosom,
    And Summer has come in my arms!

And pure as the wave of the fountain
    That wells in the moss-bosomed nook,
And breaks o'er the rocks of the mountain,
    In a free, joyous, loud-laughing brook;
But purer the blood, though it's burning,
    That thrills in my lov'd one's embrace;
For the heart-throb that trembles with yearning
    Is hallowed by Love's holy grace!

---

[1] The red, or swamp maple, *Acer rubrum*. "In spring, the appearance of the tree is remarkable for the deep crimson flowers with which it is thickly clothed." — *Wood*.

THE WITCH OF WESTMORELAND.

"A witch? God have mercy! I'll warrant a hag
  So old that the devil himself cannot tell
When the crookèd and wrinkled and twisted zigzag
  Of a wry-mouthed old spinster was first leagued
    with — well" —

"Lord! no, sir! She's only a year old to-day,
  And as round and as red and as sweet as a peach!
And the wonder is, not when she leagued — as you say,
  But that heaven could spare such a witch of a witch!"

"Well, what can she do, this quintessence of evil —
  This perversion of age in her wicked profession?
I presume she can ride on a broom like the devil,
  And crawl thro' the keyhole to secret confession?"

"No! Cæsar Augustus! she rides in a gig,
  Or is carried about in the gentlest of arms;
And crawl thro' a keyhole — why, man, she's this big!
  And the doors open wide in the face of her charms!"

"Well, seeing's believing — but what of her cat,
  With its yellow eyes, hump-back, and tail up, and grin,
As big as a barn and as black as a hat —
  The witch's select incarnation of sin!"

"Her cat? Why, my friend it is yet but a kit,
    As white as the snow and as soft as old silk;
Nor devilish, save an occasional fit,
    Which our doctor is treating with sulphur and milk!"

"Well, what of her figures in wax — I suppose,
    She has or does something of which I have read?
Can she melt off the point of a fair lady's nose,
    And open the eyes and the mouth of the dead?"

"Can she melt off the point — I have seen her myself
    Melt three or four noses to nothing at all;
And I've seen her quite often, the mischievous elf,
    Make a dummy of gum move its eyes — yea, and squall!"

"And of course, then, you've seen this remarkable witch
    Mat the manes of the horses and tie the cows tails,
Sour the milk in the churn, and give one the itch
    Till he scratch like the devil and pray for his nails?"

"Well, no; not exactly; but this I will swear,
    I've seen her tie knots and I never could loose 'em —
Yes, the tightest of knots in my beard and my hair;
    And as for sour milk, just behold my shirt-bosom!"

"Ah, yes; now I take — yes, you mean — yes, I see;
    Well, no matter — expect me to see her at dinner,
With my bell, book, and candle to save at least me
    From the spell of the witch and the hell of the sinner."

" Yes, come, and your whole end of town bring along,
    And I'll show you this witch in the arms of my
        wife —
The proudest of mothers a million among,
    And the happiest father you've seen in your life!"

OH, I WOULD LOVE YOU ALWAY!

Oh, I would kiss your lips — your lips —
    Oh, I would kiss your lips —
When warm and moist in the morning of life;
When hot and parched in the noonday strife;
When burnt out ashes at evening's rest;
When clammy and cold as the clay that pressed
    In the night that knows no dawn.

And I would look in your eye — your eye —
    And I would look in your eye —
When blue and bright in the morning's gleam;
When gray and dazed in the midday's beam;
When red and ringed in the gloaming's light;
When black and glazed and blind in the night —
    In the night that knows no dawn.

Oh, I would love you alway — alway —
    Oh, I would love you alway —
In the flash of life of the maid in the morn;
In the flush of noon by the mother borne;
In the shadow of grandmother's eventide;
In the darkness — yea, and whatever betide
    In the night that knows no dawn! .

A LETTER TO A LADY.

Nature has made you, Mary, human,
    To be by thought and feeling moved;
Nature has made you, Mary, woman,
    To be of mankind The Beloved.

But Art would make you, Mary, golden —
    An idol in your form attired,
To be by distant eyes beholden
    And in their staring The Admired.

Nature has made you, Mary, charming,
    That in seclusion you may meet
Attention in your service arming
    To lay Devotion at your feet.

But Art would make you, Mary, dashing,
    That, sex defying, you might move,
And hurl, amid your thunder's crashing,
    The lightnings of a mimic Jove!

Beware! beware! The man who kneels
    Before the golden calf of Art,
Hypocrisy alone he feels —
    Else he's a groveler at heart!

And so beware the man who falls
    Before the thunder-bolt of Art;
He but obeys the prompter's calls,
    And on the stage plays the fool's part.

A LETTER TO A LADY.

Be Nature's maiden, Mary, human,
    As youth and health and beauty can ;
And learn that he who loves a woman,
    Loves only as becomes a man.

He comes — he wooes ; but that alone
    Is but the blowing of a bubble ;
She waits — receives ; then all is done —
    Love in humanity is double.

So, step by step, mark his advance,
    That comes, as it becomes a true man —
Impelled by feeling — not by chance —
    To love as man may love a woman.

If you discern aught in his form
    That clouds futurity's clear sky ;
It is a presage of a storm ;
    Take heed in time — Let him pass by.

If not, and he come like the Sun
    Diffusing round him warmth and light,
Until, his course though winter run,
    He gleaming climbs the vernal height —

And you, another Earth, receive —
    Melting from formal ice and snow,
Until the frosts of distrust leave,
    And violets confiding grow —

Remain another Earth, in faith,
    That Nature doth your course approve ;
For there's no Joshua but Death
    To stay the climbing Sun of Love.

And Summer will as surely warm
    For you as for our Mother Earth;
For you are she in woman's form
    Evolved through eonids of birth.

Then, Mary, be yourself, the creature
    Whom Nature hath in you approved;
Incarnate Woman-Earth of Nature,
    Be, by the Sun of Man, beloved!

And let the nameless works of Art,
    In man's or woman's form attired,
Be banished from your head and heart
    To the cold moon, to be admired.

THE VOICE OF THE ANVIL.

Aye, a merry old man am I —
    And a wink is as good as a nod —
I ne'er let the rust eat into my trust
    In my anvil and my God!
Though in the grave are my wife and child,
    And I am the last of my clan,
Yet my heart is light from morning till night
    In doing the best that I can.
I work away from day to day,
And while I work to God I pray;
With my iron anvil's voice,
I worship and rejoice.

Aye, a merry old man am I,
    While I hear my anvil ring
In sweet accord, while to the Lord
    I work away and sing —
Sing in the trust of my anvil and God,
    From morning until even,
That the voice of mirth once beloved on earth,
    May still be heard in heaven!
Until I moulder into dust,
And my old anvil turns to rust,
When, among the loved and blest,
I shall forever rest.

FATE.

Ah, who can fathom the depth of Fate?
Two girls part at the college gate —
Two girls with kindred heart and soul,
Like two trees with a common bole, —
As like as twins, their chances even
For life on earth or love in heaven;
And yet before a twelve-month flies,
The one is wed, the other — dies!
The clock strikes east and the clock strikes west —
The one is happy, the other blest!
Eleven — twelve! — the nuptial kiss;
Eleven — twelve! — eternal bliss!
The bride of Life and the bride of Death —
The one bound with an orange wreath,
The other crowned with immortelle!
      While, ding! ding!
      The church-bells ring
A wedding-chime and a passing-knell!

AN EPIGRAM.

A nose, not well put out of joint,
Nor long in coming to the point.

A POET.

His model, Beauty, with the sculptor's art,
The poet shapes the marble of the Heart.

A TOAST TO WOMAN.

I drink to the woman aglow with the fire,
    That burns on the altar eternal of Love;
A spark from whose eye inflames man to aspire
    To wield for her glory the lightnings of Jove![1]

[1] Subsequently incorporated in the poem "Psappha."

A REASON IN RHYME.

To feed the ancient fire of Love,
    Required of vestal maids a corps;
So may the flame as sacred prove
    Though fanned in me by half a score.

DESPAIR.

Ah, yes; I have lived: I have loved and have lost!
The earth is but ashes and I am a ghost!

HER CHARACTER.

She was, in everything she said and did, but human —
   Her vice and virtue in these two lines you may scan :
As false as only woman can be false to woman,
   And true as only woman can be true to man.

INDECISION.

With every waver in her mind,
A quiver in my heart, I find;
My faith and doubt turn with her thought —
" I love her " and " I love her not! "
I could not change in feeling faster
Were I divining with an aster,
And felt alternate love and hate
As leaves alternate fixed my fate.

ANOTHER.

The trout in the transparent stream
Doth like the pebbled channel seem;
So changeful with her thoughts I prove —
Tell me, my heart, if this be love?

TO ———

When I was lost in melancholy's night,
With naught but darkness in my staring sight,
Afar the music of your voice I heard —
And lo! a star appeared with every word!
Until, I stood beneath a gleaming throng —
In the soft light of heaven — in your song!

TO A SILKWORM.

Spin, spin, thou silk-reeling worm,
    For our lady another thread,
That a grown may thrill to encircle her form,
    When thou art forgotten and dead.

Sing, sing, O importunate voice,
    For our lady another strain,
That an echo may live in her soul and rejoice,
    When thou art heard never again!

TO ———

When the storm of passion pervades the heart,
And the clouds crash together, the lightning will dart:
Perchance to slay, with a dagger of light,
The babe asleep in its cradle at night;
Perchance to save, like a beacon of heaven,
The tempest-tossed ship to the rock of wreck driven!
But, believe, in the calm of the head above,
The flash of the Heart has been forethought by Love!

LOVE'S RULE OF THREE.

The time — whenever it is dark is best for speedy wooing;
For many, when they cannot see, don't know what they are doing.

The place — wherever none but two can either see or hear,
Without a lantern in the hand or trumpet to the ear.

The circumstance — a man and maid, each bold a half to go it,
Forgetting that two halves will make a whole before they know it.

THE EYE AND THE IMAGINATION.

The eye lays an egg —
　Imagination hatches it;
The eye bends to beg —
　Imagination snatches it.
The eye clothes a maid —
　Imagination strips her;
The eye turns afraid —
　While imagination grips her!

KATY-DID.

Aye, Katy did and kindly,
　As alone a woman can,
In her innocence love blindly,
　A wicked, worthless man.

ASTRONOMICAL.

Nay, nay, Lenore; astronomy is not
A science to be buried and forgot;
It hath its uses — to define a kiss:
A shooting-star across the sky of bliss;
That seems a star of love to youthful eyes;
But is a meteor unto the wise,
That differs from a star of love as far
As doth a spark from an eternal star!

A FOURTH OF JULY ALTERNATIVE.

Either America's eagle on high,
In the blue vault of empyrean sky,
Or a — this glorious Fourth of July —
Musca volens in a bloodshotten eye!

THE HEART ENTOMBED.

On yonder hill, when clothed in summer's green,
There's but a leafy thicket to be seen;
But when disrobed by winter, and laid bare,
A grave's white head-stone is see standing there.

So social Mira summers to a blush,
Leaves to a smile and flowers to a flush;
While, sad and lonely, she, with blighted bloom,
Sighs for the dead and winters to a tomb!

ON KISSING.

A look may lead a lass to love;
   A hand may help with a staff;
But a lip that loiters and lingers about hers
   Will shorten the way by a half.

We were but schoolmates at finger-tips,
   And knew not the lesson of bliss,
Till, lost each on the other's lips,
   We learned it by heart in a kiss.

A LOVER'S LAMENT.

Alas! the bird, that built her nest
Within the bower of my breast,
Has flown away and left her brood
To famish in the want of food;
To flutter all in vain to fly;
To gasp a moment and to die;
To make all foul where all was fair;
To banish Hope, and bid Despair
Come, loathe the light of sun and moon,
And mourn amid the joys of June.

ON A RINGING BELL.

Ah, the heartless, cold, indifferent bell!
With loud-tongued clangor ringing as well
A wedding chime as a funeral knell —
Ding! dong! ding to heaven! ding! dong! ding
   to hell!

A LOVER'S PRAYER.

I ask what thou canst give
Alone, Almighty Jove:
As others love to live,
So let me live to love.

LOVING AND LONGING.

I've seen a maiden young and trim,
Sit down alone and sigh for him;
Day after day, year after year,
Until her eyes grew weak and blear —
Until her hair grew white and thin —
Until her bones grew thro' her skin —
Until — her hope did not forsake her —
Her corpse embraced an undertaker!

So I have seen a tender goose,
To quit her nesting-place refuse,
And, in a hopeful mother-mood,
Upon a cold potato brood,
Until — to all the world forgotten,
And the potato long since rotten,
She was too weak and numb to move,
And died in the fond hope of love.

Ah, what a blessing to creation,
A loving heart and expectation!

ON AN ENGAGEMENT RING.

It is a dainty, jeweled band
Around a finger of a hand;
And yet it is a golden girth
Encompassing both heaven and earth —
All — all, save one poor wretched part,
A slighted lover's broken heart.

LITERARY HERMIT CRABS.

There be eke certayne ermite crabbes amonge
Ye menne of letteres who indyte in songe,
And he is of them who wille back ye breeche
Of his bare witte into anotheres speeche —
Wrythe in ye convolutions of rime,
An he ye poete whelke where alle ye tyme!
But Godde a mercye onne his sillye harte,
He is swyche only in his hyndere parte!

There are, too, certain hermit crabs among,
The men of letters who indite a song;
And he is of them who will back the breech
Of his bare wit into another's speech —
Writhe in the convolutions of his rhyme,
As if he were the poet all the time!
But God have mercy on his simple heart,
He is such only in his hinder part! [1]

[1] Subsequently incorporated in "The Plain of Troy."

A SIMILE.

A fond yet fearful woman, like a moon,
Within the orbit of a jealous eye,
Revolving in impending dissolution!

GRAVEYARD GROTESQUES.

Since graveyards yawn, why may they not, then, laugh,
And Epigram poke fun at Epitaph,
Till tombstones hold their sides with bated breath,
And smiles sepulchral wreathe the skull of Death!

"Tread lightly here—" Ah, yes; pephaps,
    Our feet are shod with thorns;
Or worse than that—Jehoshaphat!
    The corpse may be covered with corns!

"Here lies James Hyer—" No further enquire,
    For the leopard cannot
    Change a single spot,
And no more can his nature, a liar!

"Here rests in peace Llewellyn Rhees—"
    I prithee read no more;
For leaving life, he left his wife
    And everlasting war!

"Tread lightly here—" What mockery!
    Addressing thyself to one
Who weighs no more than ninety-four,
    Thou stone that weighest a ton!

"She was a thrifty wife—" She was, indeed;
I've seen her in her hour of housewife need,
O'er her bare legs her husband's breeches pull,
And comb his head with a three-leggèd stool!

"Remember, man, as you pass by,
    As you are now so once was I—"
Jake Simpson, you're a wicked liar;
    You were a clerk, while I'm a 'Squire!

"Tread lightly, stranger, as you pass,
    For Samuel Greer
    Is lying here—"
Ah, yes; I remember his left eye was glass!

"Gone to meet his mother-in-law—"
    May I be curst,
    But that's the worst
Of epitaphs I ever saw!

"Here lies Jane Brown—" Don't speak so loud—
    Lest the flirt arise
    To attract your eyes,
By waving the tail of her shroud!

THE LAST KISS OF LOVE.

Confound it, Kate, Byron was crazy
    To extol so the first kiss of love,
Or worse, too intolerably lazy
    To learn what comparisons prove.

The first kiss of love!—what is in it?
    No matter if stolen and sweet,
It flashes away in a minute,
    And you cannot the first kiss repeat!

Why, any man, Kate, in his senses,
    Beginning to kiss in the past,
Continues in all moods and tenses,
    And reaches ahead for the last!

The last kiss of love's odd or even,
    The number that can't be surpassed—
In the ladder that leads up to heaven,
    Sure, the round is the best that comes last!

TO YOU, MAN.

When the lips of a woman —
    Be she lovely and wise! —
Speak falsely to you, Man,
    With the blackguard, she lies.

When the vow of a woman —
    Be she precious in pelf! —
Is broken to you, Man,
    She perjures herself.

When the kiss of a woman —
    Be she blushing to scarlet! —
Is envenomed to you, Man,
    It's the kiss of a harlot.

When the soul of a woman,
    In selfishness nursed,
Is deceitful to you, Man,
    In itself it's accursed.

Then bid such a woman
    An eternal farewell,
If you are a true man,
    And would escape hell!

JAM SATIS.

Rhymes and jingles,
    Jingles and rhymes,
Till the ear tingles
    And aches betimes.

ONCE, AND ONCE ONLY.

He that sees the same object twice, is blind in the second seeing;
He that lives the same moment again, is dead for the instant being.

He that breathes the same air twice, breathes bane in the second breath;
Opposing, the new is the habit of life, the old is the habit of death.

Earth is ubiquity changeful to man, in season, in weather, and sky;
Else with repeated sensations of same, he'd weary, then madden, and die.

Wouldst thou have proof, to the dungeon cell go, the waste of the desert or sea,
Or in thy bed lie awake in the night, and one sound and sight hear and see.

If thou, Philosopher, wouldst live, indeed, the highest existence on earth,
Let no sensation — or feeling or thought — have in thee a second birth.

If thou, fond Lover, wouldst climb to love's height, repeat not a step of thy bliss,
But, to a mile-dream prolong every thought — to a thousand leagues a kiss.

Once, only once in love's passion embrace, then nobly — most gloriously die,
Pinnacled on the most heavenly height in humanity's rapturous sky!

Or live, to totter down, step after step, decaying in pace
    with thy lust,
Till at the foot, thou art laid out a corse — a stench
    amid rottenest dust!

NIAGARA.

LOQUITUR — A suicidal debauchee, to whom the world is as burnt out without as within.

Die, like a dog with a curse-pointed kick in a
    dyke?
Die, like a hog, when the pork-market tyrant cries,
    Strike?
Die like a leper with loathesome disease —
A sewer of quackery — carrion of fees?
Die of old age with a shudder and chill,
'Mid weeping relations disputing my will?
Die like the millions of mortals that drag o'er a
Life of cold commonplace? Never! Niagara!

I that have breathed with the lungs of a fire;
I that have loved with insatiate desire —
Clasped with the strong arms of sensuous might —
Whirled in the wild waltz of maddened delight —
Whirled in the reeling of rapture to stagger — a
Vortex suspended in passion's Niagara!

I that have reveled in thrills, from a kiss
To the wallow of lust in a surfeit of bliss!
Till, bloated, besotted, and rotten with sin,
The world is as burnt out without as within! —
Save thee, O Death, in a bullet — a dagger — a
Leap in the flood of the mighty Niagara!

Save thee, Niagara! Torrent of Death!
If thou canst extinguish this passion-fired breath!
Roll up resistless thy might in one flood!
Seethe in thy rapids like love-boiling blood!
Quiver an instant in brink-edge orgasm!
Plunge! and go down with me into the chasm —
Into the thunder, the mist-cloud, and flag-array
Stolen from heaven, thou hell of Niagara!

Ha! how thou hugg'st me in love's last embrace,
Bared breast to breast, and hot face to face!
Over the breakers we hurriedly ride —
Through the swift rapids estatic we glide —
Kiss me — oh, kiss me while yet there is
    breath! —
Down, down, together we go, love, to death! —
Into the black depth, and into the blacker Aye! —
Laura-limbed, Laura-lipped, Laura-Niagara!

CHAUTAUQUA.

A SONG OF SYMBOLISM.

A lake —
As fair as only fantasy can make,
With half-closed eyes,
At even,
In the glamour of glowing, cloudy skies —
In the vision illusive of heaven.

On this lake, a boat —
As light as the leaf that is silently borne,
On the balmy breath
Of a warm October morn,

From the tree above to the wave beneath,
With neither rustle nor ripple to note
Whether breezes waft or waters float —
Nay, as light as the boat by poesy wrought
As an idle toy in the workshop of thought.

Afloat,
On this lake, in this boat,
A thing, encased in a mottled husk,
Of silk and cotton and straw and leather,
In a strange entanglement held together,
And diffusing an odor of musk!—
Fie!
An eye
Of the self-same radiant blue
That gives infinity its hue;
A lip as red as blood can stain,
When crimson art'ry and purple vein
Unite in a common mesh,
In a gauze of semi-transparent flesh;
A neck, of the upturning crucible's glow,
When the molten steel begins to flow:
As white and as clear, with a dazzled-eye hint
Of, within it, an exquisite violet tint';
A form without a single straight line,
In a series of arcs that all beauty combine;
A motion extending, with varying curve,
The lines of her form, without tangent or swerve;
A being — the wax of humanity's mold —
To be melted by love — to receive — to hold —
To shape in the pattern impressed in the past,
And turn out alternates of self with each cast;
A woman! a woman of womanly worth
As ever made heaven existence on earth.

And with this woman, one
Other,
Neither sire nor son,

Nor uncle nor brother,
Nor husband nor friend,
And yet a man — a man
To dare and do what only man can.
And here an end —
She, bending the bough, a ripe luscious peach;
He hungry — the food he most craves within reach.

It is Maud and I that, in a boat,
On Lake Chautauqua, are afloat!
Together we pull with measured oar;
Together we view the receding shore;
Together we join our voices in song,
And merrily sing as we glide along.

Away! away! o'er the waters blue!
Away! away! in our light canoe!
When the wave is calm and the sky is clear,
And the bark that floats between, my dear,
   Has only two oars in it —
     Two oars that feather
     The wave together!

Away! away! o'er the waters wide!
Away! away! o'er the billowy tide!
When, tho' death is below, there is heaven above,
And a world at rest between, my love,
   With only two souls in it —
     Two souls that feather
     The wind together!

Till our stroke, like a sledge,
Has driven
The keen prow-edge
Of our boat, like a wedge,

To the splintering heart
Of the log-like lake —
Till the lake in twain is riven,
And gapes in our widening wake;
And Maud and I from the world are apart!

A motionless speck —
An indistinct fleck,
To the eye on the distant shore;
Where the evening shadows away into night;
Where the casements lengthen to streamers of
    light;
Where the reveling's roar —
The crash of the music, the dancing, the din —
Is heard no more,
Save in the faint note of a lone violin —
A thread of gossamer sound so thin,
That sense is in doubt —
Is it something without,
Or something within?

I sit in the bow, — nay, to sit, I seem;
For I am ubiquity's self in my dream;
Maud touches the oar with a finger tip,
And listlessly toys with its dainty drip —
That touch of the girl
Transmutes the drops and the wave into pearl.
She smiles; a wavelet encircles the oar
And widens out toward the shadowy shore —
Till the lake is wreathed from a central isle
In the mirth sympathetic and play of her smile.
She laughs; the water-lap under the bow
Echoes her voice to the depth below;
While the mirth-bounding midges bear it on high,
To the stars that flash from her upturning eye.

The lake with her touch is pearled;
The lake with her smile is whorled;

While the depth below and the height above
Rejoice
With her voice;
The world — the all-inclusive world
Is intermingled Maud and I in love!

The air — so still! and the wave and the sky — so dark!
Sound and sight
Are lost in the night
That envelopes the world of love in our bark.

Closer, Maud, creep!
The heart is not hushed in the swelling breast;
The love-lighted eye has not sunk in the west
Of sleep.
Then come! — Interlocked, love, our hearing and sight
Will know not of silence, will know not of night.

Thou tremblest, love! Thy breath is warm —
Nay, hot and fast —
A feverish, full, and broken blast!
Dost fear the calm will break into storm?

Hark!
A sound
Gurgles up from the depth profound,
And startles the sable stillness around!
And now a shock!
And a rising wave that begins to rock
The listless bark!

Nay, calm thy alarms —
Thou art safe in my arms!
Our boat
Though a light and fragile shell, will float
Above

The highest as well as the lowest wave,
And save
Us in the trust of love!

In all its fury, breaks the storm,
With tumultuous force and in frensied form!
Till the ear is deaf with the thunder's crash,
And the eye is blind with the lightning's flash! —
Till our bark to the heavens above is tossed —
Is shivered — is sinking — down, down — and is lost!

Nay, lost in a swoon, Maud and I;
While the boat
Keeps afloat,
And drifts away
Quietly into a silent bay
Deep
In sleep;
Where — how long I know not — we lie,
And recover. —
The storm is over.

The shore is at hand.
And, amid the crash of the revelers' band,
At midnight, we land.

Round and round the waltzers go,
Turning on the tuneful toe,
Spinning fast or reeling slow,
    In close-clasped gyration;
Little eddies of the ball,
In the whirlpool of the hall,
In the mighty vortical
    Of the earth's rotation!

With the winding, waltzing world,
Tops by gayety thumb-twirled,
Maud and I are wildly whirled
    In the maze around us;
Round and round — the lake is dry!
Round and round — the storm a lie!
Round and round — till Maud and I
    Are as evening found us!

———

The morning is black;
The sky is ragged with rack;
The air is heavy and hot;
A feverish doubt
Runs in and out,
And is answered not —
In a cheek that blanches and burns;
In an eye that deadens and dazzles by turns;
In a heart that stifles and throbs;
In a warmth that gives and a coldness that robs.

The deck is dull; the book a block;
The song a sigh; the run a walk;
The walk a mope with hasty turn;
The look in pity half to spurn;
The ring unworn;
The letter torn;
The rose a ragged, bleeding thorn! —
A bleeding thorn that bleeds afresh,
When I draw near:
Like murdered flesh
When the murderer doth appear.

———

In the afternoon,
The hammock hangs like a horned dry-moon,
And Maud reclines in the crescent lap —
By a strangely sweet, fortuitous hap,

Blending in one symbol together,
Woman in love in the trust of fair weather.

Afar, I dare to speak.
And with my tongue, my foot keeps pace;
Nearer, nearer, till I can trace
The tears in great drops coursing down her
    cheek —
Till I can look into her eye,
And with mine ardent gaze, the tear-source dry.

The heaviness begins to lift;
And in the rack there is a rift;
The sun pours down a golden flood
That warms the blood,
Till it lightly flows,
And brightly glows.

We walk
And talk
Together.
I place a feather
Of fern in her hair;
While my tremulous fingers linger there,
Till the stem is broken.
But no matter th' inanimate token—
There's a thicket of fern
At every turn!

The rack is gone;
The faintest cloud has flown;
The sun descends in a glowing west;
The world reclines in enraptured rest.

It is even.
The earth is poised in an ambient heaven.
Every object against the sky
That listless revery can descry,

Is the haloed head of a hallowed saint,
Such as ecstatic limners paint.

The purple haze
Comes into being like a mist
Of amethyst,
And grows within our silent gaze,
Till, in one comprehending whole,
Of love impassioned, sentient soul,
Our beings dissolve and become a part —
The beating heart.

The long-curved lashes of the eyes of Day
Close the world in their shadows of gray.

Is it the darkness that makes me bold?
I dare to touch Maud's silken fold!
Close to her side I steal;
Her warm breath on my cheek I feel;
I linger on her lips, while she is pressed
In rapture to my throbbing breast.

The rack of the morn without a rift,
The clouds of the afternoon adrift,
The glamour, the halo, the haze, the shade,
In a fathomless grave together are laid —
The Past has no ghost to rise and affright
The wondrous might
Of Love encased in the black mail of night!

The boat awaits — the boat! the boat!
That in the storm kept bravely afloat!
That beat on the heaving billow's breast!
That topped the highest watery crest!

Ha! danger must take another form
To deter fond love than a passionate storm!
Thou hast no fear? Then come, Maud, come,
And the lake forever shall be our home!

Together we row — Maud and I — in the boat;
On the stormy lake again we're afloat!

A snail, in his own individual shell,
    In the torture of self writhed and whorled,
Hangs out of his window above a deep well,
    To take a wide view of the world.

Protruding a finger-like sensitive socket,
    With cautious contemplative move,
He draws out a glass from the out-turning pocket,
    And brings it to bear upon — love!

Love, deep in the circumscribed world of a well,
    In the form of a petal-like boat,
Afloat on the crest of the surface-drip's swell,
    And in it, two fire-flies afloat!

Enraptured, the snail shuts his telescope-eye,
    And sets out Parnassus to climb;
The surface is slippy, the summit is high,
    But he sticks as he crawls up — in slime!

Yea; it is true,
The lake, the boat, and Maud and I
Are but the figments of a lie;
The storm, the swoon, the dainty diction
Of the erotic muse of fiction;
And ragged the rounds
Of rhythmic sounds
That compass the sensuous dreamer's bounds;
Yet, give the poor devil his due!
The poet must writhe in his shell,
And look in a well,
And see there earth, heaven, and hell —
Yea, hopper humanity's infinite selves

To the tiniest elves
Begot
Of thought —
The fire-flies in the snail's well view,
Or Maud and I in the lake canoe.

It is an innate habit of the Thought
To mirror the great world according to
The modes in which the great world is expressed;
In halves that are as nothing when alone,
But when united are all powerful,
Omnipotent in reproductive might,
Evolving self into infinity —
In halves, or male or female — man and woman,
In highest form, down to the lowest hint —
The push and pull of every mode of force —
The in and out of every form of matter
That vortices in individuality.
And so as Man is halved in man and woman,
Each individual is halved again —
Divided thro' and thro' from brain to heart —
Into a man and woman brain and heart.

So there are male and female modes of thought, —
Philosophy and Poesy, in point.

The man, Philosophy, swells, from the one
Unto the many, with expanding arms;
The woman, Poesy, shrinks from the many,
And, with enfolding arms, clasps all in one.
Philosophy resolves the Milky Way
Into a myriad of revolving worlds;
While Poesy, dissolves the light of all
Into the lustre of a single star —
Into the soft light of a woman's eye.
Philosophy creates a quadruped,
From out the billion bipeds of the earth,
And calls the monster Man — eternal Man;

While Poesy reduces all to two,
A man and woman, who are born to die,
And who, between the cradle and the grave,
Think in one soul the thoughts that millions think,
Feel in one heart the throbs that millions feel,
And people worlds in one — Storm on the Lake.

And man and woman like, these modes of thought
May live to adult life and hoary age
And be abortive one without the other —
Each unproductive, in their work apart,
Of aught that lives a separate existence.
Philosophy, a bachelor, shoots up
Divergent rockets in the face of heaven,
That point with fiery finger to the stars,
Then burst in vain self-praise and fall as sticks;
While Poesy, a spinster, knits a sock
That ravels at the top as fast as she
Can draw the threads together at the toe.

But joined as man and wife, Philosophy
And Poesy bring forth a living being,
Wherein the aspiration of the sire,
Beyond the bourn of comprehension,
Is blended with the fond love of the mother,
As finite as an individual —
A nameless being to the wise and good;
An idol, in a thousand different forms,
Under as many names and signs, to those
Who comprehend with only eye and ear.

Here, reader, pause. Thou art Philosophy.
Look out with thy accustomed sight, that dims
Not in the dark'ning distance of the past,
And see the head-width of the wedge of thought,
That Poesy has narrowed to a point
Within the storm-tossed boat on Lake Chautauqua.

Dost see not in remotest, darkest Ind,
The mystic ARGHA, in whose ovoid depth
The stream of life hath an exhaustless fount?
Dost see not, in the mist of Hebrew myth,
This self-same argha in the mystic ARK,
That, while the world's engulfed in death,
Bears in its womb the fruitful halves of life?
Dost see not in the blue of Grecian past,
This same boat ARGOS, filled with armèd men,
Who sail away to Colchian land, and steal
The golden fleece of immortality?
Dost see not in the glamour of to-day
The symbol of the argha in the ARCH,
Through which in triumph march the hosts of men
Flushed with the glow of vital victory;
And under which, in its grand form, the dome,
The millions kneel in hope of life eternal?
Or wise Philosophy, dost see not in
The very OAR that trembles in Maud's hand —
The oar propelling the light curvèd boat —
The active AR that speaks the might of man
In union with the passive ARK of woman?
The ARROW winging from the curvèd bow
Of Cupid's self, the very god of love?
The point that EARS the mellow mould
And makes of barrenness a teeming EARTH?
The ARM of man, that in the war of life,
Strikes down the hosts of death opposing him?
The ART of man comprising all his work?
The ARDOR of consuming passion? — Yea,
An ARIAN must thou be, and freely breathe
The AIR of mystic lore, Philosophy,
To mate with Lake Chautauqua's Poesy!
Within the very words of "Maud" and "I,"
Religion from infinity has lived,
And to infinity will live — as long
As man and woman give to thought their sex.

Maternity wombs in the sound of " M,"
From " mother " to the holy name of " Mary ";
Paternity's expressed for aye in " I,"
From " John " and " Jack " to " Jesus " and
   " Jehovah "!

I come from fantasy far, far away,
To fact at hand.

         Maud kneels, and folds her hands
Together in the symbol of herself,
Before her baby in the cradle lapped,
And prays unto the Infant in the arms
Of her that bare Him — Him the finite god
Of woman thought and love concéntrated —
The Saviour of mankind a weakling babe,
Within the comprehension of a child!
In sacred sympathy with her, I rise,
Uphold my right hand tow'rd the farthest sky,
And silently extend her words unto
The infinite Incomprehensible,
Beyond the wide reach of man's aspiration!

O blessèd woman thought, sweet Poesy!
Without thee there had been no Infant Christ!
Ubiquity's too vague to be a god!

— 1877 —
THE FIDDLER OF TIME.

It was an old fiddler, as bare as his bow,
    In the arm and the time-beating leg,
And as notched as his fiddle about the middle,
    As he sate upon a keg, —

And scraped and straddled and see-sawed and scored,
    In an everchanging tune,
Now fast, now slow, now high, now low,
    The while a crash, then a croon.

And as fast as the hairs of his bow wore out,
    They grew in his long white beard;
While his strings were a part of the throbbing heart
    That in his music was heard —

That in his music was heard in the beat
    Of his bare and bony leg —
Ha! a fiddler was he as none other could be
    But Time on the Earth as a keg.

Aye, kee-squeaky-squawky-tweedle-dee-dee,
    Went the fiddle and bow of Time,
On the keg of the Earth in the mansion of Mirth,
    On the rocky ridge of Rhyme.

When lo! there appeared a succession of forms
    In the merry old fiddler's sight,
Reviewing the Past from the first to the last
    As they waltzed into the light —

Of the wick that sang and danced as it burned,
    Above the fiddler's skull,
Till behold! it shone like a golden sun
    Upon the moon at full!

Ha! this is the Maiden of Matter, ywiss,
    This shapeless, graceless mass,
In a gown of gray interstellary clay
    Diffused like a dust throughout space.

And oho! this partner that clasps her waist,
    And whirls her in his course,
Around and around till her gown is wound —
    This dashing fellow is Force!

Kee-squeaky-squawky-tweedle-dee-dee,
    Around to left from right,
Till lo! they are whirled into a World
    In the merry old fiddler's sight!

The world of Matter and Force in mask,
    In the guise of Man and Woman,
The world of naught to feeling and thought,
    Till it takes a shape that is Human!

Aye, the world without the fiddler's skull,
    And the world within, its twin;
And the twain an ape at itself agape,
    Having turned itself outside in!

When lo! as the world of Matter and Force,
    Revolved as a waltzing ball,
In the light of the sun and the mirroring moon
    That illumined the fiddler's hall —

There came and went another pair
  In the merry old fiddler's sight —
Who but Dandy Day, in the rainbow's array,
  Whirling round with the Negress of Night —

With the Negress of Night, in her gown of gauze,
  Of woven silence and jet,
With a crown on her brow, and a silver bow
  In a golden galaxy set.

Kee-squeaky-squawky-tweedle-dee-dee,
  Around in the waltz they go,
Now there, now here, until a Year
  Is turned on their tuneful toe.

When oho! ha! ha! What a jolly pair
  Is this that comes into sight?
The lady in green is Summer, I ween,
  And the gentleman, Winter, in white.

And was ever there seen such a gown of green,
  As the Lady of Summer wore,
When with golden hair and faultlessly fair,
  She appeared on the fiddler's floor?

And in what a grim guise of snow and ice,
  Was the blustering Winter dressed!
While an icicle froze to the point of his nose
  And hung down to his breast!

Kee-squeaky-squawky-tweedle-dee-dee,
  Around go the Green and White,
Till another pair in their turn appear
  In the merry old fiddler's sight.

THE FIDDLER OF TIME.

Ho! Will o' the Wind, on dainty toe,
    A filmy, fairy form,
Till, gathering force as he whirls in his course,
    He sweeps away a Storm!

While his partner, behold, the Maid of the Mist,
    In a fleecy gray gown and hood,
Till, whirling about to a Water-spout,
    She bursts into a Flood!

Till oho! ha! ha! the fiddler plays
    As never he played before,
While the lightnings flash and the thunders crash,
    And the torrent redoubles its roar!

Kee-squeaky-squawky-tweedle-dee-dee,
    Around in majestic might,
Till another pair in their turn appear
    In the merry old fiddler's sight.

Ha! Will o' the Wisp, thou wandering sprite,
    Dancing hither, and higher and higher,
Till, swelling beneath a smoky wreath,
    He rages a furious Fire!

And the Nymph of the Wood whom he holds in his arms,
    As around and around he turns,
Who is she in the sash of the hue of ash,
    But the Forest and all that burns!

Till oho! ha! ha! the wild, wild waltz
    That makes the old fiddler shake —
A Volcano of fire rising higher and higher,
    In the arms of a whirling Earthquake!

Kee-squeaky-squawky-tweedle-dee-dee,
    Around in majestic might,
Till another pair in turn appear
    In the merry old fiddler's sight.

Ah, this is the Lady of Life, I ween,
    In the morn of a summer's day,
The beauty and mirth of heaven and earth
    Involved in a clod of clay!

Her hair, the golden gleam of the dawn,
    Her eye, the blue above,
Her form, the last in the living mould cast,
    Her heart, the heaven of Love!

And this is Death, this ghastly shade,
    This greedy, grinning ghoul,
From out the gloom of a gaping tomb
    Where all is forbidding and foul.

And he would waltz with the Lady of Life,
    This loathesome leper of old;
But before he placed his arm round her waist,
    The fiddler bade him hold.

Aye, the fiddler of Time, with a quivering bow,
    And a thrill suspended leg,
With gasping breath, commanded Death
    To take his fiddle and keg.

Then away with a hop and a skip and a jump,
    He sped to the Lady's side,
And with circling arms enfolded the charms
    Of heaven and earth in his bride.

THE FIDDLER OF TIME.

And around and around in a giddy waltz,
    Went the Lady of Life and Time,—
'Round the keg of the Earth in the mansion of
    Mirth,
    On the rocky ridge of Rhyme.

While, kee-squeaky-squawky-tweedle-dee-dee,
    Went the fiddle and bow of Death,
Till Time turned about without marking a note,
    And the Lady gasped for breath—

And fell on the floor in a silent swoon;
    When Death dropped the fiddle and bow,
And, while Time stood aghast in the maze of the
    Past,
    Entombed the Lady in woe.

And behold! the wick was a ghastly hue,
    Where all was glitter and glare,
And the maker of Mirth on the keg of the Earth,
    Sate in silence and despair.

How long—how many long ages he sate,
    No human tongue can tell;
For the time-beating leg, as a motionless peg,
    Is still while the heart is in hell.

He sate until—it happened so,
    The best of reasons why—
Philosophy came to study the flame
    That cast its strange hue in his eye.

When stumbling upon the fiddle and bow,
    Of the sad old fiddler of Time,
The strings went twing-twang—and Melody rang,
    Once more on the ridge of Rhyme!

And the sad old fiddler awoke from his woe,
   And took up his fiddle and bow,
And began to play — from grave to gay —
   When the wick began to glow.

And behold! the Philosopher turned him about
   In the whirl of a merry dance,
With a partner that came with the glow of the flame,
   On an errand for old Dame Chance —

Sweet Poesy! Ah, what a winsome wench,
   In the fiddler's staring eye,
As she whirled and whirled into a New World
   In the arms of Philosophy!

Kee-squeaky-squawky-tweedle-dee-dee,
   Goes the fiddle and bow of Time,
On the keg of the Earth in the mansion of Mirth,
   On the rocky ridge of Rhyme.

And around go the twain in a wild, wild waltz,
   While the fiddler stares aghast,
As anon they assume in the gloom of the tomb
   The form of the buried Past —

Of the Lady of Life in the arms of — Himself!
   When, whirling with bated breath,
He beheld her fall in the reeling hall,
   While he danced to the fiddling of Death!

—1878—
THE LAST MAN.

He stands upon an arc of the round earth
Revolving in a triple whirl through space ;
His back, a line directing downward to
The centre of the earth — the Finite Point ;
And upward to the Infinite — the Naught,
Until, within the triple whirl of the
Revolving earth, it is involved in it,
And at its centre finite made,
       Henceforth,
To whirl, involving and evolving, till
It winds into the thought of
      The Last Man.

His eyes with the horizon form a blade,
That, whirling wheresoever may the world,
Bisects the Finite from the Infinite —
The part from an hypothecated whole ;
As it, as well, bisects himself in twain,
The part below the eyes from that above,
The mortal man from
      An immortal Soul.

Within the concave of his skull, above
The line of the horizon and his eyes —
The counterpart organic of the dome
Dividing the in-known from the unknown, —
Aye, what is the self-comprehensible
Within his skull, but the organic form
Of a self-comprehensible without —
Within the greater skull — of whom ?
        Of God !

Whence came he? From the Infinite. But how?
By the involving of the Infinite
Within the whirl of the revolving earth,
Until, made finite at its central point,
A newborn eddy set out in its course,
Involving and evolving as it turned,
Until, above the line of the horizon,
Behold! he stands revealed unto himself
The Finite Son — of whom ?
       The Infinite;
With an immortal soul, the Son of God!

But when was he begat? There is no Time
Between the Finite and the Infinite.
In the relationship between the Son
Of God and God, he Is —
      And there an end.
The soul is as eternal as its God.

But, mark, between him and the finite earth,
And other and the myriad forms involved
In individuality unto
His comprehension, there is Time — a Past
In which there are relationships
Of first and last — of sequence — Birth and
 Death,
As eddy after eddy occupies
A certain space and time in revolution.
The First Birth was the centre of the Earth;
The Last Birth was the finite first whirl still
Involving and evolving outward from
Its starting point —
     It is the Thought that gleams
Along the blade of the horizon and
His vision, that, as the earth rolls, bisects
The finite Past from out the Infinite —
. The Future — God! —
      The Heav'n of the Last Man!

THE LAST MAN.

The Thought of the Last Man a Thought of
  Heaven!
The farthest evolution from the centre,
The nearest evolution unto God —
The finite soul of the Last Man,
                          A Soul
Evolving with existence into God!

His brothers aggregate the wedge of Life
That heads with him, the highest type of Man,
And points at the horizon in the whirl
That simulates the centre of the earth;
Or heads within him as a whole, and points
At a cell-centre whirling in his blood;
Or heads within him as he stands, the Last,
And points, back in the Past, at the First Man —
The first relationship of Force and Matter
Involved in individuality
By eddying within the stream of space —
The first-born son of God —
                         Now, the Last Man.

He is the sum organic of the World.
His beating heart, the rhythm recurring of
The earth in its compounded revolution.
What has been felt, within the wedge of life
That heads in him, he feels — and more: that
  which
Is severed from the Infinite by the
Revolving blade of his far-reaching scythe —
The line of the horizon and his eyes —
And whirled into the vortex of his Passion;
And so, what has been thought within the Past,
He thinks — and more; as round and round the
  earth
Goes in its triple whirl, and the long blade

Carves out the Finite from the Infinite
With an extending point,
     In his abstraction.

Ho! ho! what thrills of bliss he feels, unfelt
Before by any other living thing,
And never felt again until a form
Attains the point of growth which he has passed!
And what bright visions of involving Heaven,
Unseen, before the sweeping scythe of sight
Has cut them from the brain of God in swaths,
And mowed them in the skull of
     The Last Man!

Aye, the Last Man — Behold the monarch of
The whirling worlds innumerable that
Have yet revolved within his recognition!
Erect upon an arc of the round earth
Revolving in a triple whirl through space —
His eyes with the horizon on a line —
The finger of the dial on the clock
That ticks within the heart-beat in his breast,
And strikes — as strike it will, whene'er the maw
Of the revolving earth will be unfilled
Within a desert of diluted space —
When, dying both of inanition, Earth
And the Last Man, their decomposing dust
Will be devoured by other orbs unknown.

Then will the clock have struck the hour of
 Doom,
And into naught have vanished the Last Man! —
A recollection in
    The Mind of God.

Unto himself no longer the Last Man,
But lo! the thought of
    The Eternal God!

— 1887 —

THE MEANING OF THE MONUMENT.

Read at the dedication of the Soldiers' Monument, erected by the Major A. M. HARPER Post, No. 181, Department of Pennsylvania, Grand Army of the Republic, at Braddock, Allegheny County, Pennsylvania, Saturday, September 10th, 1887.

Upon a height, whence the delighted eye
Opes to the sentient mirror of the mind,
A vast and varied vision of the Course
Of Empire to the Gateway of the West:
The mirky vale of the Monongahela!
Where erst the Briton in his coat of blood
Braved openly the Redskin and the Frank,
Or veiled or walled by the primæval wood,
To fall before his unseen enemy
As falls the Briton worthy of the name;
Where now a myriad of industries,
Within the inhulled acres of the stream
And inwalled mile-squares of the strath, present
A peerless exposition of the Age
Of Fire and Electricity enthralled
And bound unto their work with bands of steel,
Instead of the o'erpowered of mankind![1]
The Age, as well — (and herein hark and mark
The measure of all measures of the march
Of Man from apedom to enlightenment:) —
The Age of Many moulded into One;
The Real interwrought with the Ideal;
The human Mite made superhuman Monster;

The Finite, Infinite in time and space!
The Age of the man-monster Corporation!
Compounding, haply, thousands of mankind —
A Jove-like individuality
In comprehension and accomplishment!
The Age of Combinations without end —
The Club, the Party, the Society;
The League, the Union, and the Brotherhood;
The Clique, the Circle, and the Coterie;
The Pool, the Corner, and the Syndicate;
The Guild, the Congress, the Association —
Of Coalition and Amalgamation —
Organization and Consolidation —
Coöperation and Concorporation! —
Of Pygmy States, like individuals,
Confederating and creating thus
Gigantic Governments; of interstate
And international amenities;
Until, behold! within the blue field of
A compound nation's flag, a firmament
Of eight and thirty state-ensymboled stars!
And under it, the representatives
Of all the color classes of mankind,
The White, the Black, the Yellow, Red, and
    Brown,
Commingling their organic mind and might
In a grand continental unity!
A fateful fact, betokening anear
A union of the nations of the earth —
An age of universal comity!

Upon this height, a motley multitude,
Convened from all the airts the wind can blow,
To dedicate a monumental shaft
Unto the glory of the nation's dead —
The individuals war-sacrificed
That the United States might still subsist,

The Giant One of Many Pygmy States —
The Constitutional Concorporation —
The fateful fact forever, it has been:
The wonder and the glory of the globe!

Ah, me! the folly and absurdity!
This granite shaft, which, howsoever huge,
Of comely shape, and wrought with faultless skill,
Can be distinguished from a blasted oak
In broad daylight scarce half a league away!
The while the Union of America
Presents, in its indissoluble self,
An infinitely grander monument!
Compared with which, the crematory flame
Immountained on the rivage of the Nile
Above the dust of Egypt's royal dead,[2]
Sinks into the surrounding sea of sand
And as a prodigy is seen no more!

Nay, nay! beneath this superficial sheen
Of folly and absurdity, there is
A world of wisdom and substantial sense:
Perhaps, beyond the compass of the wright
That wrought it, building better than he knew.
While it is raised unto the nation's dead,
And glorified with their immortal names,
Yet is it raised not unto them so much
As the surrounding quick and the unborn
And unbegotten of the future's womb:
A granite-lived interrogation point —
An everlasting what? a deathless why?
To fix the sight afar, attract anear,
Incite emotion to expand the lungs,
And prick the apprehension to enquire,
What means this monument to me and mine?
That, haply, in the answer which unto

The asking is as certain to succeed,
As Truth betimes upon the heels of Try,
The questioner may see him in his true
Relations with the age in which he lives;
May learn the obligations of the most
Evolved, expanded, and exalted life
Earthfast humanity has yet attained;
And lay these lessons in his heart of hearts:

Betwixt the lowest and the highest of
The billion of the bipeds of the earth
Embodied in the mythic³ monster Man,
There are as many stages or degrees
Of growth as there are individuals;
But, for the nonce, they may be reckoned two:
Antagonistic and antipodal;
The ord and end⁴ of our humanity;
The Savage Man and the Enlightened Man.
The one — the Savage — living for himself;
But one remove above the beast of prey;
Achieving naught; accumulating naught;
His life and death, a bubble blown and burst!
The ultimatum of his ethics this —
Self-preservation is the first of laws.
The other — the Enlightened — living a
Composite and intercommingled life
Among a myriad of fellow men,
Of many-armed and hydra-headed monsters,
And such chimæras of complexity,
Compounding Man and all the elements,
Fire, water, earth, and air, — Machinery! —
As never entered a Hellenic dream!
Achieving miracles e'en to himself;
Accumulating wisdom, worth, and wealth;
Diffusing might and mind around the world;
His life and death, a gain and loss to millions!
The ultimatum of his ethics that

Embodied in the Christ upon the Cross,
Self-sacrifice is the divine behest!

And since all living things, that body forth
The fullness of their forms and complex pow'rs,
Have been developed from a lower to
A higher and more complicated state,
The ultimatum of enlightenment
Incarnate in an individual
Has been evolved — as well within himself,
As in his world of kindred as a whole —
Through a succession of inferior forms,
From lowest beast to highest savage type.

Now, hark and mark again! Albeit born
Within the range of vision from this height,
Yet is the individual not born
In the perfection of his form and pow'rs,
Like the Athenian Maid in panoply,
Burst from the cleft skull of Olympian Zeus;
And in his evolution he may stop
At any of the myriad of rounds
Between the first and last, and so remain
Or beast or savage, as the case may be!

Behooves it hence, the sire to set before
His son such monumental shafts as this!
That, moved thereby in body and in mind,
The halfling [5] may be lifted and enlarged
Into a whole of comprehension, and
Become, as soldier, sailor, saint, or sage —
As artist, architect, or artisan —
As miner, merchant, manufacturer —
As shipper, showman, chemist, counselor —
As actor, engineer, or what you will —
A vital part of one or more of the

Composite corporations of the age
Involved in and involving the great globe:
A conscious part-whole, man-world ultimate!

O instant of heart-thrilling ecstasy!
The epoch-marking moment of his life,
The youth,—involving his environment,—
Receiving an impulsion here or there,—
Attaining his full pow'rs unconsciously,—
Emerges suddenly from savagery
Into enlightenment, a round, full Man!
When, haply, he, for the first time, upholds
His oped right hand, and swears a solemn oath,
By his ensymboled manhood and his God![6]
Or when he dons his country's coat of blue,
His bosom heaving with a new-born pride,
He realizes in fast flashing thoughts,
He is absolved from self! his being merged
In the existence of his country! Aye,
His arm, henceforth, in part his country's might,
His heart, henceforth, in part his country's honor!
His life involved in and involving millions!

Aye, aye! albeit raised unto the dead,
This shaft is raised unto the quick as well!
To make the living feel heroic thrills;
To make the living think heroic thoughts;
Involve the verve and virtues of the most
Advanced and valiant in the march of Man;
And taste the glory of self-sacrifice!
To fit the player on the stage of life,
To take the Patriot's and Hero's part,
Ere he is summoned by the fates to act—
Achieve ennobling deeds, and leave his name
Engraved in granite by a grateful world!
For, surely as the flow'r precedes the fruit,
The Patriot and Hero of true worth,

Are never such in act and deed, until
They have been first in feeling and in thought!

---

[1] "The scene of this memorable conflict [the defeat of an English army, under the command of Major General Edward Braddock, by a detachment of French and Indian allies, from Fort Duquesne, under the command of Commandant Lionel de Beaujeu, in 1755,] presents one of the most remarkable industrial expositions to be found on the continent. From the bluff overlooking the valley, are to be seen in one view three [four] several lines of railway, with trestle work, river bridge, and tunnel; the Monongahela river, with lock and dam, steamboats, coal fleets, rafts, etc.; on the hillsides, the mouths of the coal pits, and, descending the steeps to the tipples at the water's edge, the railway inclines; in the valley, the magnificent plant of the Edgar Thomson Steel Works [and Furnaces,] and besides the varied works of the industrial town of Braddock near by — the only monument to the memory of the ill-starred British general. The observer of the scene cannot refrain from contrasting it with that of the 9th of July, 1755."— *Southwestern Pennsylvania in Song and Story*, 1878, p. 37.

[2] Several specious Egyptologists to the contrary notwithstanding, the word "pyramid" is of Greek origin and signifies fire-like, or rather, funeral pyre-like; and the pyramids of Egypt, accordingly, (in a country destitute of fuel and given in a myriad of ways to substitute the semblance for the substance,) are supposed to symbolize the crematory flame of India: of course, involving all the associated ideas of being cleansed by fire, purification, and absorption into the Divine Essence through the visible manifestation of the Deity which fire was and is believed to be by many millions of the people of the earth.

[3] The prime signification of the word "mythic" is verbal, or spoken: from a Greek word, signifying a word, which is the correspondent of English "mouth."

[4] This good old English phrase, of Saxon origin, signifying first and last, beginning and end, should not be permitted to lapse into desuetude; for it is of value in poetic composition, if not also in prose.

[5] Assuming the English and Scottish words, "haspat," "haspenald," "haspan," and "haspin," (signifying a youth,

stripling, hobbledehoy, half boy and half man, and variously derived by lexicographers from English "half-span" or "half-spun;" Scottish "halflin," *i. e.*, "half-long," according to Jamieson; and Welsh, "hespwrn," a young sheep,) to be the equivalents of "halfling," if not indeed variations or corruptions of the same, an effort is made here to add or restore to the language a very useful word: to supply the place of which, perhaps, there is nothing better than malagrugous "hobbledehoy."

"Since the symbolism involved in our everyday life — the silent substitute of language which we have inherited from our remote oriental ancestors, who, presumably, were approximately the same as the commonalty of India to-day — is an inexplicable enigma to many seekers after the good and sufficient cause there is for the existence of everything, the pointer, finger board, or "bishop's finger," of the poem, it is believed, will show the way to a full and satisfactory understanding of much that generally is unintelligible and seemingly void of idea in our manners and customs, our art, and even our religion. Among the ancients — the Romans, Greeks, etc., — as among the Indians to-day, the right side of the body, doubtless from the fact that the right arm is generally the stronger, was considered the man-half of the whole; the right hand, the sign and symbol of a man; and the right hand uplifted, the sign and symbol of the male principle extended and exalted infinitely, or, in other words, the silent expression of the idea of a Man-God, a Heavenly Father, and the like. With the hand opened and the fingers forming a point, the idea of an indivisible Deity was expressed; with the fourth and fifth fingers lowered, and the first, second and third upheld and parted. a godhead divisible into a masculine Trimurti or Trinity; and with the fingers otherwise disposed, other ideas, which it is not necessary here to indicate. The opposite sex ideas involved in our forms of worship are given in the preceding pages in the poems "Atlantis" and "Chautauqua."

END OF VOLUME I.

www.ingramcontent.com/pod-product-compliance
Lightning Source LLC
Chambersburg PA
CBHW051242300426
44114CB00011B/860